THE GIRL
FROM
NOWHERE

THE GIRL FROM NOWHERE

Eliska Tanzer

MIRROR BOOKS

First published by Mirror Books in 2020

Paperback edition published in 2020

Mirror Books is part of Reach plc
10 Lower Thames Street
London EC3R 6EN

www.mirrorbooks.co.uk

ISBN 978-1-912624-94-2

Typeset by Danny Lyle

Printed and bound in Great Britain by
CPI Group (UK) Ltd, Croydon, CR0 4YY

A CIP catalogue record for this book is available from the British Library.

Every effort has been made to fulfil requirements with regard to
reproducing copyright material. The author and publisher will be
glad to rectify any omissions at the earliest opportunity.

1 3 5 7 9 10 8 6 4 2

Cover image: Millennium Images

CONTENTS

THE REAL ESMERALDA

THE EDUCATED GYPSY

AWAKE

EPILOGUE

The Zlatkovs

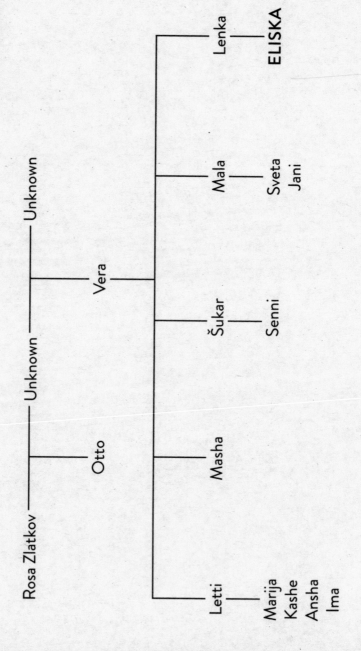

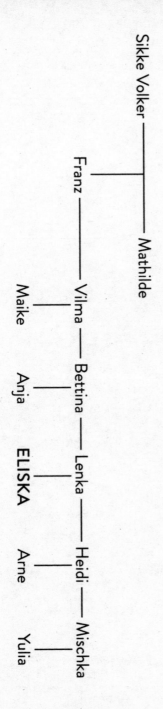

The Volkers

THE ZLATKOVS

MY DAUGHTER IS
WORTH MORE THAN THIS

My mother's side of the family are Romani. Gypsies. No baby-snatching and tambourines, just resilient souls and richly coloured skin. I look most like them, with my brown eyes and scars. I don't have the richly coloured skin, though. Instead of deep bronze or golden ochre, I came out the colour of sunflower oil and, thanks to childhood malnutrition followed by years of low iron levels, I'm now the shade of an off-brand Simpson.

I was born in the nineties to a 13-year-old girl called Lenka Zlatkov. If this were a TV series, we'd grow up like sisters, understanding each other on a deep level and bonding over common interests. Ma would sit, engrossed in me, hugging a cup of tea while I painted my nails and moaned about my friends. Maybe we'd even go clubbing together.

In reality, having a mother barely a decade older than you isn't fun. Ma was at best a frenemy and at worst the reason I slept with a penknife under my makeshift pillow.

Outwardly, Lenka Zlatkov was beautiful. Typically defiant, instead of looking haggard and rundown in the bleakest of living conditions, she flourished. All of five foot four, but with a mouth that would give a town crier a migraine, she was a fiery Gypsy woman with attitude. Her thick, glossy hair was as rebellious as she was, preferring to fall down the sides of her face instead of staying in the plaits she'd weave. The coral-coloured lipstick brightening her full lips and stolen kohl pencils lining her creamy brown eyes, combined with her wild wavy hair, made Ma look radiant. I loved watching her relaxing; she'd sit with her eyes closed, swinging her foot out of the window mindlessly as the scraps of sun that reached us bounced happily off the three gold hoops hanging from her long, wide nose. During these moments, I'd ache to be just like her, to be as effortlessly beautiful as that. Even the stretchmarks branched over her stomach, legs, shoulders and arms were fascinating to me; she was so unashamed of them that I was almost proud when, years later, I discovered the same faded vine-like marks on my own body. As if we were both part of the same tree that marked us with its long, winding arms.

As lovely as she was to look at, she was the polar opposite to be around. All the gentleness suggested by her soft coral smile vanished as soon as she spat out her trademark snide comments, and the scathing insults for which she was famed. When she was about to savage someone verbally, Lenka had a signature look: she'd raise her left eyebrow over slightly narrowed eyes and bite the inside of her bottom lip, whilst smirking enough to flash a glimpse of her gold tooth. She reminded me of a coiled viper waiting to strike. That look meant Ma was about to make someone cry.

I was never spared her tongue lashings – in fact, she worked out some of her best material on me. How I reacted to an insult determined how often she'd use it on other people. She once said I had a toad-face and I wailed for hours, only to find my cousin Sveta wailing at our Auntie Letti's feet the next day, because Lenka had called *her* toad-faced too. Sensitive soul that I was, I began weeping next to her because I felt guilty.

Lenka's hysterics and talent for verbal abuse were inherited from her mother. I'd grown up seeing my Grandma and Ma inches away from each other screaming wildly, then, minutes later, lazily chatting away.

All my aunties were treated harshly, but for Ma it was worse. While her sisters joined the "family business" in their mid-to-late teens, Ma was put to work at the age of 11 because she kept irritating my Grandma with the amount of food she ate.

It was Ma's career that was her great love. Lenka Zlatkov was, and tragically still is, an international saleswoman. India, Hungary, Romania, a dodgy month in Ukraine, and back home – Ma has worked in some exotic locations. Selling herself.

She is a prostitute. Not the perfectly coiffed, too-many-teeth-in-her-face, Julia-Roberts-in-*Pretty-Woman* type, but the penknife-in-her-bra-lining, abortion-scars and knuckle-duster-hidden-in-her-plaits type. She's more likely to knock a man out and rob him blind than fall in love with him, and all with that signature smirk on her beautiful face. It's probably how she managed to afford a set of knuckle-dusters in the first place.

At 11, Ma started to travel with my Grandma all over our city and the neighbouring ones to sell herself. She was a favourite with all the white men trawling the streets looking for some #Gypsylove.

She'd recall with glee how many men wanted her and how they couldn't even wait long enough to find a room: they'd have her behind buildings, in cars, or down rubbish-cluttered alleys. In Ma's mind, it was the ultimate compliment – that these men dressed in their clean clothes would risk the filth just to have her.

Any normal 11-year-old would be distraught, but not Ma. The few times she'd told me about the start of her illustrious career, she'd speak with a kind of arrogance. It validated her, having men pay for her. It was the reason she bounced around with that theatrical walk of hers – a cross between a shampoo advert and a salsa performance, all hair flips and hip-swaying.

It wouldn't be fair to say it was her work that made our relationship so volatile; my cousins and their mothers had wonderful relationships, despite the work. It was my permanently self-absorbed, escapist haze and Ma's resentment of me that made for such a sour mix.

As I grew older, the verbal warfare got worse and worse. Ma would say the nastiest things to me. I always kind of knew she wasn't fully serious; it was just her manner to express herself by flinging savage threats and crushing insults, her arms thrashing as violently as her words. The usual dramatics of a Gypsy mother.

"One day I will cut your tongue out of your mouth!"

"I wish I had ripped you from my womb when you first started feeding off me. Leech!"

"All you have to offer is a tight hole!"

Eventually, the shock of her banshee episodes wore off, and I stopped caring. Living where we did made us bulletproof to verbal insults in any case. We were subjected to the worst racial abuse on a daily basis and after a while, instead of gasping and recoiling at the savagery of the insults, we just rolled our eyes and sighed at the lack of originality.

This was our relationship: she'd say some foul shit, I'd either cry or be sarcastic back and it would all be forgotten within a few hours.

The physical fighting took longer than a few hours to get over, however.

From the way she'd get up in the morning and dance outside whilst oiling her hair, to the way she'd batter me with her shoe for doing the same, Ma was an enigma. There were times, I have to admit, when Ma was completely justified in battering me. I was dopey, but I wasn't a timid child, and I wasn't a well-behaved child. I spent half my time daydreaming or making up stories, and the other half being dragged by my cousins to go stealing and fighting.

I'd only ever steal food. I wish I could give you some Oxfam-leaflet line about only stealing enough to fill our starving, malnourished bodies but truthfully, instead of bread and water to survive, we stole doughy *Rožky* rolls and ice-cold bottles of *Kofola* cola.

I'd fight because I'd inherited my dad's fists and Ma's tongue – not the best combination. I took great pleasure in chasing the little white kids who were brave enough to peer around the corner to our neighbourhood and scream "Rats!" "The Nazis are coming!" "A good Gypsy is a dead Gypsy!" The look on their faces as a gaggle of dirty, brown Gypsy kids rounded the corner with makeshift catapults and pockets full of rocks ready to launch at their milky white legs still makes me cackle to this day.

So, there must have been days when Ma's flip-flop was the only way to deal with me. But there were also many times when Ma went completely overboard with the footwear. She was far from rational and administered the same punishment for stealing and fighting as she did for running too fast down the stairs or laughing too loud. One time when I accidentally knocked over the small pan of oil she'd set on the floor as she massaged it into her hair whilst humming a random song she'd heard at the marketplace that day, she snapped her eyes open as if possessed and flew into a Hulk-level rage as soon as she narrowed in on me. She rose from the floor like a demon with both hands still midway through her hair and chased after me. She clung onto one of my plaits and backhanded me so ferociously my teeth felt numb for hours afterward. She screamed at me for "not accepting my feet and having your father's *plutvy* (flippers)".

As always after these irrational fights, I'd run off to a quiet corner and lie on the ground recounting the entire argument to the clouds, as they rolled over me soothingly. I'd go into vivid detail, gesturing flamboyantly. But I would change the endings. Instead of finishing with "and that's why I'm bleeding now, because she hit me," I'd tell the clouds, "and then you scooped me up and we flew so fast, it blew the fight out of my head". This revisionist storytelling was my therapy; it was the calming cuddle that I craved whenever Ma reminded me how unwanted I was.

I've never retaliated or hit Ma. From the times when she'd be dragging me by my hair upstairs, to using strips of wood for the fire to jam into the backs of my knees, to driving her ring-laden fingers into the groove of my cheek, I never hit her back. I figured that just letting her carry on meant it would be over faster. Sometimes she'd beat the shite out of me, then give me a kiss on my forehead and leave the room, humming to herself. I'd often try to confront her after her anger had cooled, but that would end with me emotionally distraught as well as bruised and sore.

"What if you kill me one day, Ma?"

"I can do what I like with you. Cockroaches are hard to kill."

"Tch, that's settled then! You have no control when you hit me. I'm your child!"

"You are still a virgin, yes? Then I am already a better mother than my own."

I'd usually shuffle off and then continue arguing under my breath when she was well out of earshot. Some of my best comebacks were devised hours after the event, once I'd re-enacted the argument in my head several times.

To avoid a verbal scalping and losing the rest of the day to restaged arguments in my head, I learnt to just keep my mouth shut.

On my 12th birthday I suppose the memories of her previous tongue-lashings had faded slightly, because I decided to challenge her over repeatedly missing my birthday celebrations. I say celebrations, but it was just my family minus my mother, squashed in a room together dancing and drinking, whilst I was given a 50-pence-sized piece of *klobasa* sausage instead of the usual five-pence-size and had my cheeks pinched by my aunties. Then the kids would be sent out while the cheap booze took over my aunties and they'd start exchanging filthy stories, shrieking in laughter and screaming at each other in a drunken rage.

I walked in on Ma wrapping her headscarf around her hair – she wore it to irritate my grandma, who took umbrage at an unmarried woman wearing one – and she was burning some type of minty stuff, which did nothing to settle my tumultuous stomach. I worked up the courage and took a deep breath.

"So… WhyDoYouAlwaysMissMyBirthdaysAllTheTime? It'sOnlyOneDayForMeButYouNeverCome—"

I stopped to breathe, and continued, while she carried on wrapping her hair as if I wasn't even there.

"YouDon'tLoveMe—" Ma cut me off by raising her hand and sighing.

"Are you fucking simple? Don't speak all at once outside these doors, people already think I drank when I carried you. Idiot." This scene had seemed so much more touching in my rehearsals the hour before, but now I felt like apologising for boring her so much. Why do these things always go better in your head? As if Ma would have broken down and pledged her undying love for me.

Crossing her arms and turning to face me, Ma narrowed her eyes. "Eliska, don't irritate me today."

"Okay, shall I come back tomorrow?" I snapped.

"You always think you have more feelings than the rest of us. MY mother is half an hour from death and I still haven't heard her tell me she loves me without me giving her a pouch of money first. Be grateful I'm at least waiting for your periods before I send you out to work. Always fucking irritating me, I pay for you to eat and let you float around doing whatever the fuck you do. When I was your age, I'd handled half the men in this fucking place. Go to your father and see if he will treat you any better." She looked me up and down and scoffed. "*Ay* course he will! He'll pretend you're a maid or a girl he's fucking, instead of admitting to his friends that he mixed his pure white blood with filthy *zigeuner* blood. Fucking us is better than fathering us. Useless bitch. If I ever was at your birthday, I'd cover my face and weep because you have ruined me. No Gypsy man around here will raise a half *gadje* girl. You've ruined me."

Well, damn. I mean, I wasn't too well versed in the ways of men back then, but I was pretty sure no man would want to marry an unashamed prostitute, regardless of me. But according to Lenka Zlatkov, I was the reason she wasn't happily married to a wealthy man in a beautiful house with a large garden. I don't know what type of Beyoncé she thought she would have been if I hadn't been born, but she was fiercely adamant that I scuppered all of her life goals. I'd have understood her resentment if she had raised me like a proper mother, but I was raised by everyone else. I raised myself. My cousins raised me. Hell, the rats in our block did a better job of raising me than Lenka did.

In her long-ass rant though, she was right about my grandma. My grandma rarely showed any affection, so I suppose I was glad that, however volatile it was, my relationship with Ma went further than her throwing a bored "I love you" in return for a roll of money after I'd been on my back the whole day.

She was right about my father too. If I turned up at his place asking to move in, he'd either die laughing or throw me off the Rakotzbrücke Bridge and go about his day.

Ma always seemed to have a long rant ready to unleash at the mere sight of me. I often wondered whether she'd practise them, or whether that much sourness was improvised. Maybe it was a mix of both. Like everyone else in the Zlatkov family, Ma couldn't read or write, and so instead of a diary, I think she'd keep all her feelings tucked away in a separate part of her brain ready for the slightest ignition. Then god help whoever was in front of her.

Her rants and the death threats weren't ideal, but I preferred them to her crazier antics.

I started keeping potential weaponry near my pillow when I was around ten years old. Ma had got drunk because it was a Thursday or the stars were bright or she'd seen a red car – anyway, she'd got so drunk she needed help getting up the stairs to my aunties' flat, where I was sleeping with my cousins. My eldest cousin Marija had stolen a filthy rug from someone's rubbish the day before and we were using it as a blanket. Ma tottered in and shook my head with her foot. I squinted my eyes open and saw a rumpled man, who reminded me strongly of the old guy who would wear a shirt part-way buttoned with his matted-blonde chest hair peering out, sitting next to the bus stop in town whenever the schools let out. He was practically salivating at the three mud-specked little girls huddled under a dirty rug. I hate paedophiles as much as the next person, but why is it that these raggedy-looking men think that little girls are going to flock to them? It's the entitlement that gets me, standing there stained and unkempt. Put some effort into your look at least.

Ma was swaying, trying to count a handful of change. I could hear her shoulder hitting against the door every other second. I had shut my eyes tight and was trying to ignore her foot eroding the side of my head when she screeched, "Eh? What?

This is it? She's a fucking virgin! You need to give me more! My daughter is worth more than this! Even *I* charge more than this! She's brand new! You can do whatever the fuck you want, she doesn't know anything! What the fuck is this?!" The man looked petrified at this drunken squawking and bolted at the sound of people moving above us. The day after, everyone knew what had happened, thanks to the offended Ma complaining loudly about "cheap bastards". My Auntie Letti took me aside whilst the rest of my cousins were out and gave me a sharpened nail file, grabbed my shoulders and told me to keep it in my hair or under my pillow. I knew it was in case someone paid Ma the correct amount. Nobody said anything to Ma directly; she was too much to deal with. Making an enemy out of Lenka Zlatkov only ended a handful of ways, and all of them involved Ma's trademark smirk at the end.

She was hated by some of the other working ladies because of her penchant for blackmailing married men. In a tight-knit circle of sex workers, you have to be a special kind of fucking-awful to be cast out. But Lenka wasn't bothered. She had her sisters; she didn't need friends. She never saw anyone as a friend – just someone to eventually use.

Ma had a habit of collecting trinkets from some of her weaker, shyer customers. Either she'd steal it while the man was in an elevated state, or just point-blank take it from him. Her looks let her get away with a lot. Her bullying tactics let her get away with more.

Even my aunties were weary of arguing with her. I've no doubt that any of them could whoop Ma's ass – it wouldn't be easy, but still, I reckon they could manage it. But it just wasn't worth the lifelong paranoia, constantly watching out to see when Ma would take revenge.

Despite her short size, she was a ruthless fighter. I vaguely remember her almost knocking my street-fighting, Nazi father out. It's one of those moments when, whenever I think about it, I'm just a bit proud of her. My father had come down for the weekend for some racist fuckery and spotted Ma and me in town, so all three of us were driving back to Drovane in his rental car. They were screaming in a variety of languages – German, Slovak, Romanes – it was like a death-metal Eurovision in the car. Ma, as always, went too far and sang off a ribbon of insults with a smile on her face. Something about joy has never sat right with my father, and he took great offence at being laughed at by a Gypsy girl. He reached over, grabbed Ma by the hair and introduced her face to the dashboard, really hard.

I braced myself for the scream that I was sure would follow. Instead, Ma sat up, adjusted her hair a little, and wiped her face with the back of her hand, laughing. "Eh, Whiteboy? That's the best you have?" She then turned to my father and drove her decorated fist into his jaw. I was stunned at this exchange; my facial expression must have mirrored my father's, but with less blood. He was staring at her while she straightened her scarf and reached back to stroke my kneecap, soothingly telling me we'd be home soon. He never tried to hit her again after that. I think, deep down, he's kind of scared of her. He mostly just scowls and tries to turn away whenever they argue, while she pushes *him* around. The same way he does to his other women.

Ma was petty, and whenever she felt she'd been wronged she'd get her own back one way or another, be it sleeping with your husband, brother and father, or smacking you in the face with a rock. Obviously, my aunties would be watching out for the rock: none of them were married and there were no men in the Zlatkov family aside from one dead cousin and another, Kashe, in prison. Shameless as Ma was, she'd draw the line at incest.

Our dead cousin, Lukáš, passed away two years before I was born. I was told that he was my brother, and carried on believing this until years later – when I realised that Ma had me at 13, so how the hell could she have had Lukáš, who passed away at 16 two years before I was born? Unless she'd had him in a past life and reclaimed him when she came back as Lenka Zlatkov, it was impossible. Imagine being 20 and realising that my dead "brother" was older than my mother when he died, and making the most painfully embarrassing phone call to the convenience store near our neighbourhood asking for someone to fetch one of the Zlatkov women. (I say convenience store – it was really a glorified garden shed with a telephone, a couple of bottles of *Slivovica*, cigarettes and dodgy vodka. But it was Gypsy-run, and the darling lady would always let my family phone me or ferry messages from me to them).

My Auntie Mala eventually came to the phone and asked what was so important.

"Lukáš can't have been my brother, he was older than Ma when he died!" I felt my IQ dropping even further.

"Eliska. You are serious? Eliska... Eliska. Please tell me this isn't real!" All I could hear was two sets of wheezing – the shop-owner was obviously listening to us. "Lukáš, may he rest peacefully, was MY son, but you were both fed by me. You and Jani are the same age and I had milk in me when you were born so Lenka made me feed you. It hurt her too much. Eliska, you were the wrong one for an English education. You dumb child! You were brother and sister because I fed you!" Now they were both cackling. I mumbled a quick "bye" and hung up.

I know how it sounds; people would be dumbfounded that I never thought about it. But I wasn't too bright, especially back then; my nickname from both sides of the family has always been "sleepwalker", and I hung off every word Ma and my aunties said. When I inevitably stopped listening to Ma, I still held on to what my grandma and aunties told me. I believed everything; I had no reason not to. I'd just gone about my life thinking there was a dead brother of mine who kept raising hell and then got murdered. Well, at least I learnt the truth eventually. Even if I was forever known by the convenience store owner as a dumbass.

Another thing I constantly heard as I was growing up was how much money I'd make Ma one day. She'd been trying to glamourise her work to me for as long as I can remember. I must admit there were times when I'd loved the attention lavished on Ma whenever she'd bring back pouches of crumpled notes and dirty coins. She'd be the apple of my grandma and great-grandma's eyes.

She'd often have me displayed to her friends, bragging about how desired I'd be. I'd be stuffed in a small room with Ma and all her friends and sisters, who would be singing folk songs, then sexually explicit songs. I'd be dancing in the middle of everyone whilst Ma banged her hands on her thighs, making her bangles shake. She'd kick up my skirt with her foot so everyone could see (and cackle at) my faded and ripped underwear. I mean, whatever – at least I wore underwear. Ma acted as though knickers meant her vagina was password protected, and claimed it would put off "clients".

I'd be dancing for the women a few times a month from a tiny age. Each time showing off new moves Ma had taught me, throwing my hips one way and flicking my hair the other. Apart from the one time I was violently sick when Ma decided to teach me how to belly-roll, I was a generally good student. I became the best dancer in our family before I could form coherent sentences. Those are the rare times Ma would look at me with arrogant pride splashed across her sweet brown face. She'd sit with a half smirk, eyebrow cocked and head slightly raised whilst there'd be shouts of "Little Lenka! She dances like her Ma! Eliska is special! Look how fair she is! You can get twice the money for her. Imagine how many would pay to be her first fuck!" I didn't know what "fucking" was at that point but was proud to be my ma's special thing, so I stood the way I watched my ma stand: hand on hip, head tilted, and twisting one of my plaits with the other hand. I'd be beaming as Ma kissed my forehead calling me *miláčik*: sweetheart. Deep down, I know she was only proud because I reminded her of herself – and Lenka loves nobody more than she loves herself. I can't recall her looking at me with that much adoration since.

TINKLING TAMBOURINES
IN SOVIET SQUALOR

The Western meaning of the word "Gypsy" is fascinating to me. I once asked a girl why she called herself "Gypsy" when she had no Romani blood, and the answer I got was: "Well, to me it's not a race, it just means wanderlust and being free." I could have died. "Being free". *Free*. I wanted to know where we were "free". It certainly wasn't anywhere with an actual Gypsy population. It *definitely* wasn't where I was raised, in Slovakia.

Being Gypsy hasn't always been so *en vogue*. Sure, there'd be the odd weed-smoking yoga-lover who was partial to flitting between rented rooms (usually in arrears) and took issue with washing regularly, who called themselves a "Gypsy", but mostly we're a group of people that society goes to great lengths to avoid. Very rarely will someone in mainland Europe willingly call themselves one of us, which is why I found English people's love of the idea so hilarious. Pristine, clean girls with shiny hair extensions and perfectly made-up faces proudly proclaiming themselves "Gypsies", while I was thinking twice about telling anyone my heritage and wondering whether to pretend I was from Azerbaijan.

I heard the phrase "Home is where the heart is" for the first time in England. It was strange to me because home certainly wasn't where my heart was.

Home was where I was shaken awake by my drunk Ma's dirty foot getting tangled in my matted hair. Home was where I was stuffed into a bare room with two other single mothers and their kids, fighting over the thin, stained blanket the way we fought over the last piece of half-mouldy bread. Home was where I spent half my days lying face-up on the gravel, willing the clouds to take me with them, wherever they floated off to.

What I called home was generally referred to as a "dirty Gypsy ghetto" by everyone else. It's less a multiple-hip-hop-album-spawning ghetto and more of a "stepped in this puddle? LOL you got hepatitis C now" ghetto. I was born and raised in a place called Drovane. I know there is a lot of pride in countries like England and America about being from a "ghetto". When I was at university for example, I saw the video for a song called "Ghetto Refix" by an artist called Mumzy Stranger, which consisted of him and three other well-dressed, nicely made-up people strolling through a clean part of town with a few blocks of flats behind them. I almost lost my life laughing. Someone spray-painting a wall, a clean little girl standing behind a fence, and an abandoned house with no windows – that was the "ghetto" to them. Imagining them sauntering through Drovane in their expensive clothes singing "I come from the ghetto" was too much for my delicate heart.

I'm not denying that there are some dire places in the UK and USA, places where unemployment is high and the standard of living low. But the worst of these ghettos still look like luxury compared to Drovane. Believe me, nobody from an actual shitty ghetto wants to be from there.

Drovane was so violent and dangerous that even the bus drivers sometimes avoided stopping at the rotting bench at the foot of the pathway into the ghetto. There'd be times when we'd not see a bus for days. The old women would amble back up the path and send one of the teens into town to fetch the one or two items they could afford with their few coins.

We lived in huge, grey Soviet-style blocks that loomed over all the land around. The shadows they cast were so thick and dark, it was perpetual night on the entire right-hand side of Drovane. Which was a blessing of sorts; it half-hid the neigh-bouring landfill. The council had seen fit to use our home as the place to dump unwanted rubbish. The smell was bad enough, but the liquid that constantly seeped from the decaying mound of waste was the true menace. A number of kids had run barefoot through it at different points in time, and each had ended up with angry red bumps and blisters on their feet. Mothers all over Drovane would slap the back of their child's head for running around near the trash and then gently hold wet rags to their feet.

Whenever a child would wake up with itching feet, there'd always be a scramble to the next room to see if they had any water left. We had no running water in Drovane, you see. It was usually the men who would go and fill up jugs and other containers with water each morning to last the rest of the day. Sometimes it'd take five of us with two containers each, as none of the men in Drovane wanted, or were allowed, to carry water back for any of the Zlatkov women. We could never be bothered to travel to wherever it was the men went to get their water, instead opting for the nearest hosepipe round the back of the shops and filling up whilst two of us kept watch. Water was a precious commodity and we always took care not to spill any on the way back.

Without basic requirements like water, Drovane obviously had none of the luxury items such as electricity or gas. We had open fires for cooking and warmth.

Given the absence of basic facilities, it's needless to say that nobody paid rent. The borough had almost total unemployment and the government was just happy to contain us all in the one slum. It's not like the rats or cockroaches paid rent either, and they outnumbered us.

No electricity meant no television, and as a child, I didn't have toys: we played with stained old mattresses and whatever else we found lying in the festering puddles dotted around the borough. I didn't learn how to ride a bike, but I learnt how to share a cell-sized room with eight other people. Romani families are stuffed into the blocks of Drovane like sardines, though thanks to the landfill right next to us, sardines tend to smell a lot better. We were raised with no concept of personal space because, especially as kids, we were always crammed together.

Everyone else had their opinion of us, and how deserving we were of our cockroach-infested surroundings. We were always thought to be worthy of the fleapit that Drovane was, simply because we existed. A new-born Romani baby deserved to rot in Drovane because it was Gypsy. There was no help, no repairs, no attempt to give us access to running water, nothing.

Instead, the government decided that Drovane would also be the perfect pen to contain the criminals, squatters, rapists, paedophiles and other outcasts of society. So in they were moved: these white men and women, whose punishment for committing the very worst of crimes was to associate with normal Romani families.

And Drovane had its fair share of normal Romani families: the ones who were just getting by and praying for better days; who would spend years begging for a job in town and everywhere else; the ones that would prefer to starve to death than to steal. And it also had us Zlatkovs. Our family was every stereotype the nationalist groups yelled about when they came to "protest" at Drovane (their protests were really a bunch of half-drunk white men trying to fight with Gypsy men and harass the women, and almost always ended with half of them being beaten up, and more than one sleeping with a member of my family).

Drovane was worse than prison: at least in prison there are guards, and even the worst prisons on earth have some semblance of control and protection. But in Drovane the government and police left us to our own devices, and rarely ventured inside the borough unless it was to raid us for some stupid reason (I'm convinced they used Drovane as a training ground for new police officers), or when they had an unsolved crime and needed a random Gypsy to fill the role of suspect. This happened too many times to count as I was growing up. People would shield their sons as best they could when they heard sirens coming down the path. There'd be a mad scramble as the men would race up the stairs to the highest floors of the flats, and I would sob silently in terror, watching the police drag away another screaming, crying Gypsy boy.

The police would toss aside the struggling boy's mother as she grabbed at the feet of the officers, begging for them to have mercy on her innocent child.

I think that's what I hated the most in Drovane. I was always so painfully aware of my heritage. I am Romani. I am Gypsy. I am something to be spat at. I am not important enough for the government to keep me safe from danger; instead, they inject the danger into our neighbourhoods themselves by relocating the worst types of criminals into our boroughs. I am something to be hidden in grey, crumbling tower blocks so as not to disturb the idyllic White community in Slovakia.

They would not employ Gypsies in the cities surrounding us. They would not allow us to earn a living. They would refuse us entry to shops, doctors' offices, dentists and even public toilets.

This was in the mid-nineties, and even today in some parts of Europe, it continues. We were supposed to starve to death, die of pneumonia, waste away until there was nothing left of us. But we refused.

We would eat. We would drink. We would do what we had to do.

My friends, cousins and I had our games: a selection of techniques we used to supplement our parents' income. Basically, we stole shit to get money for food. One of the ways we did this was to pretend we were lost to any tourists in the nearest towns.

We'd be arranged in order of skin tone by the older kids, and as one of the lightest, I was always the bait. I was forever getting asked if I was ill. I was always laughed at by the other children, and even Ma used to tell me to put my legs away because the colour made her sick. She was such a regal brown and I was pastel-coloured. But in this game, my sandy mixed-race skin was an advantage.

Even at that age we realised what level of Ethnic most people were comfortable with. Just a hint of a shade darker than them. European features a touch beiger, but nothing else. I'd inherited a strong wide, long nose from god knows who, but my long hair was lighter than the delicious black that most of the other girls from Drovane had. In essence I looked like a Gypsy girl, but with the saturation turned low.

Any darker brown than that and you didn't exist in this corner of the world: people would barely look at you, never mind stop for you. So I'd get to borrow someone's best skirts and have my hair freshly washed and braided by my older cousins. We'd stop a tourist and while they were fawning over the cute, lost little Gypsy, the other girls would be searching through their pockets. We'd always know who the tourists were; they were invariably Americans who wanted an "authentic" experience of Slovakia. They'd go to the furthest corners of the country and walk around with huge cameras and ugly shell suits.

Another game which brought guaranteed money was me belly dancing the way Ma had shown me. On one of her "work trips", Ma stayed in a house for two months with a Turkish girl, Aysu, who had shown her all types of belly dance styles from Turkish to Egyptian. The way Ma spoke of her was always loving; I think she was the closest to a friend Ma ever had. I would dance whilst Besnik, Shandor or another boy played a tambourine. One of the drunk men of Drovane had given it to us, chortling to himself when we asked why he was so sure we'd get more money with the pretty, slightly worn tambourine. Later, I found out about *The Hunchback of Notre Dame* and realised people genuinely thought that we were baby-stealing, tambourine-waving crazies. In any case, the tourists adored the tambourine.

While I danced, jewellery, purses – and once, even a pair of shoes – got taken. God knows how someone didn't notice the shoes being slipped from their feet. To this day Pitti swears it happened peacefully, while the tourist was kneeling down in the crush of the small crowd taking pictures. I'm really unnaturally angry about this. We lived in a landfill in the bitter cold with nothing but rags and flip-flops, yet he didn't even notice the loss of a pair of shiny shoes. We ended up giving the shoes to the man who gave us the tambourine.

As a small child, I was indifferent to my Romani heritage. I knew Ma was Romani but that was all the interest I had. Before I witnessed the police ripping men and boys from their families just to close a case file, it never occurred to me that my ethnic origin was the reason I was stuck playing with flies and diseases. I didn't expect things to change; in my mind there was no better or worse life than mine. There was just life in Drovane. Living like cockroaches was all I knew, and that was the extent of my world.

Being proud of my heritage didn't particularly interest me as a child. It seemed stupid. The outfits I could fashion from the landfill next to our block of flats were something to be proud of, not what I happened to be born as. I didn't choose my heritage or do anything to achieve it, so why should I be so proud? However, it was when I was looking for still-bright crisp packets for my next dress that I got my first taste of Gypsy pride.

I was feeling fed up after discovering my hundredth faded crisp wrapper, and was ready to go home and sulk. I stopped when I heard the familiar screaming of one of the community uncles. He'd always be shouting about something when he was drunk. Nobody really paid him any mind and he'd end up shouting himself to sleep within a few minutes. But as I was walking towards the sound, I saw him standing on a crate with a smallish group circling him. I still didn't pay any attention. I was far too miserable to take part in any drunken foolishness.

His voice was scratchy as he was shouting *"SLAVERY! TORTURE! PORAJMOS!"* – the Romani name for the Holocaust. He was still raving about Auschwitz when I joined the growing crowd. I can't say I gave a shit for the first few minutes. I was more concerned about how I was ever going to finish my dress by evening, in the current crisp-packet shortage. It was only when the old lady next to me clutched my shoulder as she swayed on the spot with tears streaming down her dark face that I began to pay attention. The women in Drovane rarely cried, especially not the older ladies. It hit me that maybe these were serious matters and my patchwork crisp-dress would have to wait. There were two grown men with their eyes closed and one with both hands offered up to the sky as Uncle raged on.

Spit flew from his mouth and his eyes were fixed on a spot just above all of our heads, as if he couldn't even see us at the base of the overturned crate. "THEY MURDERED OUR PEOPLE! THEY EXPERIMENTED ON OUR PEOPLE! THEY RAPED OUR WOMEN! THEY SLAUGHTERED OUR MEN! WHERE IS OUR JUSTICE? WHY ARE WE STILL TRAPPED IN CAMPS? WE ARE TRAPPED IN THEIR CAMPS AND WE ARE TO BE GRATEFUL? I WILL DIE BEFORE I THANK THEM FOR LOCKING

US UP IN THESE NEW CAMPS!" He waved one of his arms wildly around the grey, overbearing blocks of Drovane. There was a fresh roar from the men. I felt my body erupt with a shiver at the wailing of the three women around me; they were banging their chests and one was pressing her forehead to her faded rosary so hard I was sure it was going to pass through her skull. The week earlier, someone from our community had been involved in a car accident – that was all I knew. As I got older, I realised it wasn't an accident.

I watched adult men crying and covering their faces with their hands. I watched women wrap their hair around their faces and sob. I listened intently to what Uncle was saying. He started talking about men taking Gypsy girls and selling them to other groups of men. This line hit me the hardest; I couldn't seem to shake the image out of my head. I buried my face in the skirts of the lady next to me and she clutched the back of my head. I felt tears slide down my cheek. I was only bloody looking for crisp packets.

I emerged when the woman blew her nose into her sleeve and was about to touch my head again. Uncle's screaming was drawing to an end – I could tell because his eyes were no longer wide and lost. He had the half-lidded look that my grandmother had right before her head drooped and she began snoring. He lowered his voice and half-sang out, "We are not thieves. When we take from *them*, we are not stealing. It is not a crime. We take back what was robbed from us. It is our reparations!" Uncle, being shitfaced, didn't use those words entirely but "reparations" sounds a lot better than "THEY TAKE OUR DIGNITY, WE TAKE THEIR BREAD. FUCK THEM. WE WILL BITE THE THROATS OUT OF EVERY LAST ONE OF THEM."

By the time he had finished, everyone was in high emotion. Whether it was anger, sadness, despair or helplessness, his speech had riled up Drovane and was still rippling through the estate hours after the sun had set. Uncle had mentioned something about "revolution" and waking the men at dawn to storm through town and show "them" that "they still haven't silenced us". Naturally the men were delirious, with the kind of excitement that comes when you know you're going to fuck shit up.

I wasn't so excited; I was beside myself with pity. My friends and I had the word "*PORAJMOS*" etched in our brains and we were horrified. The talk of Auschwitz had set fear in all of the children. Uncle had gone into graphic detail about what took place in the camps and whilst I didn't fully understand most of the words, the fear in the bigger children's eyes was enough to make me cross my legs very tightly so I didn't wet myself. He had spoken about "Nazis" and knowing that Ma said Dad was a "Nazi" didn't help me; he was more frightening than anyone else I'd met. I felt incredibly sorry for all of us. We were nice people, I thought. We didn't do anything to warrant the abuse we had apparently suffered.

I couldn't sleep that night. I kept waiting for huge army tanks to burst through the open door and for soldiers to lock us all in chicken cages. I was awake when the sun came in shards through the scarves hung at the glassless window. I was awake when my cousin came and dragged me up to go and get some water to wash our faces. As we made our way through the sleeping drunk men in the stairwells and landings, we passed Uncle in the entrance of our block of flats lying face down in drool and piss.

So much for revolution.

As bad as it could be in Drovane, there were also touching moments when the community would come together, help each other and look out for one another. I say "each other" because, as I mentioned, nobody really liked us that much.

Our "community" within the larger community was the prostitutes and the old ladies who had lived a hard life and were amused by the debauchery of the Zlatkov women. I think they lived vicariously through the unapologetic adventures of Lenka. Regardless, between my family and the family's friends, there were always enough spies dotted around Drovane and the marketplaces.

I first discovered this when I was caught with my boyfriend. By "boyfriend", I mean the Slovak boy in the market who chirped "Pleased to meet you, how are you?" when handing me a small bag of pears after I'd passed him the crumpled note Ma had given me. As surprising as it was that this boy hadn't learnt the same hate for us as the rest of his people, I was equally surprised when he gave me two free oranges. Unbeknownst to me, one of the Drovane spies had witnessed this little exchange, and scuttled home to tell everyone.

On my return, there were three angry women in the stairway waiting for me – my auntie's friends. I was interrogated about my "older boyfriend" and my "shameless flirting". They were so good at their job they had me believing I was Ma.

As the bigger one started rolling up her sleeves, I felt my stomach drop. She rolled up the bright floral fabric of her tunic to reveal muscled, brown arms dripping with dirty gold bangles. She bunched up her long, dark hair and wrapped her yellow headcloth around her head; a few strands of her wavy hair escaped from the glittery cloth and tumbled down the serious expression etched on her face. I was getting an arse-whopping.

Demanding my flip-flops off my feet, the three women tutted and shook their heads at my alleged whorish ways. If I'd had the courage, I would have asked them where the sense lay in lecturing me about *conversing* with a boy, when they worked as prostitutes. Deciding against it, I stood nobly and awaited my punishment.

Three swift whacks of the flip-flop later, I made a new decision. I would not be noble. I would scream my arse off.

These same women would later give me some kind of homemade alcohol as a "we had to do it, but we still love you" gesture. They asked me to go and get a glass from my room, as they'd run out. I looked at them and shrugged my shoulders. "I don't have that," I said. "Ah, you have no plate? No jar? What do you drink from?" They were baffled.

"I'm the smallest in my family. I have to wait until everyone else has drunk from the same big jar and then I get whatever's left. I don't have my own jar." I was feeling dumb, but it was true. I always had to have the nasty leftovers, with bits floating in.

Not that it was really up to us, due to the grim financial situation throughout Drovane, but we never really had "things". I learnt from watching Ma brawling with other women for their lipstick or hand-cream that possessions make you a target. During my childhood, I only had one certain possession aside from my name: a Winnie-the-Pooh teddy bear that I called Kika. I took care of Kika as if she were diamonds. As regulated as the water was in Drovane, I'd still steal some to clean the stains off her fabric arms – there would be three different hands reaching to smack the back of my head when I got caught, but it was totally worth it. Kika was a gift from an old policeman who had said something about Winnie keeping me safe and happy. Funny, as it was him dragging Ma by her hair and arm into the police car a week later, while Kika and I sat watching.

Some woman had come to Drovane brandishing a pair of men's underwear with a coral smudge, looking for "the whore sleeping with my husband". Unfortunately for the poor cow, she found her.

Ma sauntered lazily over to her, doing that dramatic walk of hers which irritated the woman more and more. She was spitting out racist insults as Ma smiled at her, biting her bottom lip. The woman decided to run up to Ma after shouting some nonsense about Hitler: these people loved to bring up Hitler as if we would melt at the sound of his name.

She ran right into Ma's vice-like grip and Hulk fists. Ma had her round the throat and was pummelling her fist into the side of her head, her nose, her ear. I felt a surge of animalistic desire to join in and beat up this woman, but I stayed with my grandma, who was shrieking with laughter and applauding her daughter.

It was my great-grandma who eventually stopped cackling long enough to bark "STOP!" at Ma. I suppose it was kind of funny to see this short woman on her tiptoes beating someone up. I felt bad when I saw the woman afterwards, though. She had fallen to the ground and was covered in dark red blood. Some of the other ladies went over to offer her a hanky, but she pushed their hands away and staggered to her feet. She was crying loudly as she swayed away down the path.

"What if her husband comes to hit you back, Ma?" I was rubbing her fist.

"Then I'll use the other fist!" she boasted back.

They all started laughing again, which drew more disgusted looks from the nearby women.

The old policeman had come back and scooped Ma up the next day.

On her return we'd decided to have a party in my grandma's room. My cousins and I went off to rummage through the bins at the back of the marketplace; that's how we fed ourselves. We'd usually manage to get some stale bread and half-rotten fruit, and some closed bottles of expired *Kofola* if we were really lucky. Unfortunately, people had got wise to what we did, so they'd started pissing in the bins and even pouring toilet cleaner all over the rubbish. We had to differentiate between the normal trash smell and the piss/bleach concoction to see if the food was good to eat or not.

This time, we managed to get some cheese in a sealed plastic bag and the usual stale bread. My aunties had got their hands on vodka, so it was going to be a real party. Ma sashayed in as if she'd come back from a world cruise. "I'm here! Where's the vodka?"

Just like that, everything was normal again. Ma was back to shouting at us to keep quiet, my aunties were dancing and shrieking, and I was watching my mother as she shook her hair free from the loose bun she'd tied and trilled, "They hate us because we are Gypsy—"

"No, they hate you because you beat up that poor white woman!"

"—but we are the flavour of this world!" Ma opted to ignore whichever voice it was that chirped in. "We gave those plain, ugly bastards music and dance! RISE, ROMA!"

Born a Gypsy. Born a crime, born to be abused, to be oppressed. Born losers, but we make ourselves winners – with a smile on our face and your purse in a Zlatkov's bra.

THE WORST PROSTITUTES
IN THE WORLD

"Legacy?" She spat on the floor. "Legacy – what legacy? You're all whores."

The entire room bristled, grumbling.

"You're not even good at that. Look at all the fucking kids in here."

I died.

"You're the worst prostitutes in the world."

Ma and I burst into shrieking laughter as my oldest aunt scowled, pushing my cousin off her lap.

Nani wasn't wrong. There we sat, my cousins and I, all but two of us fatherless. I knew my father, but the rest of my cousins didn't have a clue who they came from, although they all bore strong resemblance to the husbands dotted around Drovane – another reason why the women of Drovane loathed us. "If you're going to get pregnant, at least get a white man. They pay so much to keep you hidden away. But no – you lot get pregnant by idiots like Kama the one-toothed moron." Damn, she was on a roll today.

"She" was my great-grandma, a shrivelled, raisin-looking old thing named Rosa Zlatkov. Nobody answered her back, and nobody questioned her. Her word was gospel. My aunties held her words in as much esteem as the Christians in Drovane held biblical verses. Rosa was God in our family: she was the wisest, smartest and craziest Zlatkov of us all. In a bizarre twist, she was also the only one my father would have civilised conversations with.

Whenever there was a problem in the Zlatkov world – usually something Ma had done – Rosa would hold a meeting and decide on the best resolution. I knew she was a tough woman because her daughter, my grandmother, would flinch whenever Rosa raised her voice.

Vera Zlatkov was my grandmother, and the only one Ma answered to. But Ma could put Rosa under the same spell as she used on everyone else: a flash of her velvety brown eyes was enough to placate Rosa whenever Ma acted out. Ma was so obviously Rosa's favourite that my aunties told me of times they'd make Ma take the blame for their actions, because Rosa would never scold Ma as harshly.

Rosa had reason to be the rough, weathered woman I grew up with. She and Vera had spent time in Auschwitz during the Holocaust.

Rosa had been a young woman and Vera had been in her early teens when they were imprisoned in the concentration camp.

Rosa rarely spoke about her time there, and the only reason I knew at all was one night when Rosa had been screaming and pleading with someone in her sleep. A lot of the women on our floor of the block had trouble sleeping. Some would have nightmares like Rosa, some would sleepwalk, and some would just wait for their children to sleep and then cry. But this night, Rosa was worse than usual. She hadn't had a drink before she slept as on every other night, due to particularly bad neo-Nazi marches in town: nobody was allowed to leave Drovane by order of all the elder ladies of the families. Rosa threatened to break the legs of any Zlatkov woman who even looked outside the window, never mind leaving Drovane. It was too dangerous. So, Rosa went without her nightly sleeping potion.

She started crying loudly about ten minutes after she fell asleep. Jani and I sat up confused as we watched Rosa clawing at the air, then thrashing her left leg around violently. Vera hobbled over to her as she emitted blood-curdling screams. Vera gently shook her awake with tears streaming from her own eyes. Rosa woke with a start and backed away until she realised it was her daughter, and not whomever she was running from in her sleep. Rosa collapsed sobbing in Vera's arms whilst Auntie Šukar came and hugged me and Jani.

The next day there was a lot of hushed conversation, with either Ma or Auntie Letti poking their head into the stairway to make sure we weren't listening behind the door.

As our cousin Marija was the oldest, she was allowed to sit in with the adults. However, she remained loyal to us, and that night we all sat huddled together in a ripped blanket as Marija recounted everything she'd learnt that day.

Rosa had been dreaming of being dragged by her hair through a set of doors, with two beds and various surgical instruments on either side of the room. Two faceless men had tried to strap her to the bed; Rosa had said that her sister was on the other bed. A revelation to us, as we never knew Rosa had any siblings. Marija told us that Rosa had asked Vera to help her die, because she didn't want to live with "those animals still in my head". There were a lot of tears and pleading before Rosa managed to calm down and hug Vera tight to her. Marija began weeping at this point, and as we watched her tears drip off her chin onto Jani's hair, I felt uneasy. Marija was Auntie Letti's eldest child, the first Zlatkov of our generation. She was steely-souled and stony-faced at the best of times, so in a way, seeing her crumble was beautiful to me, because she'd never shown any soft emotion before. But it was also a sign that something serious had happened to our beloved Rosa, and I was determined to find out exactly what.

Over the next few weeks all of us made sure to sit with Rosa while she drank. In the evenings Senni, Jani and I would usually take the chance to roll from one end of Auntie Mala's empty room to the other while all the family were stuffed in Vera and Rosa's room, which they shared with Auntie Šukar and Ma. We'd roll fast, roll slow and, in daring moods, we'd try and roll over the top of each other midway. But, after her nightmare, we preferred to sit at Rosa's feet waiting for her to get drunk enough to answer our questions without slapping us around the back of the head.

After weeks of being told, "It's not for children," and Vera telling us to go away, Rosa eventually opened up.

I was having my hair washed with a damp rag by Auntie Letti and eagerly watching Marija and Sveta questioning Rosa about her life before moving to Drovane. Even Ma sat attentively, cuddling her knees to her chin. Vera kept sighing in a conflicted way as her eyes flickered from her pained mother to her desperate grandchildren. It occurred to me in that moment that we didn't actually know anything about Rosa and Vera. I knew about Ma and my aunties' childhood, but nothing about my two grandmothers.

"I was in my twenties." Rosa stood from the tatty armchair she was sitting in and walked over to her mattress. Settling down and propping herself up against the wall, she continued. "I was in my twenties and they chased us through the street. I lost Otto that day. I never saw him again."

"Who is Otto, *Mamička*?" Sveta gently asked. We all called Rosa *Mamička*, the Slovak word for mother, because she was the head of our family and mother to all of us.

"My son. I had him before I was married. I was I think, 12. We had travelled through the Black Forest and I had my fun." She winked and grinned. "I had my fun, then had my punishment when my *Daj* recognised my swollen belly. She shouted at me for hours, then slapped me and then cried because she thought she hurt my baby. *Babo* sat drinking and laughing at us. He told me I was a stupid girl, but it was okay because he was a stupid boy. I have lived many years and have never met a nicer man than my *Babo*." Rosa paused. Vera was smiling and nodding with her eyes closed. I felt pangs of sadness, because I wanted a *Babo* that I could say these things about, instead of the father I had. I wanted to meet Rosa's *Babo*. I wondered if he would like us – he probably would. He'd think we were little delights. I thought we were little delights. Little dirty delights.

"*Babo* would play a fiddle that he said he'd made himself, but I think he lied because *Daj* used to be the one who would fix anything that broke on the wagon. *Babo* would have to hold her hair while she mended everything. *Daj* was a healer-woman and that's how we ate. We had nothing much but *ay*, we were happy. I had two older sisters and three younger brothers. I can't remember their faces that well anymore. I used to help whenever I could. My older sisters would dance, the men loved them. I would take care of my brothers. It was simple but happy." She stopped and pursed her lips. "It was honest... This work I have created for all of you. It's not honest. It's not decent... *Babo* would be disappointed in me. He would hate this legacy."

"*Ay, Mamička*! It is honest. We aren't forcing these men. They are happy to pay for us!" Ma chirped. The eternally happy hooker.

Rosa smiled at her favourite granddaughter and carried on. "So I gave birth to Otto and we carried on travelling and being happy. Then my *engel* came to me! My Vera!" She clasped her hands and smiled her toothless, wide smile at Vera. Vera snatched the air and held it to both temples and smiled back.

"Otto was still small when I had Vera. *Babo* had got me married to a man who had a good business making sauerkraut. Gregor. He was a good man but useless at night. His workers were young and healthy. Vera was born when I was 13. I started bleeding that year before I was pregnant with Vera. I never bled before Otto was born." Rosa sat repeating facts and opinions as if we were no longer there and she was retracing her steps through life.

"Gregor threw me out when Vera started walking. Everybody knew Vera wasn't his. *Ay*, I'm not sure which one it was but one of his workers did a good job because my Vera was a beautiful baby. Because of her I met Karl. Karl loved Vera – he let us live with him that same week. *Babo* hated Karl, but there wasn't enough space for me, Otto and Vera. Karl didn't mind – he took care of us. But he loved to drink. He could drink more than *Babo*. So we never had a lot of money. I would clean but it wasn't enough. I would wash clothes. But it wasn't helping. He asked me to help his friend for some money, so I said okay. I didn't know what help he wanted." Rosa stopped and bit her bottom lip. "I found out that night."

I didn't like where this was going, but nobody else said anything and I didn't want to prove I was too young to be part of this conversation, so I kept quiet.

"We made enough money to eat. To live. So I carried on helping his friends and he carried on feeding my babies. I never let Vera and Otto sleep in the room with him. A man forgets

who his sister is and who his wife is when he drinks. I made sure
Vera and Otto were playing in the corner when I was working.
I could watch them from the bed. Then I got pregnant again. I
was 16, I think. Vera was three and Otto was four. Karl let me
stop working when I gave birth. The baby died. I never named
it. Why waste a name?"

I didn't like that. All we had in Drovane were our names.
But this little baby didn't even have that.

"Anyway, Karl drank himself to death. I was 22. *Babo* came
to me again. *Daj* and my two sisters were killed years before by a
group of men who set fire to the wagon. *Babo* and my brothers
were out trying to find food. They came back to ashes. When
Babo came to me, two of my brothers had wives of their own and
children. My youngest brother Adolar didn't want a woman. He
loved wearing my scarves. He was strange but happy. So, what
can you do? *Daj* would have found him disgusting but *Babo* didn't
really care. He'd say that 'all we can hope for is happiness'. So, it
was me, *Babo*, Otto, Vera and Adolar. Then came… I never saw
them…" Rosa started breathing hard.

"Never again." Vera finished sadly.

"OTTO! ADOLAR! *BABO!*" Rosa suddenly shrieked, and
half of the room jumped. She wept and banged her chest.
"OTTO! ADOLAR! *BABO! BABO! BABO! BABO!*" Sveta
grabbed her and held her to her chest as Rosa kept screaming
for her father. I backed away into Auntie Letti's chest. Ma kept
her eyes on Rosa but patted my knee.

Rosa was subdued for a few minutes, then shook her head and sat up. "We were eating when we first heard screaming. A man had run past and banged on every window he could, screaming, 'RUN, THEY'RE HERE!' I had been ill that week and didn't know what was happening. All I saw was *Babo's* eyes, and then I pulled Vera with me, he pulled Otto, and we ran. We got separated pretty quickly – all I heard was *Babo* telling me to run. So, I did. I ran and ran with Vera. Vera, do you remember?"

Vera was motionless. "Yes, *Mamička*. We ran right into their arms. My hair still hurts to this day, the way they dragged us." She turned to us, "They punched her so many times because she wouldn't let go of my hand. Then finally one of them shoved their knee into her and she fell. *Mamička*, why didn't you just let go?"

"Would you let go of Letti? Masha? Šukar? Mala? Lenka? Who would you let go of?" Rosa smiled. "It's impossible. I wish I'd taken Otto. But then I think maybe I should have left you with *Babo* too. I never saw Otto again. He must have been killed instantly. He didn't suffer." The words "I hope" lingered in the air.

"What was it like in those places?" Tactless Senni strikes again. I heard the slap that I half-hoped for. Senni was Auntie Šukar's oldest daughter, and had a habit of never reading the emotional vibe of a room. She was infamous for asking inappropriate questions and pushing on with a conversation when someone was clearly not willing. Although half the time she was only doing what the rest of us had too much manners to do.

Rosa looked at Senni for a few seconds before spitting on the floor. "Hell. It was hell. No, it was worse than hell. In hell, you'd know why you were there. You'd know what you'd done. Yes, I had a baby before I was married. Yes, I cheated on a dried-up old man. So what? I deserved to be treated that way?" She was asking herself these questions, it seemed. Like she was searching for something that justified being treated so wretchedly. "If I deserved it, what did Vera do? She was what? Nine?"

"Ten, *Mamička*," Vera mumbled.

"She was ten. What can a ten-year-old do to deserve that?"

"Deserve what?! Tell us!" There goes Senni again.

"Your fucking mouth!" Auntie Šukar was getting annoyed.

"I just want to know what happened." Senni was persistent.

Rosa held her hand up to Auntie Šukar as she rolled up her sleeve, probably to slap Senni back to Rosa's youth to apologise.

"What happened there was why you never trust white people. Because there is something wrong with them... What they managed to dream up to torture us with isn't normal, Senni. It's not human. They are... just... it isn't normal. I remember parts of my time there. I've spent 50 years trying to forget. Now you want me to tell you... There was a guard there who loved the little girls, the ones who looked frail and the ones who would jump at the slightest sound. He would say filthy things to them in front of all of us. He'd tell them what he was going to do to them. He said he loved to hear the sound their young bones would make when he'd play with them. One of his favourite girls went insane. She eventually came back and she'd sit there stuffing her sleeve in her mouth. Just sat there, putting fistful after fistful of fabric in her mouth staring straight ahead. Nobody cared. I didn't. I was just grateful it wasn't Vera. You couldn't let yourself care too much about the others. I only had enough tears for myself and Vera. You know, some of the others would spy on us and tell the guards if we even turned our head the wrong way. Bastards."

I was stunned. This was too much. Simple as I was, I only understood half of what was implied. It was only as I got older that I fully grasped the horror of what Rosa told us.

"Let me show you something." Rosa pulled up her tunic to reveal a long, gnarled gash on the side of her torso. There were a few gasps and Ma tapped my knee again. "They hated us enough to lock us up and treat us worse than animals. But they admired us enough to perform experiments on us. There was a man, he looked like that thing Eliska and Jani found at the neighbours'." She cackled.

She was referring to the broken garden gnome we found at "the neighbours'", which was the affectionate name we gave to the oozing landfill. The face was cracked, which gave the gnome's eye a leaking effect, like it was slipping downward.

"He was obsessed with twins. People would pretend to be twins because they thought it would make life easier. Me and another woman pretended to be twins, stupid idea. We looked similar and had the same birthmark. I have this here," she pointed to a black beauty mark by her lip, "and she had one by her eye. That was enough, I suppose. Stupid idea." Rosa fell silent again.

I kind of wanted Senni to ask what had happened, but the room was silent. It was a few minutes before Rosa spoke again.

"They injected something in me. It felt cold, I could feel it moving in me. I could see *Daj*. I was back in our wagon. *Daj* was angry at *Babo* and he was trying to make up with her. He was nudging her, saying, 'I haven't killed nobody, why are you punishing me?' *Daj* smiled. Then turned to me and my sisters and told us she loved us. I felt hot pain in my side, I couldn't move, Vera! The men were talking about my bones, I think. They were laughing. I was thinking about you, Vera. I thought about Karl and whether he ever touched you. The other woman, *ay* what was her name, she was whimpering. Like a little puppy. Then one of the men rushed over to her and the noise stopped. I felt them zipping up the hole they cut in my side. I was back with *Daj*. She told me she loved me."

Vera inhaled a ragged breath. Rosa was so fragile in this moment. Lying back against the wall, her eyes looked tired. "*Mamička*, Karl never touched me. You kept me so safe."

"Safe? Vera. Slitting your throat as soon as that man banged on our windows warning us, would have been keeping you safe."

"*Mamička*! As if you could, you could barely cut vegetables without hacking off your own skin." Vera started to chuckle; the rest of the room followed suit. It was the first time we'd laughed since Rosa had started her tale. It was pitch black outside and one of the women above us banged the ceiling. The laughter died down and once again we were perched eagerly, awaiting Rosa's next line.

"Oh, my sweet girls. I am grateful to my simple mind that I have forgotten everyday life there. I just can't forget the feeling. The feeling that any time, any place, something evil would happen. It was evil. Evil place. They would piss on us. Some of them would piss on us. Vera, do you remember the way one of them would grab your feet and the other would piss on you. It'd go into our mouths, our ears and our eyes. If you'd try to wipe your face, they'd hit you. A few times they'd shove themselves in our mouths and then piss... Evil place." Rosa spat on the floor again.

"How did you end up in Drovane?" Senni was back at it.

"Ask Vera. She dragged me here. I don't remember anything until the day she was pushing out Letti." Everyone turned toward Vera.

"There was a group of Bulgarian Jews who told us about places in Bulgaria that were safe for Jews and that we'd be accepted there too. So we went to Bulgaria. Which ended up being Slovakia."

"What?" About three different people spoke together.

"We got lost. We ended up joining a group of Gypsies that came to Slovakia. We came with them. They left Drovane or died, it's been so long. Drovane wasn't so bad at first, these blocks weren't built. There were little houses and about two families in each house. It was a close community. We helped each other. When I was pregnant with Lenka, that was when the government ripped down our homes and pushed us into these blocks. Senni, that's why your ma and your aunties except for Lenka are nicer and have more shame. Lenka was raised in Drovane and is Drovane. She is the degradation and harsh life we've had ever since."

Vera was blunt. She was also right. There was a stark difference between my aunties and Ma.

"We had no jobs because, well you know why. The fucking doctors here don't even let us in if we're bleeding to death. They'd more likely send your next of kin the clean-up bill."

"Bullets are cheaper. Save more dignity too," chimed in Auntie Letti.

"There was only one way that *Mamička* knew how to make fast money. We did it. Nobody has enough of sex." Vera smiled at Rosa.

"We weren't even good at that. Look at all the fucking kids!" Repeating herself, Rosa was the first to snort with laughter as the rest of us joined in.

Something amazing happened that night: Rosa looked younger. She had shared all the hurt and bile that was rotting in her heart, and it took the roughness away from her. Since that day, she started talking more about her experiences and then, in true Gypsy fashion, began to make the most outrageous jokes. For many Gypsy women, humour is a form of self-healing.

The first few times my cousins and I had tried to cook sausage on a roughly constructed grill over an open flame, failing spectacularly, Rosa threw her head back and squealed with laughter. Banging her hands on her thighs and taking a deep puff on her cigarette, she exclaimed, "IT SMELLS LIKE THE BURNING GYPSIES AND JEWS HERE NOW! *AY DEVLA*! I THOUGHT I'D LEFT THE CAMP." We stared at her with our jaws dropped open and eyes wide in shock, which only made her laugh harder. "I THINK THEY SMELT BETTER! YOU IDIOTS WILL STARVE YOUR HUSBANDS TO DEATH!"

That night was bizarre for a number of reasons: finally hearing Rosa and Vera's story, sitting in one room that long without arguing, and witnessing the human side of Vera.

Vera Zlatkov was a formidable woman. While Rosa started the Zlatkov vagina merchantry, it was Vera who honed it. Rosa only allowed my aunties to work once they'd started their periods. But within weeks of Rosa succumbing to age and preferring to spend her days praying and sleeping, allowing Vera to take over, most of my cousins were on the streets working. Vera thought waiting years for periods to start was a waste of time and earning potential. Jani and I were the only ones who didn't get slung onto the streets as soon as we were able. In Jani's case, she had a weird vagina. She had trouble pissing all the time; she'd end up on the floor pissing and crying because it would burn her so much. As we were inseparable, being the same age and all, I'd hold her hand as she pissed over the both of us. Then she'd end up with an angry red rash all over the insides of her thighs. I was kept off the streets due to the threat of reprisals from my father and, perhaps more importantly, my failing of Vera's special classes.

Vera had opened the Zlatkov School of Hoecraft and Hookery before I was born. She put her daughters through it, then my older cousins, and then she tried to put Sveta, Jani and me through it.

We'd gather at her feet, listening to all the tricks to use to squeeze every drop and penny out of a man, so they'd continue to use the Zlatkov girls. From two-hands to no-hands to sticking fingers in uncharted territory, we were disgusted and fascinated at the end of these classes.

After the theory, Vera would make us do the practical. She'd gather a bunch of bananas, and one by one we'd be on our knees shoving the banana in our mouths and seeing how far the banana could go down our throats before we gagged. Sveta managed to train herself not to gag until her eyes were streaming. Jani looked like a professional sword swallower and I – I had the Virgin Mary's throat, apparently. Even thinking of the banana curriculum my grandma delivered made me heave. Out of all the Zlatkov girls, I was the worst in those creepy classes. I would go forth with such determination to tickle my lungs with the tip of the damn banana, but each time it went the same way: I'd end up wetting myself and then crying wide-mouthed with no sound. Vera had zero fucks to give, and would instead berate me for opening my mouth so wide after I had already wasted all the bananas.

Eventually Vera had enough of me and told me I was a useless waste of light skin and bananas, and threw me out. It's still a sore spot for Ma that I was slung out of Hoe School. When it happened, she swore at me and choked me, telling me I was born with a tight throat and a loose pussy.

I found out that Sveta had been able to move on to preparing other places of herself for men with filthier appetites. I do not and never want to know exactly what the hell Jani meant when she told me that. Jani had been kicked out of Hoe School a couple of weeks after me when her piss-rash was discovered. I think we both got lucky. Sveta began working on the streets as soon as she graduated from Vera's school.

Vera was always like the grandfather of our family, in the sense that she was the stricter one, the one we were threatened with as punishment.

Her favourite pastime was grumbling about food or the lack of it. During one of their infamous blazing rows, Ma had confronted Vera about her constant niggling. "YOU COULD GO AND CLEAN. IF YOU TRIED WORKING, YOU'D KNOW IT'S NOT FUCKING EASY! THERE ARE WOMEN WORKING UNTIL THEY DIE ALL OVER DROVANE! BUT YOU'RE SAT UP HERE LIKE YOU'RE A FUCKING PRINCESS. YOU EAT LAST FROM NOW ON. YOU. EAT. LAST. YOU DON'T FUCKING WORK!"

Ma's eyes were wild, and she was gesticulating madly. Vera sat perfectly still, save for her left leg, which was shaking violently.

"Finished?" Vera asked.

"YOU ARE. YOU'RE FINISHED. YOU ONLY EAT BECAUSE WE FUCKING LET YOU! YOU WOULDN'T LAST—" Ma stopped as soon as Vera lunged for her. There was hair flying, faces being slapped, Vera's hands around Ma's throat and Ma's hands entangled in Vera's hair. During the scuffle, Vera's top had managed to tear and expose her breast. They both stopped and started laughing hysterically.

"She wanted to join in," Rosa chuckled, pointing at Vera's tit as we sat on her mattress watching Vera and Ma fixing each other's hair and praising each other on their fighting skills. Within five minutes they'd gone from trying to rip the other's eyes out to marvelling at the scratches all over their arms and faces.

Vera walked over to our mattress and pushed me off with her foot.

"When are you going to earn your bread? This isn't a church. We don't keep for free," she barked. I tried to think of something to say whilst Rosa cackled but Ma spoke before I could.

"Leave her. I'm saving her. I'm not wasting her for a few pennies. I'll get more for her." Ma motioned to me to leave the room while Vera carried on griping about me.

Vera was gratuitously stern. Half the time we wondered if she genuinely hated all of us. The way she'd treat us was insane. The only one who got gentler treatment was Auntie

Letti. Vera's oldest daughter, Letti was level-headed, maternal and affectionate. She made the least money because she didn't really have what it took to be the brazen hooker the rest of the Zlatkovs were, but somehow Vera didn't mind. Vera would consult her over everything, and only Auntie Letti could make Vera second-guess a decision. Auntie Letti had saved Ma's life from Vera and her battered old penknife a number of times. Vera would lunge at teenage Lenka with such ferocity that Letti had an untold number of scars all over her forearms. I enjoyed the stories behind her scars because it warmed me knowing someone loved Ma enough to sacrifice themselves for her. I'd wonder if Ma would do the same, then laugh hysterically at the notion of Ma doing anything that wasn't going to benefit her.

SECRET
SISTERHOODS

Auntie Letti was mother to Marija, Kashe (my imprisoned cous-
in/brother), Ansha and Ima. Most of my aunties had a series
of miscarriages and abortions. In a few harrowing incidents,
Vera had been the engineer of the miscarriages and abortions.
Marija was to us what Letti was to our mothers. She was the
level-headed one who made the important decisions on our
behalf. Granted, nobody really gave a shit about our opinions,
but on the rare occasions we had a say in a matter, it was Marija
who would guide us. Kashe was dragged off by the police after
a known racist had been brutally beaten minutes away from
the entryway to Drovane. By all accounts, Kashe was definitely
responsible for the Nazi-beating. I'm indifferent towards him:
he did something bad, but then a Nazi minutes from Drovane
isn't good for anyone involved. Ansha was a self-important cow,
and she and Ima would meddle in everyone's business. I wasn't
particularly close to Letti's children, because the age gap was
wide enough to knock us into separate interests. They were
an extension of my aunties, I felt. In Drovane life was already
very secret. We had our own Gypsy world in the midst of the

dirt, prejudice and oppression. Especially as children, it was important for us to create games, fun and laughter to counteract the doom and gloom. People like Ansha and Ima were hell-bent on currying favour with elder relatives, as they thought it meant more food, a larger share of the water, or life made a fraction easier. All it really did was make the Drovane children loathe the tale-telling shits. Anybody trying to police the fun we had or make an attempt on our harmless shenanigans was instantly an enemy forever. In an already bleak pit like Drovane we needed unity, not junior officers.

Directly under Auntie Letti was Auntie Masha. Despite working on the streets since her early teens, she had never been pregnant. Not once. No miscarriages, no abortions, she was just never pregnant. There was obviously something medically wrong with her, but the "No Gypsies" rule imposed by the medical facility near us, twinned with Vera's nonsensical insistence that Masha was just lazy, meant she remained undiagnosed. I got closer to Auntie Masha as I got older. I noticed she never really interacted with me or my cousins until we were no longer considered kids by her. There's always been an air around Masha; I'd believed she was a copy of her mother, all meanness and insults. But I realise now, it was sadness. She was sad. She didn't want to be near us because we reminded her of what she could never have. In Drovane she was deprived of basic human essentials such as food and water like the rest of us, but she was also denied something everyone else had: a family of her own. Something that people like Ma either didn't want or took for granted. She felt wronged to be born in a life like ours and then deprived of the flickers of joy that could have eased the pain.

Ma would never fail to use this against her when they argued. Masha had a special knack for "finding" makeup, and Ma had a special knack for "borrowing" Masha's makeup. This led to fierce arguments, all ending with Ma scoffing, "WHY DO YOU CARE? ARE YOU GOING TO PASS THEM ON TO YOUR CHILDREN WHEN YOU DIE?" and Masha falling silent with wild eyes. The day would end with Masha sat at Ma's feet whilst Ma would rub her head with oil.

My third auntie was Auntie Šukar. She was Senni's mother. Senni's big mouth was inherited directly from Šukar. The loudest one after Ma, Šukar would lean out of the glassless window of her room and yell down to any one of us to go run chores for her or to come upstairs and give her something from the next room. She was a tall, asparagus-looking woman with a straight silhouette until you reached her roughly cut hair. She used to keep it jutting out at random lengths. She had a very boyish body according to Vera, and according to Rosa that was why Šukar got the "weirdest men" paying for her. Vera would joke that Šukar was the first hooker with a "virgin pussy", as her clients seemed to prefer other entrances. She would only need to work a few days a week to earn the same amount as the others. Aside from Ma, Šukar was one of the better earners in our family. She was also renowned for morphing into a demonic entity each month when she had her "special week". Nobody would want to go near her when it was her period. Expensive sanitary towels weren't considered vital in Drovane, so she had "period rags" that were every bit as horrifying as they sound. These unsanitary towels were a pile of rags cut from worn-out clothes and old fabric and kept in a filthy box each month until they were needed. The uncomfortable wedge stuffed in her knickers and the excruciating pain rendered her unbearable until she'd shout out of the window, "SENNI, COME AND SEE YOUR MA." Then all Zlatkov shoulders would sink in relief.

Second to last of Vera's daughters was Mala. Auntie Mala. My precious Mala. She was mother to Sveta and Jani – my eternal playmate Jani, and Sveta who was always leading us in and out of mischief. Mala had Rosa's dimples and the best smile I've ever seen. Practically toothless, except for the handful of rotting teeth holding on for nostalgia, her dimples and gummy mouth gave her the look of an overgrown baby. You couldn't help but smile when you saw her stretch her lips to reveal her chessboard mouth. She was the one I slept with and she was the one who took the most notice of me. She'd make sure to rub a wet rag over me when she'd finished "bathing" Sveta and Jani. She was the one who found me sobbing and feeling sorry for myself when Ma had beaten me for being kicked out of Vera's Hoe School. She soothed me and sang folk songs to me while I picked out the knots in her hair. Mala's relationship with Vera was interesting. They barely spoke. Marija had told us that it was because Auntie Mala's father was the only one Vera loved. Auntie Mala was the one who christened Vera with the nickname *Lon*. Behind her back, of course. Due to the excessive dandruff that shook from Vera whenever she moved, Mala called her "Salt".

Then the last of Vera's daughters, Lenka. Ma. She revelled in being the youngest: it made her feel as though she could get away with anything. Rosa adored Lenka. She'd watch Ma with a mix of fascination and pride. Ma's unapologetic ways were impressive to Rosa. Vera wasn't quite as easily swayed, but she also found it hard to hold a grudge against her youngest daughter. Lenka could always be forgiven. Ma knew it and would demonstrate it regularly with her outrageous actions and vicious tongue.

Watching my aunties and their interactions with their mother used to make me grateful that Ma wasn't more like Vera. I've always known Ma's not the full pack of crayons, but whatever we have is much better than what any of the aunties had with Vera. While they were left at Vera's mercy in the cramped rooms we had hidden away in Drovane, I at least had other family that I connected with.

THE VOLKERS

DON'T WASTE
MY BLOOD

In stark contrast to the vibrant Zlatkovs were my father's family: the Volkers. Pure white Germans. Well, apart from me.

My father, Franz Volker, was and remains as dirty-dicked as my conception implies. He was 23 when his friends paid for 13-year-old Lenka as a birthday present for him. Ma admits she'd lie about her age whenever she was asked. She claimed white men never could tell if a brown woman is too young or just naturally youthful-looking. Dad has always maintained that if he'd known she was 13, he'd never have gone near her. Who knows? He currently has five children by five different women, and has cheated on every woman dumb enough to be with him.

Despite living with Ma the majority of my childhood, I've always had more to say about my dad. One of my earliest memories of Dad was looking up at his eyes and crying. His eyes were a rich, deep blue. I was used to the brown eyes of the Zlatkovs and the other Gypsies in Drovane. To this day, his eyes make me feel uncomfortable. It's not the colour of them, it's the coldness.

To anyone who didn't know Franz, he was a gorgeous-looking man. He still is. I can concede that; he is very striking indeed. He's always towered over me at six foot (something I disliked intensely: I too could have been tall, but instead I took after the short Zlatkovs). Full, healthy hair that he usually wore Young Stalin style, unless there was some racist meddlin' he needed to do with his friends; then it was shaved and/or bleached for extra Aryan effect. He had a chiselled bone structure to match his carved physique, and a mean scowl that was his face's natural shape.

To anyone who did know Franz, he was gruesome. A violent nutcase who should have been in prison, but — thanks to friends in high places and a talent for intimidation — was instead free to roam the world, inflicting his hate on whomever he wished.

He made the vast majority of his wealth illegally. From a young teen, he'd been competing in underground prize-fights in East Germany. He would earn money from the organisers of the fight, just pennies to start with. I mean, nobody was going to pay a 13-year-old a fair price, but after he'd proven himself as a fighter with a natural flair for beating a man into an unrecognisable mess, he was taken under the wing of Felix Strauch.

Franz didn't have the most stable of childhoods: the Volkers have never been short of money, but they've long been short on humanity. They had a long military history of which they were immensely proud, and my grandfather, Sikke Volker, worked hard to maintain the ideals of the Nazi regime he held dear. Growing up in the seventies, Franz was all too aware of the impact the

Nazis had on the world but, like his own father, he refused to feel shame or guilt. Sikke ensured his son knew that as White German men, they were the ideal. The world may have wanted them to feel shame at what had been done to create a race of men just like Sikke and Franz, but they would not. They would be proud of their race, their heritage, and the display of strength the Nazis had shown to the rest of the world. This is what *Opa* would babble out whenever he was drunk or feeling extra-feisty.

Dad would say the same stuff whenever I asked him about why he did what he did. He grew up with Sikke teaching him how to draw swastikas and other Nazi symbolism, then burning the papers when they were finished. The way Hitler and the Nazi rule were explained to Dad was in Sikke's delusional, brainwashed, fantastical terms. According to Dad, Hitler was a man pushed too far by "others" forcing him out of his own land and hoarding wealth whilst white people starved. All Hitler wanted to do was liberate white people, reclaim their land, and stop "others" from taking over white countries. The Camps were necessary; it would have been whites in the camps unless Hitler got there first. Then Dad would usually veer off onto the state of multiculturalism in Europe, how it was getting worse each day and white concentration camps would soon be a reality. For someone who was so astute in other ways, Dad was surprisingly gullible when it came to his father's version of history.

Because of the nationalist views in the home, my grandparents only mixed with people who thought the same way.

Being branded a "Nazi sympathiser" was dangerous, so my grandparents' circle was small. Dad never interacted with kids his own age, and spent most of his time being trained by Sikke and being guided into the grip of bigotry. By the time of his first fight, Dad was already a fully-fledged racist psychopath.

His first fight was in the middle of the night, in the front room of a carpenter's house, against a 15-year-old boy who had been fighting for a year already. It was over in minutes; Dad had won, though not without eating a few punches. My grandmother told me how Sikke stormed into the house afterwards and went straight upstairs. Franz followed a few minutes later and sat next to her in the kitchen.

"I won."

Oma said she had to repeat the two words to herself, because Dad's manner didn't match what he'd said. They sat in silence, waiting for Sikke to come downstairs. Eventually they heard him stomp into the living room, barking for my dad. *Oma* says Dad faltered for a second, then strode inside. She followed. Sikke was standing with a bag of weights at his feet.

"You embarrassed me. Letting him fucking hit you. Pick up those two plates, hold them out until I say so. If you put your arms down or say one word, I'll smash them in your face".

According to *Oma*, Dad didn't say a word; he just picked up the plates. He held them out and maintained eye contact with *Opa*. There was sweat pouring off him, his arms were shaking, and his left leg dipped slightly before *Opa* flicked his hand at Dad.

"He didn't drop them straight away, he slowly bent down and put them on the floor and stood back up, staring at your *Opa*. Franz was always strong-willed. Even then." *Oma* always sounded impressed when she'd tell me of Dad's resistance to authority.

My *Oma* was from a wealthy background. She was the most tolerable in the family, and hadn't been so keen to champion Hitler as her husband. Mathilde Volker had been bullied by Sikke Volker all her life: whatever he said was law. She'd gone from enjoying a healthy relationship with her father and watching her mother have an equal place in their household to sitting in the kitchen until her husband wanted another beer. Then she would pour it for him and be banished to sit in the kitchen again.

When my dad was born, it was worse. Mathilde didn't work much, as she suffered from arthritis and sciatica after the birth, and *Opa* would reward Dad for telling him what she got up to each day. Dad figured out that if he had something to report to his father then he got a treat; if he didn't, then no treat. So Dad started making up lies to get his father's approval, and whatever bottle of drink or sweet was offered to him. Mathilde told me herself that Dad would threaten to tell Sikke about her "secret boyfriend" unless he got his own way during the day. Dad would sit with his treat as Sikke beat Mathilde in the bedroom. Dad himself began hitting Mathilde when he was eight years old, after *Opa* invited him to the bedroom because Mathilde had accused him of lying.

"He had his father's fists." Telling me this, with a proud smile on her face, she looked almost deranged.

The next fight saw Dad rearrange an 18-year-old's face. That night *Opa* let Dad drink beer with him in the front room as they sang patriotic songs. It was Dad's fourth or fifth fight when Felix Strauch sought him out. Dad and *Opa* were sharing a drink with some happy gamblers when Felix appeared. That's how Sikke described it: "appeared", as though he materialised from the shadows like some suave Al Pacino-style gangster, instead of a chubby, short middle-aged man stuffed in a tight suit.

Felix Strauch was universally known as being untouchable in my grandparents' community. He was described in the vaguest of terms as a "businessman", whatever that meant. All that was clear was that he was an anomaly. In the GDR, Felix was somehow thriving. There'd be jokes that Erich Honecker, the East German Head of State, called Felix for advice or for a ride. Felix had a car. In the GDR, it was nigh-on impossible to get a car within a decade of first hoping for one. Felix was respected by some, feared by some, and low-key hated by all. But he had power and possessions, so nobody was going to make their disdain known.

Felix admired my dad's fighting skills and asked him if he wanted to make real money. *Opa* answered for him: "Who doesn't?"

I met Felix a handful of times as a young girl. He gave me a pink headband with embroidered roses. I couldn't imagine him doing the things he'd done when I saw him; I know he was older, but he looked so... pathetic. Dressed in an old sports jumper and jogging bottoms that barely contained his huge belly, he looked more likely to damage the pantry than another human. Especially my psychotic father.

Dad had been driven by Felix all over East Germany to fight in bigger rooms, with more notable members of society in attendance. Dad rarely lost, and when he did Felix would be easier on him than *Opa* was. *Opa* would punish Dad in the most sadistic ways. It went from holding the plates to lifting weights naked outside in the unforgiving weather to whipping him with a heavy belt and trying to choke him with the belt if Dad yelled out.

Through Felix, my granddad connected with more people who were interested in preserving the ideology of Hitler. I wasn't as surprised as I perhaps should have been to know how many people in positions of power held the same beliefs. Corruption and undercover racism were always a part of my life: the jagged scars on my neck awarded to me as a child by an over-zealous policeman during a nonsensical raid on Drovane can attest to that.

Some of the men who followed each fight in East Germany had been having whispered discussions about forming a type of club that could keep track of the "outsiders" in their little world. They wanted to know who didn't belong in glorious Germany. Then they wanted to let those people know they didn't belong. There was plenty of Russian influence growing up in the Volker household. Russian food, cultural habits and even language seeped into the Volker home. Dad learnt the German-Russian fusion that Sikke spoke, and used it to communicate with other members of the "We Are Totally Not Nazi-Sympathisers, We Just Like to Gather and Discuss the Extermination – Oh, Sorry, Integration – Of Races" group. There were only a few "low-level" men willing to speak about it. The paranoia was intense, by all accounts. Nobody knew who was Stasi, and many people preferred to keep their views to themselves. From what I've been able to gather, it was a small group of drunk white men with nothing better to do.

The important "higher-ups" in Felix Strauch's world rarely had anything to do with the other racists, outside of the meticulously organised fights.

The plans rarely came to fruition. However, Dad was pulled deeper and deeper into that world.

Dad continued fighting for most of his teens. He trained as a mechanic alongside Felix's brother as a respectable cover for the illicit bare-knuckle fighting. He rarely went to school. *Oma* would tell me that Franz never got on with people who told him what to do. In the day care centres that he was sent to when he was younger, he'd always get spanked for misbehaving and sometimes have his lunch confiscated by the staff.

"School was not for him – it is not for everyone," she'd say.

It was whilst working at the garage that Dad met Felix's niece, Vilma Strauch. Dad first met her when he was 14 and she was 24; he described her as a miserable woman with a bad acne problem. He never found her attractive, and hated it whenever she came to see her father, Felix's brother, at the garage. As the years progressed, her acne cleared up a little, and as her Uncle Felix took care of them, she was eating more.

Almost clear-skinned and with a cushiony body, she was suddenly more appealing to Dad. She was 28 and Dad was 18 when she got pregnant. Dad told me with glee how he had sex with her in one of the cars, and went to get her a towel to clean up but left instead, as he saw Felix and his brother pull up at the garage. They caught her waiting for Dad in the car.

"What did Felix do?!"

"Nothing. I was fighting every other week. I had money riding on me – he had people that he had to keep happy. It was only his niece."

He had been enabled all his life. From my grandparents to Felix, Dad had the same skill at manipulating people and escaping potentially dangerous situations unscathed as Ma.

Vilma was pregnant and pressuring Dad to marry her. He refused. My grandmother told her to "have some dignity and stop begging for marriage". How did they know it was even Franz's baby? If she could take advantage of a young boy like Franz, then who knows how many other men she'd slept with?

Felix arranged for his niece to get married to a young police officer who was in his pocket.

She gave birth to a healthy child at her father's house. The little girl was named Maike.

Dad had some semblance of a relationship with Maike, thanks to Vilma's infatuation with him and her willingness to accept him into her life whenever he showed up, regardless of his actions.

"Maike had the same look on her face as Vilma, that scowl. I waited until she was a year old until I saw her again, to see if she grew out of it," Dad explained. No love at first sight for this guy.

A year after Maike was born, a Russian divorcee caught Dad's eye. From all accounts, she was too polite and sweet for someone like Franz Volker. He wasn't good for anybody; he'd leave them broken. But like every other woman before her and after her, by the time she realised it she was already in love with him. A blonde woman with blue eyes and a skin tone that made her look like one of Hitler's visions of the master race, Ana had been left with a small inheritance from her husband's death. Not many people knew, but Dad did.

He married Ana in 1989 and had a peaceful two months with her. Long enough to squirrel away the lion's share of her inheritance. Within a year, he'd impregnated a receptionist who'd never known danger like Franz. Ana forgave him, but agreed to live in separate homes on Dad's request. She stayed in her parents' house and Dad lived alone. During the day, at least.

The receptionist's name was Bettina Metzger. She was a quiet lady who lived with her parents and kept herself to herself. At 26,

Bettina hadn't been married before or had a boyfriend. She was painfully shy, and preferred to sit at home with her parents instead of partying like Franz. She was older than Dad by five years, but he was light years ahead of her in terms of life experiences. They met where she worked, and Dad waited for her to finish her shift before turning on the Volker charm.

Bettina told me she was sure he wasn't serious – "He was so attractive and had a car. I wasn't attractive and had elderly parents to care for". Nevertheless, within the month they'd slept together, and she found out she was pregnant.

She gave birth in 1990 to a lovely blue-eyed baby, Anja. Bettina and Anja lived with Bettina's parents, and Dad would visit as rarely as he visited Maike.

Bettina didn't find out about Vilma and Maike, or Dad's wife, until Anja was a year old. Dad was in Slovakia, but my grandparents had kept in touch with both of his daughters in Germany. They invited Bettina for dinner and invited Vilma, too. Their intention was just to see their granddaughters; they hadn't even thought about whether or not the two women knew of each other.

Bettina arrived at my grandparents' home to find Vilma in the kitchen with *Oma*, and Maike being ignored by *Opa* in the living room. Instead of a Jerry Springer-esque uproar, it was a teary affair for all involved. They remained friends, Vilma and Bettina; they became the other parent for each other's daughters whilst Dad was in Slovakia.

Dad came to Slovakia with Felix in the nineties. Felix had been making contacts all over eastern Europe since the fall of the Berlin Wall. He took Dad along with him on Dad's insistence; Felix had been haemorrhaging power and control since the wall came down. He wasn't as intimidating as he used to be. The small measure of threat he held, he exercised as often as he could. But he wanted a fresh start elsewhere. He'd tried Poland in 1990, but they already had their own organisations; he'd managed to arrange a few fights there for Dad and a handful of other men who were still loyal, but it only served to make the fighters respected and welcomed, rather than Felix. Dad was asked along to many underground meetings involving nationalists, and he quickly made friends. Dad and Felix were growing further and further apart.

Moving on to Slovakia and setting up white pride groups couldn't have been easier, according to Dad. They had enough hatred, just not enough organisation. So when Felix and the few associates he had in Slovakia joined forces, they created their own personal band of racists. They'd raid the homes of non-whites and terrorise the Romani families living around them.

Eventually a Romani man decided enough was enough and slung a rock in one racist's face, catching him in the eye. A brawl erupted. The police were called: Dad said they watched for a few moments, until the Gypsies overpowered the whites, before moving in. In the confusion, Dad swung at one of the policemen, earning himself an arrest and subsequent time in a

Slovak prison. It was only a matter of weeks, but the prison time netted Dad even more praise from his fellow fascists.

In the few weeks that Dad was imprisoned, though, Felix all but abandoned him, heading back to Germany without him. So, on his release, Dad moved in with a few of the men in the east Slovakian group. Near Drovane. Near a family of prostitutes – the Zlatkovs.

Lenka was 13 and working the streets when "a car full of ugly, bald white men came shouting through the streets". They'd seen her and beckoned her over. She told me that she was driven to their home and, after giving them oral sex, she was sent to a bedroom. After ten minutes, they'd led in Franz with his eyes closed. They were cheering and yelling things, but Ma told me she wasn't bothered what they were saying. "All I could think about was him. He was so sexy, Eliska! It was probably the first time I really looked forward to sleeping with a white man. His skin wasn't lumpy like the others, and he looked clean."

They had their moment.

When Ma was a couple of months pregnant with me, Dad went back to Germany to visit his parents and spend a few hours with Maike and Anja. Vilma had been taken in by her uncle Felix after her father had been murdered – possibly due to her precious uncle Felix's dodgy business dealings – and her husband had unceremoniously packed up and left whilst she was visiting her mother. To say she'd fallen on hard times was an understatement.

Dad visiting was the highlight of Vilma's year. She'd been at home with her cousin Heidi Strauch, Felix's daughter. Dad and Felix had had little interaction since his release. Never one to let a disloyalty slide, I'm convinced Felix's desertion during Dad's imprisonment was in the back of Dad's mind when he slept with Heidi that day.

Heidi was 25 and lazy. She'd been in limbo since Felix lost his influence. She wasn't as popular or adored as she had once been. With Vilma downstairs tending to a bratty Maike, Heidi and Dad conceived my brother, Arne.

"Vilma knew what happened – she was sat downstairs crying, but what was she going to do? Hit Heidi? She'd be kicked out. Hit me? I'd have broken her jaw. I kissed Maike goodbye and left. She still had that scowl of Vilma's. Ugly child."

Vilma moved away from East Germany before I was born. Heidi never heard from her again, even though Felix maintained contact with Vilma and Maike and sent them money regularly. Maike eventually went away to Russia after marrying a Russian man at 18. From the contact we've had from her via Arne, she's had a happy life over there.

Felix was infuriated to find out Dad had impregnated his daughter, but what could he do? He was well into his fifties and Dad had barely hit his mid-twenties. Felix was done, and Dad knew it. He didn't have to do anything but let nature take its course. Nobody trusted Felix anymore, and the intimidation he'd used to control so many had been turned against him. Grown sons wanted to return the favour after their parents told them of the ways Felix made a hard life harder. Felix moved away to Stuttgart, taking Heidi with him and leaving Arne behind with relatives.

During Lenka's pregnancy, she heard nothing from Franz and continued working. It was when I was due to be born that she found out he was back in prison. Some of the other prostitutes had been back to the house the men had been staying in to do some "investigating" for Lenka. She had assured them that nobody else had been allowed to finish in her, but "he was too good for me to stop him".

Lenka and Vera travelled to the prison, which unfortunately was known only too well to Drovane, as half the men were rotting inside its walls. They waited there to try and see Franz, but were inevitably turned away. They received news that on the latest trip to the house, one of the prostitutes had come face to face with Franz's mother, my grandmother. Vera apparently cackled and told Lenka that their days of working in the alleys were over.

The first meeting between Mathilde Volker and Vera Zlatkov went as Vera expected, by all accounts. My polished, pristine German grandma was scared shitless by my beautiful, bold and unashamed Gypsy grandma. All Lenka needed to do was sit there, heavily pregnant. *Oma* told me how she was so frightened that she didn't question what Vera was saying – she agreed with her just to get her out of their house. I always roll my eyes at this; I knew *Oma* had been bullied into submission by my grandfather all her life, but she wasn't as fearful as she made out. I suspect she knew Dad was the father, due to his reckless fathering habits in Germany. She told Vera she would speak to Dad when she next visited him.

"I didn't fucking believe your mother," Dad told me. "It's obvious why she wanted to pin the baby, you, on me. Look at me. I had money, too. She—" During this modest speech, I interrupted him and asked how the hell Ma could have known he had money? They hardly had a conversation, she hadn't said "show me your bank accounts".

"I look like I have money, Eliska."

Oh, okay then.

"I told your *Oma* that if she had any contact with Vera or Lenka again, I'd beat the shit out of her first and the other two after."

"Did she listen?"

"No, she carried on meeting them. She's always had a soft spot for Lenka. She believes all the 'it's not their fault the way they live' bullshit."

I ignored him: explaining to a rich, white man about the plight of the Gypsies was a futile effort.

"She was supposed to meet them the day you were born."

I knew how I was born. In Drovane, with Vera and Rosa easing me into the world and Ma half pissed on vodka and plum brandy to numb the pain.

Ma was so disgusted with me causing her so much pain that she refused to hold me for a fortnight, so Vera took me to meet Mathilde.

"I knew you were his straight away, *liebchen*!" Mathilde told me. "You both had the same lopsided face when you were born!"

Thanks.

"He had a mean face, but his face did the same thing as yours, it was like someone was pulling your lips upwards."

I got the message the first time.

Despite her lack of backbone her entire marriage, she sprang into action when forcing Dad to see me. Neither one of them tells me what she said or did to make him begin those frosty trips to Drovane, but she got her own way.

Without her I would have been another fatherless Zlatkov child.

He returned a handful of times to visit Arne at my grandparents' house, but that stopped when we were both around ten.

Arne was left behind with an auntie, a cousin of Heidi who couldn't have children. She and her husband moved to the Black Forest and have taken care of Arne ever since.

I'd always had a good relationship with my siblings; they'd come and visit me with Dad sometimes. But the moment Dad started taking me to Germany, with the help of Maike's baby passport, lax border control or bribery (who knows?), and sometimes stuffing me in a trunk until it was safe enough for me to sit in the front seat, my relationship with Anja and Arne truly flourished.

Flawed as we all were – what with Anja's refusal to speak up for herself against Dad lest he cut her off, Arne's laziness to do anything but wander aimlessly around Berlin and the Black

Forest, and my Drovane-induced feral behaviour – we loved each other fiercely.

Dad spent his years setting up garages all over Germany, fighting on occasion when the price was right and participating in right-wing racist groups across Europe. He had girlfriend after girlfriend after girlfriend, and was faithful to none of them. More times than I can count, Anja, me and Arne would be in our room playing when we would hear Dad and whichever woman he was seeing that week having loud sex. To begin with we were horrified, jamming our fingers in our ears, but after a while just lazily knocked the door shut and turned up the television.

Even in our twenties it continues. We start daring each other to knock on the door and tell him to shut up. Which Arne tried once, and ended up being boxed round the ears.

One girlfriend as resilient as the long-forgotten Ana was a Russian woman called Mischka. She had been holding on to Dad since she was 26 and Dad was 32. Mischka was a promising student from St Petersburg; her mother was Tatar and her father a Russian man. The two gave Mischka the same yellow-tinted skin as me, brown eyes and full lips.

Despite his white pride and long-standing views on "the master race", Dad has never been able to resist an ethnic-looking woman. Dad subjected Mischka to the same harshly dismissive behaviour he displayed to his other women. He spoke about her in the most vulgar manner and was as physically abusive as he was to every other woman in his life except Ma, but she refused to relent. She would be there every other month arguing with him, begging him to give up the other women, giving him ultimatums, and generally wasting her beauty and intellect on him.

Anja, Arne and I were dumbfounded as to why Mischka, who would read us poems and tell us about Russian literature and Tatar culture, would be chasing after Dad. He wasn't ugly to look at, but he was rotten inside. He had his own homes, business and money, so I guess that was all it took. She could have done so much better, and become so much more than Dad's back-up plan for when he couldn't be bothered to go outside to pick up women.

Because of this, the three of us were beyond disappointed to find out that Mischka was pregnant with Yulia. Dad told us one weekend when we were all in his large kitchen, playing Monopoly and eating our body weight in *Soljanka* (spicy Russian soup) and *Spezi* (basically cola and orange soda mixed together). Okay, it was just me doing the eating, but I didn't have access to this deliciousness all the time like the other two.

"Mischka is pregnant. You'll have another brother or sister soon," he said as he walked in. He busied himself with pouring a bowl of *Soljanka* from the pot I used to heat it. I didn't think I'd heard him properly, but when I saw Anja and Arne's faces, I was sure.

"What?!" Arne was the first to speak.

"Yes, she's having the baby in the next few weeks, probably." Dad was blasé.

"I thought you were with that other woman? The ballet one," Anja asked.

"Yeah. So?"

"So when did you get her pregnant?" Arne was determined to get answers.

"She said something about being pregnant when I told her to leave. I thought she was lying. She wasn't." He began eating his soup.

"Where has she been staying?" Arne pressed.

"Not with you, so why are you upset?" he laughed.

"Because she's... she... I don't get how you do this. You're in your forties, when are you going to stop?" Arne's tone was low.

"I'm *almost* in my forties, and so? It doesn't mean I stop working. I'll keep going until there's no women left. Even after that, Mischka will still be there. Even Bettina or even Heidi, remember her?" He was laughing as Arne's face soured at the mention of his biological mother who had nothing to do with him.

"Doesn't it bother you that—"

"YOU BRING ALL THESE KIDS INTO THE WORLD BUT YOU CAN'T BE A GOOD DAD TO EVEN ONE OF THEM!" Anja's shouting muted us all. Arne and I exchanged "what the fuck happened to her" expressions.

"Shut the fuck up." He looked bored as he watched his three children trying to take him to task.

"I'LL SHUT THE FUCK UP WHEN YOU STOP FUCKING WOMEN ALL OVER THE PLACE!" Anja was impressing me; I didn't know she had it in her. As she stood up, Arne and I followed suit.

"I'LL STOP FUCKING WOMEN WHEN YOU CAN PASS A FUCKING CLASS IN SCHOOL, YOU BRAIN-DEAD IDIOT!" He hit on Anja's sore spot. She wasn't thick, just lazy and used to Dad's money, so her schoolwork wasn't the best reflection of her intelligence. She hardly ever attended compulsory education. She'd eventually got enough grades to be granted access to a photography degree, in which she had just failed all of her end of semester exams. She looked visibly stung, and left the room with tears running down her face.

"DON'T FUCKING SHOUT AT HER!" Oh great, I'd started now. There was a voice in my head telling me to stop escalating the situation, but then there was a different voice saying, *but how will these people know you are Lenka's daughter? You must make everything worse!* "SHE'S TRYING! SHE'S DONE BETTER THAN YOU. YOU ARE A SHIT DAD. WHERE IS MAIKE?!" Aaaaand there was *his* trigger. I really had Ma's talent when it came to provoking Dad. "SHE'S IN MOSCOW DOING GREAT WITHOUT YOU! ANJA NEEDS TO GET AWAY FROM YOU! WE ALL DO!"

I also had Ma's talent for never knowing when to shut up. I realised this as Dad slapped me in the face. I didn't fall, as Arne held me upright from my armpits like a shitty marionette. We looked ridiculous.

Dad strode back to the counter and resumed eating.

"I don't understand why you needed to pay for a prostitute when you have women who wanted to sleep with you for free? Why bother Ma? Why drag me into your life?" I argued, clutching my stinging cheek.

"Eliska, don't. Leave it alone." Arne tried to drag me out of the kitchen.

"I didn't pay for her; she was a birthday present." He was so un-arsed that I wanted to slap him back. "If I didn't want you in my life, you wouldn't be, Eliska."

That was true. I didn't have anything else to say, so I let Arne pull me away.

I couldn't answer him because he had made more effort than Ma to help me during my childhood. There were occasions when he'd seemed so determined to break me out of the Drovane cycle of oppression that it'd drive him to be the best father he could be in terms of acting on my behalf.

One time when I was around six-ish, he was coming to Drovane for our regular "going to the same three shops and struggling through a conversation in broken German and Slovak" meet-ups. He'd take me to the market to look around. I'd unwillingly march back to the car with him after accepting he wasn't going to buy me anything.

This time, I wanted to call him *Babo*, the way the other Drovane kids referred lovingly to their fathers. I wanted something to be special between us, even if it was just one word. As I sat watching for his car to come, I practised different ways to drop *Babo* into conversation. I didn't want to make it a big deal; even at that young age I knew Dad had to be handled delicately. His car came up the path – he'd hired the black one again. I liked the black one, it smelt nice. He pulled up next to me as I sat on the wall waiting for him. He'd told me off last time for jumping down by myself. I'd fallen and spent the entire visit crying.

He got out the car and walked over to me. He'd left the door open. Unlike everyone else, he was never afraid of Drovane. He never felt the danger of the place.

"Hello." His voice was monotone as usual.

He'd almost reached me when I looked up at him. I was swinging my legs, trying to act natural. "*Babo*, can I have some *Kofola?*"

He was reaching out to pick me up and stopped. Looking at me as if trying to figure out which side of my face would yield a better sound, Dad clapped me in the left cheek with the back of his hand. Immediately I let out a yowl of pain. He looked at me icily as he waited for me to shut up. He lifted me by the chin until I was facing him.

"Don't call me that again." He'd leant down so I could feel his hair dangling on my forehead. He got back into the car and drove off.

Auntie Masha found me, still crying on the wall, sometime later. I was afraid to get down. She picked me up and cradled me all the way back to our rooms.

The next visit Dad had decided I needed more out of life, to make sure "my blood wasn't wasted on you". He decided

I needed to go to school. I needed to learn to read and write and how to behave like a human and less "Gypsylike". He had spoken briefly to Ma about it on the phone, who laughed it off and told him she wasn't going to waste time going to schools on someone as simple as me. I was inclined to agree – I wasn't the brightest of the bunch. I preferred lying on the ground and watching the clouds for hours to actually figuring out ways to get food and money like the other kids.

But Dad was adamant. I was going to be educated and that was that.

So once again, I was sitting on the wall in a T-shirt miles too big for me that covered almost all of my long skirt. The T-shirt kept dropping off my skinny shoulders, leaving the entire right side of my chest exposed. I sat shivering with my two plaits, cleaned down earlier that morning by Auntie Mala, falling forward, as I had my head bowed. I wasn't going to speak to him until he apologised to me.

"Where are you going, ladybird?" It was the woman who used to sneak me little sweets from the shop she cleaned. "You look so sad!"

"I'm going with my dad. He slapped me last time." I was feeling extremely sorry for myself. My shoulders slumped further.

"*Ay*, the German?" She looked sympathetic as I nodded. "Well, I'm sure he won't slap you today. Look how sad you look! Cute girl! When you come back, I'll get you some more sweets."

She winked and kissed my hands. As she walked back to the blocks, I wished she'd take me to the market.

The door slamming made me jump, but I carried on looking down. He didn't deserve my attention. I closed my right eye so that I could look out the side of my left eye better at him.

He'd come in a newer, shinier car. I was almost impressed. I was still sullen as he walked up to me and said "Hello". He pulled up my drooping T-shirt and scooped me off the wall. I didn't say anything and kept my head down, sighing miserably every few seconds.

He didn't notice and continued carrying me to the car. Setting me down, Dad waited for me to climb onto the seat. I still hadn't mastered it. I'd use both of my elbows to climb up with my bottom in the air, then my skirt would get caught under my knees as I struggled to sit up. He ended up coming to my rescue, lifting me onto the seat properly. He fastened my seatbelt and slammed the door shut. I watched him walk around to his seat and wondered whether he even remembered what he'd done the last time we met. He got in and gave me a tight smile.

We drove to a nearby bed and breakfast type of place where many of the prostitutes from Drovane would go, Ma included, with the "fancy men who didn't want to get their suits dirty in the alley," according to my grandma. It was a dirty two-storey building with overgrown hedges surrounding it. There was rubbish stuck in the branches and a battered old car half-claimed by the vines.

I was still trying to struggle down from the seat as Dad went to the boot and brought out some bags and a large suitcase. He hung the bags from my arm and then held my hand, making the bags slide and weigh down on my shoulder, digging into my bare skin.

As we entered, I almost gagged on the smell of perfume and bleach. A large Gypsy woman with several teeth missing smiled down at me as Dad was speaking to the man behind the rickety desk; she reminded me of my grandma. She gave me a small sweet in a multi-coloured wrapper as the man handed Dad a set of keys. Dad grabbed my hand again and gripped it, so I wasn't able to unwrap the sweet until we had entered the musty-smelling room with stains on the walls. Dad noticed me unwrapping the sweet with my tongue out in hungry anticipation, and snatched my little treasure from my hands. He said something in German and shoved the sweet in the half-full wastebasket on the floor. It took everything I had not to bite him.

He took the bags he had decorated me with and set them on the bed. He nodded towards them. "I bought you something". I couldn't understand his fast, mumbled German, so I carried on staring at him with a hateful expression. I had the quintessential "God give me the *zor* to deal with this fuckery" expression that Gypsy girls master as soon as they're born.

He sighed and pointed to the bags, then to me. "*For you. You.*" That's all I needed. The feud was over. I rushed over to the bags and shrieked in delight at the mass of pink ruffles and frills. He had brought me a new dress! A clean, new dress!

It was marshmallow pink with ribbons and beads and buttons. The kind that little blonde girls wore. I was elated. It was the best day in the world for me. It was the first item of clothing I'd ever had that was brand new.

Instantly, I forgot the sweet. I loved Dad fiercely in that moment.

He had brought me a dress, new socks, underwear and a pack of hair ties. I was in heaven. It was Drovane Fashion Week in that room. I wasn't confused at all by this sudden windfall; I knew that sometimes men would take Ma away and she'd come back with gifts, so to me this was natural. I imagined all those men being Ma's fathers. I kept looking through the bags despite Dad telling me to stop.

He eventually dragged the bags away and told me to take my clothes off. After seeing my hesitation, he picked me up and sat me on the bed and began undressing me himself. He seemed more uncomfortable than I did. This made me feel bad for him, so I tried to help by pulling my arm through the large T-shirt.

When I was completely naked, I got my first ever taste of absolute freedom. I wriggled down off the bed and proceeded to run around the room, laughing louder and louder. I jumped off the chair in the corner and shot between Dad's legs to run around the shaky bedside table. My father chased my naked bottom with a towel, half laughing and half scolding me. I knocked over the wastebasket and kicked the papers and tissues around. "Eliska! Stop!" But the smirk on his face made his tone softer, so I carried on. Eventually he caught me as I tried to do a forward roll the way Jani could; after seeing too much of his daughter Dad wrapped me up and carried me to the bathroom.

He set me down as he went back to the room to grab another bag. He pulled out a spray bottle and a packet of sponges. He began cleaning the bath as I sat on top of the toilet. He rinsed the bath and began filling it. He pulled out another bottle and poured some of it under the running water.

I'd used a toilet before. But I'd never used a bath. I stopped swinging my legs happily as soon as I saw it filling. He beckoned me over. I stood next to him. Dad hadn't noticed me shivering as he carried on filling up the bath. I began panicking as the water sloshed around the tub. I clung to my father's belt and moved directly behind him with my eyes shut.

To think that I was going to be slung into this watery-filled coffin chilled me from head to toe. Seeing the swirls of steam rising from the tap reminded me of all the stories I'd heard my cousins tell, about the Devil. Unfortunately, this bone-chilling terror made me look as though I was freezing cold and couldn't wait to be put into the cauldron. Dad stirred it up with his arms, adding a bottle of purple liquid that made the bath froth up like a rabid mouth.

My father evidently had no time for this. He commanded something in German and dragged me off him when I ignored him. He took the towel, placed it on the rickety hook behind the door and lifted me into the bath as I tried to wriggle away. He shouted something else in German, which I didn't understand but was enough to make me sniffle quietly to myself and actually wish my mother was there. The water was very warm and felt surprisingly nice; it was a strange sensation. I felt like the carrots my grandma would slice up and throw into her scratched steel pot. Knowing how mushy the carrots got in the water sent a fresh wave of fear over me and I started sniffling again. Dad sighed and put his fingers to the bridge of his nose. "Eliska, shh." He finally opened his eyes and looked down at me. I sat in the water with my lips slightly open, ready to channel my best ear-piercing air-siren screech if he stepped out of line.

He knelt down and smiled at me. He stroked the side of my face for a few minutes and pushed his fingers through mine as he entwined our hands. He pressed against my small hand as he lowered our hands into the water, holding them there for a few seconds as I got used to the water. Gently he began to wash me, all the while speaking softly, almost whispering, in German to me. Apart from a jolting moment when he cleaned my bottom, it was very relaxing and comforting. As he scrubbed my dirty skin and shampooed my matted hair, I was on the edge of falling into a blissful sleep. I had tingles all over. Eventually it was time to get out, and I was truly upset when he stood up to reach for the towel.

I was lifted up in the cold air and began shivering again. He had taken his own top off and my wet skin slid slightly down his chest as he hooked me in a vice-like grip with one arm whilst pulling the towel onto me with the other. He had none of the softness that Ma's chest held. Ma was a peach – her heart was stone, but her petite body was soft. But Dad was too muscly and hard. It was like trying to cuddle a plank of plywood.

In the room, I was red and raw from my father's idea of drying me. He'd dried my feet, then stood me in the middle of the floor whilst he wrapped me in the towel and vigorously shook it until I made an involuntary "uhhhhhh" sound as my voice box danced along with the rest of my organs. He put on my underwear whilst scowling uncomfortably at me, as if it was my fault I was a girl. Then came my favourite part: the dress!

Dad wrapped my hair up and tried to jam the dress over the top of my makeshift turban. After almost snapping off my neck, he inspected the dress and discovered a zip hidden behind the ruffles at the back. Swearing viciously, he slammed the dress into the mattress a few times, then finally eased me into it. Letting my half-dried, clean hair cascade down my back, he looked at me with a rare expression of tolerance. He even kissed me on the top of my head, and instead of barely touching me and instantly recoiling, he left his lips on me longer and rested his cheek on my head. It couldn't have been more than a few seconds, but to me it felt like years. I shook him off, eager to show the world my new dress. Sometimes I wish I'd stayed still longer; it's one of the few moments in my life that he's touched me out of love instead of duty or anger.

He slipped on my flip-flops after wiping them down with wet toilet paper: he'd brought new pink socks but forgot about new shoes. He made me wear the frilly socks with my flip-flops.

He had unpacked a new comb and was looking at my hair, perplexed. Where to start? I turned my back to him and pushed all my hair behind me. He pushed the comb through the middle of my head, pulling it towards him. He didn't know how easily my hair got tangled. He found out when the comb didn't move, instead bringing my whole body crashing into him. He tutted and rubbed my stomach as an apology.

"Can you do this?" he asked.

"*Ja.*" I turned back round and started combing my hair the way I did at home. Parting it to put it into plaits. He saw what I was doing and stopped me. He combed my hair all the way through after I had sectioned it into two and left it loose.

He dressed himself in a new pair of black trousers, black shirt buttoned at the collar and a black suit jacket. He had wiped over his shoes with the same bit of tissue paper he'd used for my flip-flops. After combing the top of his own hair over so it fell over the left side of his face, managing to graze the top of his ear, he pulled the gold necklace he always wore out from under his shirt. He later told me my *Opa* gave it to him after he'd bought my grandparents a house. He sprayed some stuff that made me choke, and then we locked the hotel room behind us. I watched him as we walked. The hair on the sides of his head was shorter than the hair on the top – I didn't know if he knew – and the hoop he always wore in his left ear was thicker than the ones the women at Drovane wore.

Off we went, back towards the car, and then to a primary school near where I lived. I had my head held high and was doing my Princess walk, which was really my normal walk but with every third step, I'd whip up my pink dress and let it float around me. The flip-flops forced the socks to contort around my toes, but that didn't bother me.

We pulled up outside a grubby building. The gates we'd driven through were peeling and looked as if one more strong winter would finish them off. The pathway to the entrance was bumpy and poorly kept. It seemed ridiculous to waste such a delightful dress on this place. But as we got closer and closer, the sounds of children playing made me feel like I'd arrived in paradise. I couldn't wait to show off my dress now.

Dad looked me over before he got me out of the car. Carefully lifting me out, he smoothed out my dress and did that nasty thing that parents do when they lick their finger to fix stray hairs and smudges. He held my hand tightly and half carried me to the door.

A tall lamp-post of a woman met us at the door with a folder in her hand. She surveyed my father with a smile on her face and a slightly raised eyebrow. Then she looked down at me. Her smile soon disappeared when she saw my mug smiling up at her. It was as if a marching band had gone past singing "I'M A GYPSY AND I'M GONNA ROB YOUR SHIT!" She turned and mumbled something as we followed her inside. My Dad's grip tightened.

We sat in the reception for an age. It was sparsely furnished, with one brown sofa, two wooden chairs and a dying plant on a coffee table. There was a bundle in the corner that looked like the remains of another chair. Dad was watching me as he sat, leant back, manspreading with his arms outstretched on the top of the battered brown sofa. I was twirling around in my dress, then dancing the way Ma had shown me with my hips, making my dress swish side to side. My flip-flops were squeaking on the floor.

The woman at the desk was staring at Dad with a weird look on her face. She kept staring at his crotch; he must be taking up too much space on the sofa, I thought.

I was playing with a broken chair leg when an old white man with pin-straight hair came marching up to me. He was about to say something when my father held out his hand and introduced himself whilst dragging me in front of him.

The man looked from me to my dad and back to me. I gave him my best smile. It was the same lopsided smile as my father's. The man didn't smile back. He continued looking from me to Dad. Mixed race babies were hard for people to understand in this part of the world, I guess. He stammered a little and then delivered a fast line of Slovak. My dad said something in his broken Slovak and then pulled me backwards, closer to him. My dad's voice was getting slower and lower whilst the man's voice was getting higher and faster. My dad then bent down, picked me up and spat some rapid German at the man and the lamppost woman, who was looking disappointed, and left.

We drove back in silence. I knew we wouldn't be coming back. The few words that I'd managed to make out from their exchange weren't positive. *Cigáni* (the Slovak word for Gypsies) and "No" were brought up more than once. The look of disgust on those people's faces stayed with me for a while afterwards. I remember telling my grandmother that we must really be awful for them to still hate me, even in my pink dress. She told me she'd shit on their mothers' graves if she could.

Driving back, Dad reached out and tapped my knee stiffly. I had picked up on the atmosphere between the man and my father and the disappointment and anger in the car, and I wanted to be back with my family. They would be jealous of my dress, even if nobody else was. I suppose my dad was tense about what he would say to Ma, who had warmed to the idea of me getting an education, once she realised she didn't need to do anything about it herself.

She was already waiting for us when we drove down the dirty brown paths into Drovane. She was looking anxious and had three different rosaries hanging off her wrists. She'd got them off a Christian couple who had come to preach to the people of Drovane when I was very small. She was sitting swinging her legs off the same wall Dad scooped me off every visit, dressed in a bright yellow skirt and plain greying-white T-shirt, with a pink scarf flying out to the side of her.

I heard my dad take a deep breath before parking the car. We sat in silence for a few seconds just watching Ma sat swinging her legs. Dragging me into his lap, he opened the door and got out. Setting me down and smoothing my dress out, he kissed the top of my head and smiled at me. The same tight smile I'd see for the next 13 years. The why-did-you-happen-to-me smile.

He took my hand and walked to Ma, who was facing the other way. She heard us coming and turned her head, a small smile on her face. "So...?" She was wide-eyed and excited. Then she saw the look on his face and looked down at me. "You were born to torture me." Rolling her eyes, she pushed me towards the blocks. Dad slapped her hand away from me and said goodbye to me.

I waited for Ma to follow, but as I turned back, I saw her talking to Dad with a smile on her face. She was twirling her plaits and leaning on the wall. Dad was smiling back. I watched him follow her as she led him to the car. My parents drove off as I searched for someone to admire me.

I wore my new outfit for two full weeks until the dress was ripped beyond repair.

He didn't try again. Instead, he began driving me to Germany, and got Anja and Arne to sit with me, making me repeat words and sentences in English and German. None of us thought of teaching me how to read and write; we didn't have the patience for it anyhow. Within ten minutes of improvised language classes we'd be off on another activity. We were always aware of the limited time we had with each other and tried to stuff in as many adventures as we could.

The first time I went to Germany, I fell in love instantly. Dad was driving me out of Slovakia; he'd brought a blanket and a pillow and swaddled me into the front seat. I was awake for most of the journey – for some reason I felt like sleeping in front of Dad would annoy him. And the music blaring from the speakers didn't help, either.

Dad's music taste was eclectic, to say the least. As I've gotten older and developed my own identity, I've realised we're similar. My fondness for Depeche Mode comes from the times he'd be driving us back and forth playing *Strangelove*, *Everything Counts* and the *Violator* album on repeat. The heavy metal and rock music he'd play mixed with random synth tracks were fine for me – I enjoyed them. I managed to get a few laughs from him by dancing along in the front seat. But I disliked the other stuff: nationalist bands that he loved to play as we drove though Romani-heavy areas. A song that got constant play during our road trips was called "*Weisse Wut*" or "White Rage". I couldn't understand what they were saying; this was hardly a talent-heavy band in my opinion. But it was songs like this that used to sour the mood in the car. Dad would either be singing along or having a conversation with the song about "the state of Germany".

The trip took longer when Dad took the route through Poland. He had many friends there who were as heavily involved in white pride groups as Dad was. We'd make stops at various houses for hours at a time. Being told I was a pretty little girl as Dad sat in an armchair, smiling smugly as if he owned the country, was one of the highlights of the trip. They were all older than Dad and treated him as the golden boy who could do no wrong; they'd heap praise on him for being "the future" of their race. At the time, I was soaking up the attention. As I got older, I realised how surreal it was being picked up by a topless man with a swastika tattooed on his chest, giving me sweets and telling me how much I'd grown. Even as a teen, on a visit to Drovane, Dad would drive back to those same houses and I'd sit amid aging Nazis, all complimenting me and telling me how I was growing up to be a lovely young lady. I noticed I wasn't always the only mixed-race child there.

I enjoyed those moments with Dad, just us driving for hours. He'd hardly speak to me but periodically he'd tap me on my head or knee and ask if I was okay.

CLOSE THE CURTAINS AND DANCE FOR ME, *LIEBCHEN*

My relationship with my father's parents is complicated to say the least. My *Opa* has always been very vocal and upfront about his issues with my race and heritage. With my *Oma*, it's very subtle and barely-there hints at her natural belief that I'm somehow inferior to her fully white grandchildren.

I can say with confidence that they both love me. As much as they can love people – love isn't something most Volkers feel. To the male Volker, outward emotion is weakness, a chink in the armour of a real man. To the women, love means relentlessly waiting on their precious sons, vigorously training their daughters, and subserviently morphing into whatever their husbands need at any given time – maid, cook, prostitute.

It's from my grandad that my father inherits his arrogance and self-serving attitude. Both think they can do what they like regardless of others, simply because they have always done what they wanted regardless of others. Consequences just aren't a part of life to them.

Sikke and Mathilde Volker married in a simple ceremony with no more than four people present. Sikke's family lived in a different city, and instead prepared a celebratory piss-up a week later. Mathilde's family were banned from the wedding, and also from contacting their daughter unless they were sending money.

Sikke was the prototype of my father. He was as charming and controlling as Dad, and made women do whatever he wished. He certainly was able to make my grandmother obey his every command. She was forever whizzing around their home, fixing him food, mending his shirts, washing his car, or lost in another task that Sikke just couldn't pull himself away from his beer to do. When he'd run out of jobs for her, she would sit for hours smoking at the kitchen table, staring at the mustard curtains with a dim lamp behind her.

My grandmother and I never shared much in the way of physical traits. Maybe our eyes – but the darkness of hers always felt morose to me. She could never maintain eye contact with anyone, including us. On the odd occasion we'd lock eyes, I'd see an intense pain that made my heart sink. My dark eyes have always looked "simple" according to anyone who spends time with me. Both my Gypsy cousins and white siblings agree that I always look like I'm in my own world; as if there's nothing behind my brown irises, just empty space I've filled with fairies and clouds. One thing my grandmother and I undeniably share, however, is our intense dislike of sunlight.

Daylight and any other harsh light have always made us both feel physically sick. As a child I rarely saw the sunlight. I'd lie under grey, swollen clouds praying they could squeeze me in somewhere and carry me with them. When shards of sunlight managed to cut through the Drovane gloom, I'd instantly get too hot and run off to find shade. Maybe it was because of my escapist nature that I preferred the darkness: you can see what you like in the darkness, whereas in broad daylight you're forced to face reality. My grandmother and I have never been fans of reality. Me for obvious reasons, and her because her reality was as bleak as the dulled, mustard curtains she spent over half her life staring a hole through.

Whenever I'd stay with my grandparents, it was always with Arne and maybe Anja. Dad would make sure he'd have me and Arne at the same time so he could drop us both at his parents' whilst he continued with his shenanigans. Arne and I have always been called "the twins" by our father's family, as we're both the same age – and also because they find it hilarious that a short, Gypsy girl and a tall, German boy could be "twins". We fully embrace this title, as we've spent so much time together and have such an intense bond that we feel connected in the way twins sometimes do.

Our time in eastern Germany with our grandparents was never boring, despite the house being swathed in the dullest of beige and wood panelling. The only splashes of colour were the blood from my grandmother's lips when Grandad would smack her in the face in his drunken rages. He'd launch plates and cups at mine and Arne's heads, but he always used his fists for *Oma*.

Each visit would start the same: we'd walk slowly up the path to the faded front door and wait a few seconds before knocking. Then we'd hear Grandad scream for my grandmother to open the door, despite her being in the next room. The kitchen chair would scrape, and she'd take exactly eight seconds to answer the door. Arne would count loudly through the letterbox when we were younger – something he stopped after he heard Grandad berating my grandmother for taking too long to answer, and the whole street knowing he had a lazy wife thanks to his big-mouth grandson.

My German wasn't brilliant, and I always managed to drop in some *"Zigeuner-Scheiße"* (Gypsy-shit) as my beloved grandad used to call it – but with Arne's help and my penchant for speaking with my hands, we all half-understood each other. It wasn't like Grandad sat and had profound conversations with any of us anyway, and my grandmother had all the patience in the world when it came to sitting in front of me with a gentle smile as I struggled through nonsensical sentences about what my cousins had done in Drovane. She could listen to me and Arne for hours. She'd sit, head resting on her fist with her free hand stroking Arne's hair as we eagerly tried to outdo each other with tales of "back home". We were the only entertainment she got.

The neighbours barely knew my grandmother as she rarely left the house. They knew Grandad. He had a voice that carried. Most of the men were friends of his and loved going to his house for a drink and an illicit bitch about the state of Germany. Some of the women would smile at him and walk by quickly, some would raise their voice an octave higher and tilt their heads when saying hello. One particular woman on my grandparents' street would glare at him and pointedly turn her head. She was a tall, Rubenesque woman who had a husband the same size as her with half the assured assertiveness. She walked with her eyes fixed forward constantly; she never looked down or to the side. Just straight ahead. Arne would try and imitate her walk whenever we'd see her and end up tripping over his own feet.

My grandmother laughed when we told her that the "big woman with the eyes" kept giving Grandad dirty looks. The three of us and Dad were sitting around the kitchen table waiting for Grandad to come down; my grandmother just shrugged and said, "Maybe he tried to take a flower from her garden." Arne and I had no idea what she meant, but Dad chuckled and shook his head.

My grandmother had a beautiful way with words. The way she'd speak was poetic, be it sexual innuendos, begrudged scolding, reciting a plain Kartoffelpuffer recipe, or telling us mundane stories about her day. Arne and I would sleep downstairs at their house, in the front room on the sofas, and each night she'd come in with a wooden tray and perch on the floor between the pair of us. Her wooden tray had a worn bird pattern on and some words we never understood at the time, and she always had a terracotta bowl with a baked apple topped with nuts and whatever else she'd managed to buy without Grandad knowing, two spoons and a shot of vodka each "to help you sleep". We'd sit hanging over the sofas, digging into the small apple with both of our spoons as our grandmother watched us with a dreamy smile. She'd start speaking in something neither of us understood, so we'd exchange "she's drunk again" looks and carry on fighting over the poor apple.

During the days my grandad would make Arne go to work at the allotment the neighbours owned. They were considerably older than my grandparents and had good-for-nothing children, according to Grandad. I would stay with my grandmother at home and do housework and whatever other errands Grandad had left for her. It was such a contrast to my life in Drovane in the sense that I'd be in a house with functioning plumbing and food, but the grind of daily life seemed to weigh on me harder in Germany. In Drovane I'd be with my cousins, I'd be with my aunties, I'd be with Ma when she was in a drunken good mood. I'd largely be left to my own devices, watching the sky and ignoring my stomach growling and my whole body itching. But in Germany it was chore after chore after chore with the curtains drawn and the looming threat of Grandad's violence if the tasks weren't done to his satisfaction.

I never minded the constant darkness my grandmother kept the house in, but I certainly minded the constant furrowed brow and look of panic she'd get when working. It was as if her whole life was a series of panic attacks. Her fear of Grandad added an extra layer of terror to him; she would shake physically when it was half an hour before his homecoming, and we hadn't quite completed the housework or started cooking his tea. Her face would gradually redden brighter and brighter, and her breathing would be heavier. She'd watch the clock and sporadically stand in the middle of the room, flailing her hands as she looked from the clock to the stove. This would cause my heart to beat fast and I'd start rushing around with carrots, potatoes and whatever else I could find to thrust in her hand and help her start cooking something, anything that Grandad would see when he came home. More than a few times Grandma would be boiling salted water when Grandad stomped inside; he rarely ventured into the kitchen, so just hearing or smelling food cooking would be enough to placate him. Grandma fooling him this way would give me some comfort when I'd be in Drovane, wondering if she'd managed to finish her chores and dinner before he came home.

Of the pair, Grandad was the one more subscribed to the idea of a White Master Race. His prejudices were born from racism and hatred. I feel like he was so utterly sub-par in everything he did that he took it out on those who were "beneath him" both in his own mind and by social standards. He revelled in telling stories of meeting Hans Pfitzner – a composer during the Nazi era who desperately tried to curry favour with the Nazi elite and had his own complex prejudice towards "foreign" Jews. He told us how he regularly would watch Li Stadelmann and Elly Ney (two harpsichordists who practically salivated at Hitler's treatment of Jews by all accounts) play to crowds of "patriotic Germans", and he and his own father would be amongst the first to embrace all that the Nazi party implemented and stood for. I doubted all of his stories from this time of his life. In actuality, I think he was a man with nothing to show for his "master race" status, so he resented and adored my father in equal measure to compensate.

My grandfather was barely in his twenties when the Nazi era came to an end. There was always a sad longing whenever he spoke about his father's "achievements" and his own brief experiences. It was as if he felt cheated that he hadn't been able to fully enjoy the fruits of Nazi atrocity. One thing my grandad held on to from his father was the strict, vigorous exercise regime he'd been following since he was a child. Grandad wasn't a young man when my dad was born, but physically he was as fit, if not fitter, than most of the men half his age fathering kids. He has always had an insane routine, involving lifting weights, running laps and doing cardio, all before dawn broke. The men in the Volker family never seemed to age as rapidly as their peers; I suspect it was because all the stress and strife that caused so many to look like wrinkled, ashen-faced zombies with puffy eyes was laden on their wives, sisters and daughters. The men sailed through life whilst the Volker women rushed behind: polishing, panicking and placating. My grandfather's sprightliness and youthful attractiveness seemed usurped from my grandmother when the two stood together.

My grandmother was in her mid-thirties when she married my grandfather and gave birth to my father. An "older woman" by the standards of that age, she aged faster than most. My

Drovane-hardened grandmothers were ageing like wine, whereas my *Oma* aged like milk. She seemed less enamoured with the idea of eradicating all brown, black, disabled and homosexual people, but more in favour of class segregation, regardless of colour. Her prejudice was born from snobbery and elitism.

The first few times I went to my grandparents' house, I was wearing the same oversized T-shirt and faded floral skirt that I wore in Drovane. My father had scooped me up off the wall, bundled me into the car and driven me back to Germany without stopping for an outfit change. I'd eaten lukewarm tomato sandwiches and drunk so much water and fizzy drinks that my legs were crossed tighter than Ma's when a dusty Drovane man tried to flirt with her. It was the same every time: I'd be hopping from heel to heel as my bladder threatened to tornado me into the air, while Arne tried to poke my stomach – as if we both wouldn't have got smacked up by Dad if I'd wet myself. My relationship with my grand-parents was still quite new, so I was painfully aware of not "embarrassing our name" as my aunties had told me. My grandmother would open the door to a sullen-faced Arne, a gritted-toothed Dad who was still muttering death threats to the both of us, and me doing a weird Hammer Time-meets-Moonwalking dance whilst trying to look charming.

She'd look down at me as Dad pushed past her with me under his arm and wrinkle her nose slightly. I prefer to think it was because of the few drops of piss that leaked out as Arne jabbed my stomach. I prefer never to think of the times afterward when I'd stand on her doorstep as a teen, piss-free. It was as if she could smell Drovane on me, even when I'd gone to visit Germany straight from England.

Her opinions on the "poor" and "lower classes" were out of the ordinary for me as a child. She was so much quieter and mellower than Grandad's loud racist ramblings and drunken instigating. She would shake her head softly whenever he would make me take my plaits down and put my hair up in a bun. Even the length of my hair offended him. She would wipe Arne's tears gently, kissing his cheeks whenever Grandad would beat us both with his belt, with Arne trying to push him away from me, earning him an extra backhand in the nose. She regularly asked me to show her my "funny little dances" and sing some of the songs I was used to hearing back in Drovane. I'd stand there, hair loose and free, belting out an Esma Redžepova song whilst she stood watching adoringly. She never seemed to have any mean thoughts about anybody who didn't deserve it. So, when my grandad would talk about the family on the next street, who had one child and a rusty bicycle, it would startle me when my grandmother would viciously rant about "peasants" and "shameless reproducing". She'd have a snarl on her pretty, worn face, dragging furiously on her cigarette.

*

It was during my late teens that Anja, Arne and I were staying in Arne's Black Forest home, as per our newly established Christmas and summer traditions. It was gorgeously black outside, and we could barely see faint outlines of the dipping hills and Bob Ross-style trees. We sat on Arne's balcony with a huge cheeseboard, *Schwarzwälder Kirschkuchen* and vodka. All the lights in the house were off, but the string lights Anja had made Arne put up were twinkling over us like stars. We had enjoyed a full day of my picnics, Arne's construction tutoring ("you never know when you need to fix things, you can't rely on men") and Anja's dulcet tones reciting the stories our grandmother would tell us.

"Do you guys remember some of the other stories *Oma* would tell us?" Anja broke the silence.

"The ones we never understood?"

"Yeah, it was Russian," Arne answered.

"Where did she learn Russian from?" I always wondered why she could speak that unknown language so fast and beautifully when I was younger. I assumed it was fast German with the added bonus of *Oma* being a little drunk when she was tucking us in to sleep.

"I don't know." Arne turned to face us with a dumb grin on his barely illuminated face. "Where the hell did she learn Russian from?"

The three of us started laughing at this ludicrous idea that our grandmother was somehow a fluent Russian speaker behind our backs.

"We should ask her! Let's go tomorrow and ask her!" Arne pulled out his phone and typed in the postcode, trying to plot a route. He'd been driving since we were 14 but had legally obtained his licence a year ago, so was desperate to do longer car journeys.

I was always up for a spontaneous road trip, but the idea of seeing my grandparents without Dad's permission made me uncomfortable. He'd get angry; we'd get angry, Anja would get upset and then me, and Arne would end up retreating into our mother issues as Anja went back to the bosom of her maternal family. "But Dad…"

"Oh, so what. He was fine with dumping us there whenever he wanted to 'see us'. Fuck him. I don't give a fuck what he says." Arne shrugged.

Anja was biting her lip nervously as she always did whenever she anticipated trouble. "Well, if I text him and just say 'Eliska is here and we wanted to see *Oma* and *Opa*, meet us there?' wouldn't that be better than just showing up? Maybe *Oma* and *Opa* are going out?"

Arne stayed silent. I waited a couple of minutes before agreeing that texting him would be the best solution.

Arne and I started planning the trip and arguing over the best places to stop for food as Anja clutched her phone, waiting for Dad to text back.

It was when Arne and I were engaged in a hand-slapping match over a quaint inn that Arne decided was too out of the way to stop at and I decided we all HAD to go to, as their dumplings looked to die for, when Anja's phone chirped.

"He said, 'Why didn't you tell me you're all at Arne's?' What shall I say back?" Anja resumed biting her lip.

"Say 'Oh, I'm sure I did? But we can meet at *Oma*'s tomorrow? We're going to drive down'." Arne's tone was noted by Anja, who silently typed out his response. Dad responded instantly with a simple "okay".

"Now the Führer is satisfied, we—" Anja slapped the back of my head, cutting me off mid-sentence.

"Don't say things like that! Stupid!" Anja never got used to my sense of humour, whereas Arne was cackling in the background.

So off we went the next day, leaving at ten instead of the agreed time of seven, much to Arne's irritation. Anja had her duvet, and settled down in the back of Arne's car as I sat in the front.

We drove for hours in a haze of laughter, arguing, comfortable silence, angry silence, and scoffing the snacks we'd packed in a frenzied attack on the poor carrier bag. Our grandparents' home was just under eight hours away and we drove the whole way, stopping only twice to stretch our legs and use a bathroom, and at a Turkish restaurant to placate me after Arne drove past the turning for the little inn from the night before with a shit-eating smile on his face.

We were near Berlin when Dad texted us in a group chat Anja had set up. "Where are you? Have you left yet?" He knew Anja and I were late to everything even when we gave ourselves extra time to prepare. The both of us seemed to always manage to be late. We were working out what to text back when Arne's phone rang. It was Dad.

"Answer it Eliska, I'm driving!" Arne motioned with his chin.

"No! Here, Anja, you answer!" I passed the phone to Anja who burped in response after inhaling half the coke bottle she'd been drinking when Dad rang. "Eurgh! You dog, Anja!"

I answered the phone with a soft "Hello?"

"Who is this? Where is Arne?" Dad sounded angry already.

"Eliska... Arne's driving."

"Oh, hello. When did you get to Germany? You didn't tell me." If I hadn't met Franz Volker, I'd have thought he sounded hurt.

"Ah... sorry. I told Anja to tell you." Anja pulled my ponytail. Ignoring her, I continued. "We're in Berlin almost, so we should be there in a couple of hours. Are you there already?"

"No, come and pick me up. I'll go with you. Do you guys want any food?" He was rustling around with something and I wasn't sure I'd heard him properly. Nevertheless, I asked the other two if they wanted any food. They returned my confused expression with their own.

"No, we're... okay. Erm, we'll see you soon then." I said my goodbyes and hung up.

"Why did you ask us about food?" Arne asked.

"We've got to pick him up and he asked if we wanted food." I felt as weird as the sentence sounded. Arne's jaw clenched and Anja sighed as she sat up.

"He always wants to control everything. All the fucking time." Arne shuffled in his seat.

"He's going to complain about this, look! The duvet! Eliska, can you put it in your bag? Please!" Anja started picking up the strewn crisp packets, sweet wrappers and magazines she'd had all over the car.

"Calm down, I'll pull over by the library and then we can tidy up the car." Arne reached backward with a spare arm, as his eyes were fixed on the road, and waved around until Anja clutched his fingers. "Don't worry, you can sit up here. We'll let the Gypsy girl deal with Der Führer!"

"Fucking idiots! I've had enough road trips with him, it's you lot's turn," I protested.

"See, you've had loads of trips so you're better at it!" Anja stroked the side of my face and then said the magic words. "We'll take you to a bookshop on the way back, yes Arne?"

"Yes, we'll go to the inn as well." Arne poked my stomach.

Arne pulled off the road near the library and we all exited. He left the doors open as Anja went around scooping up all the litter whilst I wrestled the duvet into the boot. We sprayed some perfume in the car and once it was fit for a military inspection, we took our new seats and set off towards Dad's home.

We pulled up, and he was at the door beckoning us in within seconds. The three of us sat staring at him, whilst arguing and trying not to move our lips at the same time.

"You just go and tell him it's getting dark," Arne muttered to Anja.

"Someone do something before he gets pissed off." I shuffled in my seat so that Dad thought we were coming.

"Let's just go, come on." Arne unclipped his seatbelt. "Thanks for all your help there, Anja," he snapped as he exited the car.

We walked up to Dad, who stood there with his arms crossed. He stepped aside as we walked in and were met with a delicious smell.

"Go to the kitchen. I got you some food," Dad shouted behind us as we exchanged looks.

He'd brought some currywurst and fresh bread. We devoured the food within minutes as Dad finished getting ready.

He came downstairs with a duffel bag and a bag of material. The material was for *Oma*'s embroidery habit; she had an intense passion for embroidery and would embroider anything she got her hands on.

I was washing up our plates when he popped his head in the kitchen and asked if we were ready to leave. Anja cleared the table as Arne was doing his best impression of a pretzel, stretching out his back.

"Yeah, let's go." Arne twirled his keys and set off for the car.

Anja, me and Arne were sitting in the car waiting for Dad to lock up when Anja turned in her seat. "Are we going to ask *Oma* about her Russian in front of him?"

"I completely forgot about that. That's the whole reason we're going," Arne laughed. "No, we can't ask with him there. Him or *Opa*."

Dad walked toward the car with his bags, so we sat silently. He put the bags in the boot before taking his seat in the car. "I'm in the back?" he asked as he plugged in his seat belt.

We drove silently for about 20 minutes before any of us spoke.

"So, was that Anja who had the duvet?" Dad asked stoically.

I saw Anja's shoulders tense up slightly as I racked my brains for something to say to stop an argument starting.

"Lazy, lazy girl," Dad chuckled. "Were you sleeping here too?" he nudged me.

"No, she was navigating here with me." Arne smiled.

"Yeah, her people are good for navigating. Free spirits." He had a smile on his face as he looked out of the window.

I was as bewildered as the other two looked. Why was Dad acting so… nice?

We continued in silence for another half an hour. Anja nodded off and Arne put on music. He loved rap music, in stark contrast to his friends and family in the Black Forest. Their taste was more commercially palatable to the community and Arne was regularly teased for his tastes. He found the lyricism interesting. He enjoyed meaningful poetry in general and this was just an extension of that.

Dad put his hand on mine. "Need some Depeche Mode," he whispered, and I smiled up at him.

He returned to staring out of the window with a grin. I instantly felt teary and looked out of my own window in case anyone saw. Maybe it was him implying we had a bond between us that my other siblings didn't have. We had our "song", our "band" and our journeys. Whatever it was, it made me long to hug him after everything that had happened during my teens. I wanted to stay with him and feel safe forever.

We arrived at our grandparents' house in darkness. We drove down their street as Dad gently shook Anja awake.

"Why did you want to see your grandparents anyway? You barely go when I make you." Dad leant back as Anja woke up startled.

"She speaks Russian," Anja said blearily.

"Yeah, she's half Russian. Obviously, she's going to speak Russian." Dad looked from Anja to me, and to Arne who'd stopped the car and turned around. "What?"

"Who's fucking Russian?!" Arne was the only one who answered.

"Your *Oma*. How do none of you know that? I told you!" Dad looked amused.

"Yeah you told us the same time Anja told you Eliska was coming to Germany." Arne rolled his eyes.

"So, when did she become half Russian?" I was fascinated.

"When she was born, idiot." Anja rubbed her eyes. "When did she become fully German, more like."

"Go inside and ask her," Dad shrugged as he exited the car.

"This fucking family," Arne scoffed.

"The most interesting thing in Mamma's family is that my cousin became vegan," Anja laughed.

We all greeted our grandparents and left Dad with *Opa* as we sat around the kitchen table with *Oma*. We politely ate the food *Oma* prepared after Dad had told her we would be visiting. Anja helped with the dishes after we ate, as Arne and I sat squabbling over some nonsense.

Dad came in and said he and Grandad were going out for a beer at a friend's house. I didn't know what friend or why they were going so late, but I was secretly happy. *Oma* was always more relaxed when *Opa* wasn't breathing down her neck.

When the clearing away was complete, we were all in the front room and nattering away about nothing significant.

"*Oma*, are you Russian?" Arne blurted out. He was never one for patience.

"Yes." *Oma* carried on talking to Anja.

"No wait, why are you Russian?" I didn't care how distorted my German was getting. It was so bizarre that it made the Zlatkovs look normal.

Sighing, she set her tea down and smoothed her dress. She still dressed like she was from a vintage advert, not always out of choice – mainly because *Opa* rarely allocated any money for new clothes.

"My father is… *was* Russian. Don't you know this? Your papa didn't tell you?" she laughed.

"No, nobody told us anything. It is serious? Or are you joking?" Anja half-smiled as she asked the last question.

"No, it's not a joke. It's always been our secret. Nobody here knows. Or if they do, they've never said anything." *Oma* looked at the clock and hesitated slightly.

"But why is it a secret?" Anja asked.

"My grandparents were wealthy people. High-class people. Some of the clothes my mother said she'd seen and the jewellery… ah, I wish I could see her closet." She looked sadly at her own dress.

I admit, I believed she was a fantasist. If your grandparents were so wealthy and had closets full of grand clothes, then how did you end up an abused wife sitting in a decades-old dress in East Germany? Then I thought of all the times kids in Drovane would laugh at me and think I was a liar when I spoke of my rich, white family in Germany with fancy dresses and televisions. How dare I doubt her?

"What happened? How did you end up here?" I didn't mean it to sound so beneath her, but her life now surely wasn't what she'd dreamt of as a child in Russia? I was also pressing harder because *Oma* had such a talent for storytelling. She'd tell Dad about mundane activities we did with her with such vim and delicious language that our day sounded more like a movie than a few hours spent baking, gardening and cleaning. She had ways of dripping droplets of wisdom, the type that comes to tired, older women, in the middle of winding, endless stories in her soft, scratchy voice.

"Like I said, my grandparents were wealthy. They were Germans who had moved to Russia only years before the unrest. They had made a good life but then the revolution happened. They managed to escape Russia with my mother and her four sisters. I never asked how or even why. Questions weren't for little girls in those days. My aunties never spoke of it, and my mother would rather act as if she was deaf whenever her parents were brought up. She never had a good relationship with them. She'd call them traitors. My aunties were different, they were kinder about them." *Oma* settled in her seat and there was a twinkle in her usually lifeless eyes. "I don't remember much; I've never spoken about this with anyone for so long! I spoke a little with Franz, but he wasn't so interested."

I didn't want to ruin the mood by saying "actually it's your fault he's so uninterested in anyone else because you and your husband raised an arrogant, selfish man and continue to baby him to this day," so I stayed silent and waited for her to continue.

"My grandparents still made a good life in Germany. They had and did more than most. Each of their daughters had a passion that they indulged in from time to time. My aunties loved painting or sewing or writing or cooking. My mother's passion was my father, however. He was a Russian by blood who had escaped through Crimea. They met during a small dinner party my grandparents had. It wasn't a grand affair, but it was traditional Russian food, and so that attracted some of the Russian community around them. He worked with his uncle. My father's parents were killed in Russia when he was a little boy. An accident, apparently. He was like my mother and still had a strong pride for Russia. It was like they were brainwashed sometimes when they'd talk of Russia." *Oma* paused to drink her tea, which had gone cold. She winced and went off to make some fresh.

"They act the same way about Germany." Anja was the first to point out the obvious.

"What is going on? What is the 'revolution'? Why did they need to escape? What the fuck is Crimea?" My head was pulsating.

"Google it later. Just let her finish before they get back." Anja glanced at her watch and at the wall-mounted clock to make sure the times matched.

Arne was silently staring at the carpet from his seat on the sofa. My grandmother came back in with tea and some apple cake she'd made earlier.

"I need to talk fast before your grandfather comes back. He doesn't like me speaking about this." She smiled tightly as she passed us slices of cake. It was as if she'd read our minds about Grandad, but then did she need to? She'd been married to him for so long. She knew his mood swings better than anyone. "So, they met each other at the dinner party and my father said he asked for Mother's hand within the week. My grandparents said yes, because he had Russian blood but a good work ethic, and so they married. They carried on working for their respective families and living apart for three years. Then on her 28th birthday they moved into his uncle's home to take care of him. He was getting older and needed constant help. A week after they moved in, the uncle died. My father used to tease my mother and call her bad luck – she'd get so embarrassed. He was like that, a joker. He always said to me 'nothing is more valuable than happiness.' He heard it from a priest once after his parents died, and it stuck with him."

I had so much to say, but she was speaking a thousand words a minute and I didn't want to miss a second of it. She had closed her eyes as she spoke as if she was flicking through the memories of her life and picking out the important bits.

"I was born the next year, and my father said that's when his life was complete. Every night he'd ask me if I was happy. And I was, you know. I really was happy as a child. I had a comfortable life and I had more than most, even during the war. I never felt anything but happiness. I used it all up then and have none left today." She smiled softly. "Marriage was something beautiful for my parents, but for me it was not so… fortunate."

Oma sitting there telling us about her past reminded me of when I'd sat years before at my maternal great-grandma's feet as she told us her own story. The differences were obvious between the two, however. There seemed to be more despair in *Oma's* story. No, she hadn't suffered the atrocities my Zlatkov grand-mothers suffered, but they at least survived enough to carve out some sort of life in Drovane. Bleak as it is. Whereas *Oma's* story was so horrifying to me because it was so… achievable.

How many women her age suffered through abusive, passion-less marriages out of simple fear that "people would talk", or because they hadn't been allowed to develop the life skills to make it on their own? How easily could it still happen? Women and men trapped in abusive relationships with no real means to escape? The slippery descent into decades-long misery and resigned acceptance was terrifying.

"How did you meet *Opa*?" Anja put her hand on *Oma*'s knee.

I certainly wanted to know how the hell he'd managed to get his mitts on my happy grandmother.

Arne was still burning a hole in the carpet.

"He was in his forties and handsome. He was so good at building things; he made a bench with this little bird carved out for the neighbour. I was in my thirties and lazy."

"Why didn't you get married? Didn't everyone get married at like 12 back then?" Anja interjected.

Oma broke out into a singing laughter, showing all over her teeth. "Not quite 12 but yes, I was an old, old woman back then when I got married! Nowadays women think 35 is the perfect age to start thinking about marriage. Good for them – we aged ourselves so prematurely. After 30 we were all considered to be 'expired', but men were 'refined'." *Oma* ran her fingers through her hair. "You've heard it all before. It's all women talk about now. As if it makes any difference. The only thing that matters is looks. If you make enough effort with yourself then you can easily be 50 and take a man from a 22-year-old."

She fell silent and picked at her dress. "Of course, you need money for the potions and the positivity to find happiness in little things. Like you, looking at clouds all day when you come from… that." She looked at me. I felt the joy from the clouds but the disdain in the way she spat "that".

I shrugged with a smile. What else do I say? *Yes, even dirty Gypsies rotting in ghetto coffins can find happiness* or *Don't worry Grandma, I know you don't mean to say "that" in such a way, and I know you didn't mean to avoid introducing me to Grandad's friends when they popped round once when I was younger, and I know you didn't mean to just let Arne be the main topic of conversation while I sat upstairs with your old dresses.* What could I say to a woman who would cradle me and feed me baked apples after Grandad beat me, but would make me dance in front of Grandad's drunken workmates as she laughed along at "the little dancing Gypsy"?

"I never married because I didn't need to. I didn't run away from strict parents or marry, because I couldn't survive financially. I stayed with my parents. People thought we were weird all around the neighbourhood, but who cares. People have talked about others since there were three people on Earth. Nothing will change. I only wanted to marry when I found someone who I could share a bond with like my parents. Then I met Sikke. And I thought I'd found it. I watched him deliver the bench. I sat in the garden pretending not to see him. He came over and asked if he could have some water. And that was it. I've been with him ever since." *Oma* took a crumb of the cake in front of her. "Obviously there was more to it. He told my parents he had a successful business with his woodworking. He owned this, he owned that, and he made so much money. My parents were pleased that I wouldn't need to work hard and then the marriage was fixed. We didn't even go on a date. Nowadays you all go on dates and move in and have children before you decide to marry. Even then people don't. Disgusting. There's more prostitutes than virgins nowadays."

I ignored this comment and continued to stare at her.

"He told my parents he was a traditional man and expected them to pay for the wedding. My father had doubts but Mother pressed ahead. She just wanted to make sure I was married to a well-to-do man so I could continue lazing my days away. I think she was also sick of people wondering what was wrong with me. A single, unwed woman at my age was ripe for gossip. So, my father gave him the money to make the preparations. But Sikke didn't make any preparations. He used the money to pay off debts. My father found out he didn't have a business and he'd lied about having so much money. But I was already in love by then. I used the same line so many stupid women have used: 'I don't care, we'll get through it.' I stopped talking to my parents after Sikke threatened to leave me if I didn't stop contact with them. We didn't speak for five years." *Oma* ate some more cake. "We got married and drove back to Sikke's family home. It was all done within hours. I was making him his first meal at the end of my wedding day. He's the one who called me 'Mathilde'. He hated my Russian heritage. He let me keep a few things I took from home like my tray, my hairbrush and things. But I wasn't allowed to tell anyone I was half Russian. I had to pretend I was just German. Sikke didn't want anyone to doubt his love of Germany. But he'd let me cook Russian food, he'd let me teach him some Russian so he could keep his… meetings secret. You know the ones he had with the… other people who believed what your grandfather does."

She finished and sat silently before we had time to register the last rapidly spoken portion of the story.

"But why did you let him do that?" I couldn't fathom loving someone that much who hated my heritage.

"Because I loved him. I don't have any explanation. I just… loved him." *Oma* shrugged and glanced at the clock.

"Do you still love him?" I wasn't satisfied with her response, but it was the only one she had.

"It's not important. Love only matters the first five years, ten if you're lucky. Then it's about your children and after that your grandchildren, and after that you're too tired to leave." She got up, stretched and carried the tray to the kitchen. "I can't believe you didn't realise, you've always had Russian food. I've told you so many Russian stories in Russian! I've got Russian things all around the house! You silly little kids."

Anja, Arne and I sat in silence as we took in all that had been unleashed in a matter of half an hour. She'd condensed years, no, decades of her life into one long monologue that we couldn't even question her about, because *Opa* would return any minute. I went and helped *Oma* in the kitchen as Anja went to have a bath. Arne remained in the front room lost in his head. There was no talking to him when he was like that. Those were the times he'd usually go and sit in the trees with a flask of tea and his thoughts. Both of us were feral in our own ways.

I felt awkward around *Oma* as we cleaned the dishes. I just didn't know what to say to someone who'd allowed herself to be erased by a man. I wanted to ask when she started talking to her parents again. Did she talk to her aunties? Where did they live now? Was anyone still in Russia?

That evening we didn't discuss anything that had been said. *Oma* said goodnight to the three of us as we played card games in Dad's room, until he came and kicked Arne and Anja back downstairs to the sofas. I slept in the same bed as Dad.

"You get to ask your *Oma* what you wanted?" Dad asked softly.

"Yes!" I shrugged him off as I sat up. "Dad, what the fuck?!"

He laughed a little before he put his finger to his lips. He shut the open door and put the main light on before settling back into the bed. "Wild story, yeah?"

"There's so much stuff I don't understand, she was speeding through so fast. How did *Opa* manage to get her to stop talking to her parents? Why did *Opa* let her teach him Russian but never tell anyone she was Russian? She's right, we've always had Russian stuff in the house. So why is it still such a big secret?" I was babbling, but I didn't care.

Dad ran his fingers through his hair just like his mother did earlier in the evening. His hair was still thick and grazing the top of his ear like the day he'd taken me to school as a girl. He didn't look anywhere near his age, and I understood why *Oma* would have fallen for Sikke if he looked anything like Dad.

"Your *Oma* was a spoilt woman who spent all day baking cakes and selling them slice by slice to the neighbours. She had a fucking boring life. Then she met your *Opa*. Money is great and doing nothing is great, but sex is amazing. She took one look at your *Opa* and that was it. Her parents weren't going to do what my dad was doing to her." He laughed as I pulled a sickened face. "It's true."

"Have you met her parents?" I wondered how they would feel about him. From what *Oma* told me, her parents were kind, gentle creatures. I didn't see them liking this arrogant, violent man who openly laughed about his parents' sex life.

"Yeah. They've been here a few times. I never liked them. They were just boring, unrealistic people." He leant against the headboard. "I know she's had a hard life with my dad. Sometimes I feel sorry for her. I feel bad for my part in it."

"When you used to lie to *Opa*, so he'd give you sweets and beat her up?" I leant back next to him.

"Yes, stupid. I feel bad about that. She never needed the extra hassle. I was greedy, though. I tell her sometimes to leave him. He's fucked half the street and he's definitely got kids over in Munich. Mum's life isn't over. She can say what she wants about age but if she gave herself a makeover, she'd be the best-looking woman in this whole city." Dad had a small smile on his face. It was nice hearing him be so sweet about *Oma*.

"Are they still alive?" I knew it was unlikely.

"No, they died years ago. But some of her aunties are alive and her cousins and their kids. She's got a huge family in Russia. Some are in Moscow; some are spread out throughout Russia. Do you know how big that place is? I should take her there. She's never been." He fiddled with his earring as he spoke.

"You should. It could make up for… you know." I kissed his cheek, not knowing if he'd push me away and lay back down in the bed.

He sat up a little while longer and then switched off the light. I felt him get back into bed and sigh heavily. He stroked my back as I fell asleep.

FREEDOM

THE WHORE'S DAUGHTER
GOES TO ENGLAND

No-one in my family really spoke about leaving Drovane. Not seriously. It was accepted that Drovane was where they'd all die. Sure, they'd speak of visiting exotic places like Bratislava when my aunties were drunk on cheap vodka, but it was mindless talk. We couldn't afford to get into town on the erratically appearing bus, never mind going to the other end of Slovakia. Drovane was our lot.

By the age of 13, my trips to Germany with Dad had shown me a glimpse of a life I preferred. I didn't necessarily want all that my dad had; it hadn't done anything to make him happier, I thought. But I wanted the safe feeling I always had in his home. I could sprawl out on the queensize bed I shared with Anja, I could have endless amounts of fresh, cold water in fancy glass-glasses all to myself, and I could have shiny clean hair whenever I wanted. The televisions, computers and other gadgets weren't too important to me. I'd spend my days drinking water and twirling my glossy hair as I watched the clouds from Dad's bedroom window.

In an ideal world, I would live in one of Dad's homes with Anja, Arne and all of my Zlatkov family.

I dreamed privately of leaving Drovane – I'd never even tell Jani. My dad barely tolerated me; he'd never let Jani come and live in Germany. That was what I planned to do: I would wait until I was older and then I would move to Germany. Anja would definitely help me, and so would Arne.

It was a week after coming back from a weekend in the city near Drovane with Dad that Ma said the greatest thing I'd ever heard her say.

"I'm going to send you to England."

I was speechless. I stared at her in complete confusion.

"Close your mouth, idiot. You look slow." Ma flashed me a dirty look before continuing to wipe the old, damp rag between her thighs. "I want you to learn to read and write. You can come back and buy me a house. I want to be able to breathe without getting three other families stuck up my nose before I die. Now fuck off. I'm going to sleep."

She didn't need to tell me twice; I shot off to brag to all my cousins. I was going to the regal, grand country of England. I would wear huge dresses and clutch a handkerchief to my nose. I would walk with my lips pursed and eyebrows raised. I would be just like the drawings of English people I saw on biscuit tins at my dad's house.

I found Sveta, Senni and Jani walking across the rubbish-strewn "courtyard" of Drovane. They were going to beat up

Ansha and Ima. Apparently, the duo had snitched to Vera about Sveta and Senni flirting with some white boys in town. I decided to go along and watch: after the violence, I'd be able to tell my news to all of them together. Also, watching those two being slapped was always good for the soul.

We went off to find them and bumped into Marija, who had returned to hand Vera the money she'd made so far. She asked where we were all marching to, and Sveta told her. Marija rolled her eyes and told her not to hurt her sisters too much – they were just stupid, not malicious. She came with us, nonetheless. This was great! Aside from Kashe, all of my cousins would be there when I delivered my news. I imagined them weeping and begging me not to go as I insisted I would come and visit them whenever I got a spare minute. I imagined I would be very busy in England.

Eventually we found Ansha and Ima plaiting each other's hair in the stairwell leading up to our rooms. Ansha laughed at us and asked whose wedding we were going to in such a hurry.

"Not a wedding – your funeral, bitch!" Sveta lunged forward as Ima scrambled to her feet, laughing. Ansha scooted backwards, cackling just like Vera.

"You shouldn't have brought shame to the Zlatkov name." They were both sneering.

I was waiting for Sveta to attack them. But when Marija walked forward and back-handed Ima round the face, then dragged Ansha up by her hair to do the same, we all gasped.

"You know how hard it is here! Why the fuck are you two making everything harder! You all need to be there for each other. Don't be like Auntie Lenka. She's always shit-stirring. You want to be alone like her?" Marija's tone was low and cold.

I decided not to defend Ma's honour in this instance. Marija knew more about Ma's antics than me; she must have good reasons to say what she did. Ansha was still sniffling from being slapped, and Ima was looking down at her feet.

"Sorry," she mumbled, as Ansha sniffed in agreement.

Within minutes everything had calmed down, and we were all sitting on the stairwell chatting lazily. I waited until Ansha had finished drying her eyes as Marija cradled her before I spoke.

"I have something to say!" I got to my feet and stood in front of all of them.

"Yes, my little dancer?" Marija beamed at me, probably to make up for insulting Ma. I was 13 years old, but still looked 10 thanks to the pitiful scraps I ate.

"Ma said she's going to send me to England!" I finished with a wide smile.

I watched all of their faces. I wanted to see who would be the first to cry. My money was on Jani. We were practically twins. Same age, same height and only a few shades between us. What I hadn't prepared for was all of them, save for Marija, exploding in ringing laughter. Jani, the disloyal cow, was clutching her stomach as she laughed. Senni was pointing at me and laughing. I stood expressionless at the insensitive bitches.

"Stop it. Stop laughing!" Marija was trying to shut the girls up; she shot me a sympathetic smile. Why did everyone find this funny? They wouldn't laugh when I left and didn't see them ever again.

Marija managed to quieten them down whilst I stood neutral-faced with my hands by my sides.

"What did Lenka say?" Marija nodded at me to continue.

"Nothing else. Just that I was going to learn to read and write so I could buy her a house." I felt as stupid as my cousins thought I was.

That night, as we were all stuffed in Rosa and Vera's room with Ma and my aunties, shit-eating Ansha decided to announce to the room that I was leaving for England. I braced myself for more laughter and was more than surprised when Ma snapped at Ansha.

"Yes, so? Don't blame me if your mother's pussy is too dried out to do anything decent for you. You're like the fucking old women in this place, lonely and bitter. My Eliska has always had more potential than you and that other cross-eyed beast." She nodded her head at Ima.

Apart from Ansha, Ima and Auntie Letti, the entire room burst into raucous laughter. Ma looked at me and winked. I was busy snort-laughing with Jani. Ma's vicious words were the only solution in some situations.

Rosa held her hand up as she wiped tears from her eyes. "Silly girl!" she playfully chided Ma. "Hopefully our Eliska will be going to England. We've spoken about it and it could happen. We just need to talk to Franz when he comes. I think he will be coming next week. Anyway, it's late. You should go to sleep now. I'm tired." We all said our goodnights then went off to shiver our way through the night as usual.

I lay peacefully in between Auntie Mala and Jani that night. I was too excited to worry about the hard floor we were sleeping on or the thin fabric masquerading as a blanket.

"Eliska," Jani whispered, "What does your *Babo* have to do with you going to England?"

That was an interesting question, and one that I should have asked Ma.

"Maybe he will drop me off," I whispered back.

"Oh that's right! In his car! It's not that far, I think." Jani kissed my cheek as we settled in to sleep.

The next day I found Ma before she set off to work. I was apprehensive about asking her too many questions. She'd end up either changing her mind or smacking me for being too nosy.

"Ma…" I tried to gauge her mood.

"Mm?" She was stretching, she seemed okay.

"How am I going to England? Is Dad driving me?" I didn't stand too close in case she was in a smacking mood.

"No. You'll get there. Don't worry how. You are allowed to be uncomfortable. There isn't a rule in our family that says Eliska must wander about like she's slow whilst everyone else works," she snapped.

"Wander about? Oh yes, look how beautiful this place is. I love to wander about. I am so comfortable sleeping on the floor and wearing second-hand knickers!" I snapped right back, and then darted down the stairs when she swore at me and tried to grab me.

I ran across the yard of Drovane, and when I was sure she wasn't chasing after me I sank down. I wasn't going with Dad. I would be uncomfortable. I wouldn't be going alone, would I? And, hold on, who the hell did I know in England? Where would I live?

I never got a straight answer from Ma about how I would get to England. But I was told one day, a couple of months after it was first brought up, that I would be going to England the next day. During the weeks leading up to this, I'd become aware that there were three others going with me to England from Drovane. I knew all of them, and felt a little more at ease. I spoke to Besnik and Vlasta, the daughter of the family above us, often – but Dušan rarely spoke to us. Senni and Dušan looked so alike. His mother hated the Zlatkovs.

I never questioned how Ma was able to send me; I was just happy I'd be going with some people I knew.

"Do I need any clothes?" I asked Ma as she sat with her feet dangling out of the window.

"Yeah, take a suitcase and make sure you fold your dresses nicely. Then you can go and get your shoes, make sure you don't scratch them, they're designer. Oh and don't forget your designer bags. Do you want to take the solid gold toilet roll too? Just in case?" She rolled her eyes, "What do you fucking have to take? Eliska, fuck off."

"I'll miss you too!" I barked.

She turned around and swung her legs back indoors. "I'll say what I want to you. I've done more for you than ANYONE has done in this whole. Fucking. FAMILY!" She banged her fist on the floor with every word. "You're an ungrateful leech. You should miss me. You fucking should. I'm glad I won't have to see your fucking face every day."

I walked away. What was the point of arguing with her? She was just being honest. She wouldn't care that I wasn't there. Why would she? She'd probably only notice I was gone when she was angry and needed a punchbag.

Ten minutes later, I was sitting at Auntie Mala's feet having my hair cleaned with the hair-cleaning rag. She told me she would do a nice bun for tomorrow. I was thrilled. Ma came storming in.

"You think you're better than us. You always have. You have the same look HE has. Your three drops of white blood don't make you fucking BETTER THAN ME! YOU'RE STILL THE WHORE'S DAUGHTER. Go to England. Go to Germany. Go wherever the fuck you want. You'll always have WHORE'S BLOOD!" She was breathing hard, on the verge of hyperventilating. Auntie Mala had frozen, with my plait in her hand and the rag still on my head.

Nothing in the world could have made me answer her back. I was staring at her in disbelief.

"DO YOU KNOW WHAT I HAD TO DO TO GET YOU TO FUCKING ENGLAND?! I'VE HAD SO MANY

MEN TO PAY THAT FUCKING FLESHLESS BASTARD, MAY HIS BONES ROT, I'M SO FUCKING LOOSE NOW MY PUSSY IS FUCKING SAGGING AND YOU'RE STILL STUCK IN YOUR OWN WORLD. NOBODY HAS IT WORSE THAN YOU. NOBODY SUFFERS MORE THAN YOU. DO YOU KNOW WHEN I LAST HAD A BATH? YOU CAME HOME FUCKING CRYING BECAUSE YOUR FUCKING FATHER MADE YOU HAVE A BATH!"

Spit was flying everywhere and her eyes were frenzied. Vera had come running in after hearing the commotion, and was trying to calm Ma down. I didn't know what she had done – I didn't know who the fleshless bastard was.

"Forget it. You're a useless fucking bitch." She spat on the floor and let Vera guide her out.

Auntie Mala tapped my head and carried on doing my hair. We didn't speak until a whispered "Goodnight" when we were ready for bed.

I lay awake for a while wondering if that was the last thing Ma would say before I went. I didn't think about the journey: the lack of details bothered me. I would only work myself up into a panic expecting the worst. But surely it wouldn't be too bad. Driving to Germany wasn't too bad. Maybe England was further. It would be a squash with four of us in the back, but we were used to being bunched up in Drovane. I must have fallen asleep at some point because Ma's toe poking my forehead jolted me awake.

"Come on." She was halfway out of the room when she saw me blinking up at her.

I was allowed to refresh myself with the small cup of water someone had left me in Vera's room. Rosa was sitting up, beaming at me.

"Look at you. On your adventure. You'll be okay, won't you? Our little dancing girl." She looked so hopeful, in that moment I wished I had spent more time with Rosa. Sitting massaging her feet instead of hiding until she roped in another one of my cousins to do it. But it was too late. I wasn't sure when I would see her again.

Ma took me to the foot of our block of flats. It was still dark outside. Besnik, Vlasta and Dušan were waiting with their mothers. Besnik looked as upbeat as he always did; his sister and mother doted on him, and he had as happy a life as one could have in Drovane. Vlasta looked nervous and confused and Dušan looked as sour-faced as his glaring mother.

Besnik was the first to speak. "I hope the Queen has some decent *slivovica*".

His mother hugged him and buried her face in his hair. Ma chuckled and then resumed her taunting smirking at Dušan's mother. We heard a vehicle pull up, and Ma told us to start walking.

Ma hadn't spoken to me since her whispered 'Come on' earlier in the morning, and I didn't know what to say to her. I was feeling anxious about this journey; I wanted her to tell me it would be okay, although hearing her say something like that would probably have made me pass out.

We all walked up to the entrance of Drovane as a van with blue writing on the side pulled in. A scruffy-looking man hopped out. He had a ring of shabby hair around his head but was glisteningly bald on top. He wore a greying white T-shirt with a cracked black Adidas logo and stained Puma track-pants. Something about his hair and his T-shirt tucked into his track-pants was too much for me. I felt my stomach tense up as he observed us, his eyes lingering over Vlasta.

He spoke with Ma in a low voice and looked us over once more. He motioned for us to get in the van. I looked at Ma. She was adjusting her hair under her headscarf.

The other three were being pacified by their mothers with kisses and hugs.

I looked at Ma. She finally made eye contact with me.

She gripped the sides of my face. "Be good." Then off she went.

The other mothers exchanged shocked looks as Ma flounced away. We sat in the back of the windowless van. We could hear the other three mothers saying "Bye!" right until we turned the corner.

I was behind the driver with my back against his seat. Besnik was next to me and Dušan and Vlasta sat against the sides of the van. The four of us were silent.

We had been driving for what I thought was a while. I was tired but something told me to stay alert. The van slowed down and came to a stop. We looked at each other quizzically; I half wanted to ask if we were in England yet, but visions of Ma rolling her eyes and calling me a simple idiot stopped me.

Suddenly the doors swung open and the driver stood puffing on a cigarette. He looked at us all and then cleared his throat. "I can do anything to you. Nobody would know. If you told anyone it'd be too late, I'll be gone. So if you fuck about, get too loud, don't listen to me or try anything…" He grabbed his crotch and smiled at me and Vlasta. "Don't think I won't," he directed towards Besnik and Dušan. He looked so stupid, grabbing himself in his clothes that were worse than ours, that I bit down on my lip to stop myself laughing. His little "give me no shit and I'll give you no rape" threat was so ineffectual that I felt bad for him. He must have thought we were scared of him. Poor guy: he looked like one good sneeze could end his life.

Due to being in the back of a windowless van, I'm not sure exactly what the journey was. We made one more stop hours after the first stop where the driver was clawing at himself like a meth-addicted cat. He made us all go and pee in some woods. There were a few cars going past, but we were well hidden; Vlasta and I didn't need to pee but took the chance to breathe fresh air and stretch our aching legs.

After that we drove for an age. I fell asleep for half the journey. When I woke up, the others were all asleep. My bottom was sore and my neck was stiff. I never thought I'd miss the old mattress in Auntie Mala's room so much.

We stopped again and the driver told us to keep our heads down and shut the fuck up. A man leaned into the window and the driver seemed to be handing him something. They spoke some more, and then we were off.

Nobody was speaking in the van. It was as if we were still trying to process what was happening. We were going further and further away from Drovane. It was daunting.

The next time we stopped it was pitch black again outside, and we were in what I now know to be the Netherlands. The van was opened by a man who looked less like his name should be on a sex offenders' register than the driver. He smiled at us and asked us something. We didn't speak what he was speaking, so we stared dumbly at him. He laughed and did a thumbs-up sign. Dušan returned the thumbs up; I carried on staring.

Mr Thumbs-Up turned to the driver, and they spoke for a while. Then he gestured for us to get out of the van. We got out one by one and realised where we were. It wasn't England, as we initially thought. We were surrounded by gigantic rectangular boxes, in multiple colours. We could hear birds and an overwhelming smell was making my stomach churn.

I wanted Auntie Mala, Auntie Letti, Jani or even Ma at this point. I was confused. I hated this whole thing. I didn't want to go to England anymore. I wanted to go back to Drovane.

Mr Thumbs-Up gently ushered Besnik toward a blue shipping container. I had seen shipping containers before, when Arne went through a sailor phase and had glossy pictures of all things sea, port and boat related. It was open and there were loads of boxes with a picture of a washing machine on. I recognised the washing machine; it was like the one Dad had.

There were two boxes lined up in the middle, with their lids sticking up in the air. Mr Thumbs-Up pointed to us and then pointed to the boxes. I panicked. Small, confined areas weren't my favourite things in the world: I had flashbacks of being made to sit in Dad's trunk. The terror must have shown on my face as I was lifted and shoved into the box. Vlasta was lowered above me, her blackened toes dangling millimetres from my lips. She slid down and adjusted herself, so her foot wasn't poking in my arse. We tried to link hands but settled for linking fingers after lunging at each other's palms and scratching each other. The lid flaps were pressed down, making us tuck our necks into our shoulders. The box was pushed until we slammed into the side of the shipping container. Someone leaned on the side of our box and had a brief conversation with a voice I didn't recognise, followed by some fake-sounding laughter.

We heard the other box, containing Besnik and Dušan, slam into the wall. I could hear heavy breathing through the cardboard. I wanted to vomit and cry so badly, but I clamped my jaw tight. I could hear Vlasta sniffling in the darkness.

After a few minutes we heard the doors slam shut. I imagined Dad bursting in and saving me. I imagined Ma beating up the driver. I imagined suffocating to death in this washing machine box. We felt ourselves being lifted up, the container groaning as we were carried through the air. We landed hard on a solid platform. I had never been so frightened in my life.

There was more movement, a sort of swaying motion. Vlasta popped her head out of the box and beckoned me to do the same. I looked around and there were a few shards of light from two holes in the ceiling of the container.

"Vlasta? Eliska? Is that you?" Besnik's voice came from the box next to us.

"Yes, come out, there's nobody here." Vlasta sounded excited.

We all scrambled out of our boxes and scurried across the container, where there was space on the floor to sit. The four of us looked at each other, wide-eyed.

We didn't speak. We just sat, swaying. Looking back, I suppose the sea was choppy. It wasn't a rough ride, but it wasn't smooth. It was enough to keep my stomach on "just-about-to-puke" alert. I was contemplating the day's events. Maybe I should have given the family business a chance. Everyone else was working on the streets – why shouldn't I? Maybe I should have asked Vera if I could re-enrol in the Zlatkov School of Hoecraft and Hookery.

I had fallen asleep again, and was shaken awake. I looked around expecting to see Ma, but it was Vlasta.

"What?" I was annoyed at being woken up.

She didn't say anything. She was crying.

"What's happened, Vlasta?" I couldn't see her clearly; she had moved herself opposite us. She was struggling to tell us something, then I saw it.

In the slits of light we saw her legs, stained with a burgundy liquid. Blood.

I knew all about periods. Vera was always talking about me working when I started my periods. So much so that I believed she would just drag a cloth over me, shove rags in my knickers and plop me in the alleyway half an hour after starting. I didn't know, however, the workings of a period. I assumed that it was like urinating – you could cross your legs and it would go away. So when Vlasta was sat there with blood trickles on her already filthy legs, I felt she was nothing more than a drama queen who couldn't keep it inside the way I was keeping my vomit in. I admit I considered her weak in that vulnerable moment.

Vlasta was crying and asking for her mother. She could barely speak through her sobbing. She was in the middle of asking for her mother again when she suddenly fell silent. She leant forward and cuddled her stomach. I heard her stomach gurgle and then the stench hit. Vlasta had soiled herself. I pressed my back against the container wall as far away from her as I could. The smell was getting stronger and I was fighting back vomit.

Luckily the boys had stronger stomachs than me, or they were just plain nicer. Besnik ripped one of the cardboard flaps off the washing machine box. He scooped up whatever had leaked out of her skirt. Dušan gave Vlasta his jumper to wrap between her legs, and she tied it around like a nappy. Vlasta wept for a while, whilst we tried cheering her up and tried to make her laugh. It didn't work.

She eventually cried herself to sleep and made those shuddery sobbing noises that children do when they've cried too hard. I wondered how such a weak little thing had lasted so long back home. My sympathy for her only registered years after, as a late teen, when I started my own periods and stood in the shower crying from one end and bleeding from the other with vice-like cramps in the middle.

It seemed like years had passed before another unknown man opened the container doors. I certainly felt like I'd aged. The man pulled back immediately and gagged. We must have looked like a damn sight. One was covered in shit and blood, one was in a stained vest with a hole in the front, one had stained arms from trying to scoop up the liquid shit Vlasta had spilled out, and I must have looked thoroughly traumatised with puffed out lips, trying not to projectile vomit everywhere.

Keeping his distance, he herded us off the boat and onto a wooden platform. I wish I had taken in more of my surroundings; all I remember is biting the insides of my cheeks so hard to stop myself chucking up and walking as fast as I could to keep up with the new man leading us to this stupid promised land. We were taken to another van, oh joy. This van was in the middle of overgrown grass and looked totally suspicious, but whatever. I wasn't the people-trafficking mastermind. It was dark again so maybe it wouldn't look so bad.

The man opened the doors and there were washing machine boxes. Only two. I knew what was coming. Within minutes I was struggling into the box again, and then Vlasta got in after me as I pressed my eyes tight shut.

More time passed, the van stopping and starting, the smell of diesel mingled with that of shit, and the effort not to gag. I heard tyres swish through some water, then, finally, the engine noise stopped. I couldn't ignore the cold, slimy feel of Vlasta's legs. I hated this so much, and I felt awful for being so unsympathetic. But I just wanted to be away from Vlasta. Of all the days to start her period.

I heard the man get out of his seat and slam the door shut. Footsteps approached and the doors to the van opened. I shot up through the cardboard flaps and earned a slap around the back of the head. I couldn't care less; Ma's slaps hurt far more. I swallowed mouthfuls of clean English air.

We were in a field. The man reached past us and pulled another box to the forefront. He told us to "geh awt". We figured he meant we had to get out of the van. As we exited and leant against the van half-famished, he was pulling out clothes and passing them to us. I was over the moon. Fresh, clean clothes! I had a T-shirt with the same Adidas logo as our original driver. With pink leggings. Besnik and Dušan had matching jumpers with a small tick in the corner and black jogging bottoms. Vlasta had green leggings and a plain black T-shirt.

The man gestured towards the front seats of the van. I would have sat on top of the roof if it meant not being shoved into that nasty box with Vlasta. I felt so much better in my new clothes. I sat next to the driver and watched him put his seat belt on. He saw me watching and winked.

We drove through the field and onto a road, the four of us squashed over two seats and this hulking, bald man driving us. We were on the road for a while, watching the different buildings zipping past. The driver was chattering away as if we understood what he was saying, and I was grateful it wasn't silent.

We pulled into a car park. There was a brown woman standing with her hands on her hips watching us pull in. She had on a baggy red blouse and plain, black trousers. She smiled at us as the van rolled to a stop. The loud man said something else and pointed to the door. He got out, then reached for my hand to pull to his side. I recoiled and inched closer to Besnik as he was waiting for the other two to get out. The driver laughed and shut his door. Eventually we all got out and the brown woman looked us up and down, then paused when she got to me. She said something to the driver, who shrugged his shoulders and held his hand out.

She gave him a brown envelope and he tucked it into his belt and pulled his T-shirt down, concealing it.

She held her hand out and then motioned for us to follow her. We walked through a little alley and into a clean yard. There were three big blocks of flats like Drovane, but that's where the similarity ended.

It was stunning! The windows ALL had glass in! There were pretty curtains hanging in almost every window. Some even had vases and other colourful items in them. I forgot the pain and discomfort of the journey there; my sickness had vanished. This was the height of luxury. I didn't know the name of this place yet, though we learnt it eventually.

It was glorious.

It was South Shields.

WEAK-WILLED TRAFFICKERS AND FRENCH FANCIES

The brown lady said we were her family. If the two walls either side of us asked, then we were to say she was our auntie. I didn't understand why, and I'm positive none of us would have remembered to say, "She is our auntie." Nevertheless we nodded our heads obediently.

Vlasta had bled a little through her new clothes and was getting teary again, desperately stuffing her fist into her mouth. The lady gently took her by the shoulders and led her through the living room door, grabbing her handbag on the way. The three of us waited awkwardly and let our eyes dart over the white walls, black sofas, slightly marked coffee table – anything that meant we avoided each other. We'd all shared such a life-changing, intimate experience on the journey from back home, yet the atmosphere was tense and strange.

The lady finally led Vlasta back into the room. Vlasta was walking strangely, in a different pair of leggings. We were told to "relax", and that was it. We sat on the sofas like guests and waited for whatever else the lady told us to do. She switched on the black television and left us for a few hours as we stared at a nature show. Personally, I loved it – the programme had lots of cloud shots and it was soothing to see something so familiar in such an unfamiliar setup. And that was it: the week was full of everything we expected England to be. Bountiful, limitless and dripping in unnecessarily wasteful excess. Or maybe I was just bitter that I could have lived like this in Slovakia if I hadn't stupidly been born the wrong race.

We had been at South Shields for roughly a week when the attentive, affectionate manner of the brown lady disappeared. We had been given more new clothes, food, baths, and we were allowed to watch television sporadically. I didn't know what I'd done to deserve this life, but I was grateful. The four of us eyed each other suspiciously the first few times steaming hot plates of food were placed before us, wondering if we were to make the food last all day or if we were permitted to stuff our faces to near suffocation right then and there. After the first couple of days, the introduction of three full plates of good ol' British stodge had wreaked havoc on our poor guts. I was used to eating regularly whenever I was with Dad, but the food I ate in Germany was very different. In Germany I'd have a pancake with fruit salad in the mornings instead of a heaving plate with eggs, sausages, bacon and a lumpy red soup that had the faint taste of tomatoes. My stomach would cramp awfully and I'd be convinced it was going to explode. All was forgotten, of course, whenever the thickest sandwiches in the world were laid out in front of us at lunchtimes, stuffed with chicken, salad, crisps and salad cream.

Throughout this week of goodies and treats, the lady never told us her name. When we'd first stood in the middle of the plain flat we were led to, she had given us a lengthy speech of which I only understood a handful of clearly enunciated words. The similarity to German and the few words Arne and Anja had taught me helped me grasp the general gist.

But within no more than a few days, the lady morphed into a psychopathic entity. Our first taste of this was when Vlasta had stopped bleeding and was able to wear underwear without the sticky-backed monstrosity that the lady had been helping her stick to her knickers. She came inside beaming and announced that she had finished her period. We were relieved. She started dancing in the middle of the room, spinning on her feet with her hips pushed out and bent arms around her circling the air with her hands. The two boys and I watched her in admiration and unspoken reminiscence; it was so like home, this dance. My family made our entertainment with dance, storytelling and dark humour. The boys, I'm sure, had seen their mas, grandmas, sisters and aunties dance in a similar way. Our eyes were back in Drovane.

Out of nowhere the lady appeared and went ballistic. She took her shoe off and whacked it around Vlasta's bottom. The boys looked terrified, as did Vlasta, but I was still in Drovane. Flip-flop fuckery was a daily occurrence in my family, so the horror of the moment was lost on me. She began whisper-shouting at us whilst pointing at the floor and "shushing" us aggressively several times. I didn't have the vocabulary or courage to explain that Vlasta was hardly going to make enough noise for anyone to hear us: she was a frail girl who'd recently been acquainted with menstrual diarrhoea. I doubted there was enough in her to make a sound even if she'd been jumping off the table. The lady raised her hand as if she was about to slap us, but held it in the air as she put a finger to her lips and shushed us one final time. Vlasta had tears dripping off her chin as we were left alone in awkward silence.

We were given the grand tour of the kitchen later that day, and the lady showed us where all the dishes were kept. Up to this point, the lady had been the one who cooked for us and cleaned our dishes. I knew eventually we'd need to do something. After all, I was raised by whores, not wolves; I knew pulling my weight was expected of me, and feeding myself and cleaning up after myself was my own responsibility. So I was grateful to go a week on the lady's generosity. I had a basic understanding of kitchens, as Dad had made me help him with chores as he swore at Anja for being good-for-nothing.

But Vlasta was lost. She had that permanent look of confusion and fear that was beginning to annoy me. I knew it wasn't her fault really – she'd had a wonderful family and had had the privilege of being a child, whereas in the Zlatkov family we were raised to scrap for what we needed or starve. Nothing was done for us just because we were kids. Even by the nothing-age of 13 I'd been in countless fights and scuffles. And that was my cloud-worshipping self. My less "dopey" cousins had been fighting like it was their job since they could walk. Vlasta being so terrified at every little thing was alien to me. How did she manage to make it to this age in Drovane with such a weak constitution?

The lady said something about "brake fast", which I knew was the English way of saying *frühstück*. She took out some bread from an open loaf – my dad would have belted her for leaving the wrapper open for the bread to "go hard and fucking stale. Who the fuck wants hard bread? Anja you're one useless idiot, fuck off inside."

She put the bread into a red box and pushed a button on the side. She waited a few seconds, then pressed a different button, which instantly stopped the bread and it shot out. I nearly lost my life. The button had made the bread fly out back to Drovane, it seemed to us; in reality it just jumped up slightly as she pulled it out and laid it on the table and began spreading butter. We watched her explain something none of us understood, and then we were off on our next "tutorial". She'd just left the toast on the table, buttered and wasted.

That day we learnt how to make toast, how to hoover a carpet, and how to pretend we understood exactly what she was saying.

The next day we were given more clothes. I was given a pair of jeans to wear for the first time. I hated them. I couldn't move properly, and waddled like a penguin until I got used to them. I caught the lady giving me the same weird look she'd given me when we first met. Sort of curious. As if out of this whole experience so far, I was the only strange thing. She stared at Vlasta with a half-sneer, as if having to deal with her period had made Vlasta an enemy for life. She barely looked at the boys; when she did it was with an indifferent blank expression. That afternoon, when the other three were taken to another van as I watched from the window, and two new girls arrived, I realised what the issue was.

Vlasta glanced behind her and we made eye contact for a brief second. She had the same terror on her face that she had been wearing ever since we left Drovane. I gave her a tight smile. What could I do? How was I going to reassure her and give her the strength that a life of hardship in Drovane should have already instilled in her?

The two new girls arrived with another brown lady, but she was lighter than the first lady. The girls with her were lighter than Besnik, Vlasta and Dušan. Standing in the front room, the four of us looked somewhat believable as a family. That was the issue: I was too light for the "family façade". I wondered if it was worth telling them that my grandma, aunties, cousins and even my own mother were darker than all of them. My sickly pastel skin was a blend of races, nothing else. People could surely understand that in England? With their education, high society and larger-than-life breakfasts?

The new woman introduced herself as Gunjan. She asked what our names were with a bored look on her face. The tallest girl in the room said in almost perfect English, "I am called Dagmar. I am from Czech Republic." Dagmar had hazel eyes and a few freckles on her nose, and she was the same yellow shade as me.

The other girl muttered, "Rayaan," and kept her eyes to the floor. She was a touch darker than us, and had jet-black hair with thick eyebrows.

I answered, "Eliska. *Slowakei*."

The differences between us weren't noticeable enough to rouse suspicion. We genuinely looked like a little set of sisters.

Gunjan grunted and began unzipping the massive suitcase she'd lugged in. She pulled out a bunch of books with "ENGLISH" written on them; they looked like the books Arne and Anja had used to try and teach me.

When she pulled out a packet of pens, I realised what was happening. I would finally learn how to read and write! This was what I'd come for!

The first week we practised tracing our names, then we started on simple phrases. Gunjan seemed to be concerned with us learning as fast as possible. None of us noticed that we hadn't left the house at all since our respective arrivals.

By the end of the month we were able to conduct basic introductions unaided. Dagmar had already learnt some English during her time in the Czech Republic, so she helped me and Rayaan with pronunciation and word order. The three of us would communicate in basic English, which helped us practise.

We watched television and practised repeating what they were saying. We watched *Home and Away* so much that we could all say "stone tha flamin' crows" just like Alf Stewart. Gunjan caught us and made us watch the news bulletins instead. During one viewing, Rayaan pointed to a story on Afghanistan and said "Home. Is my home!" We watched in silence as they showed the aftermaths of car-bombings in Kabul.

The English lessons continued for a few weeks presumably until we were proficient enough to conduct a basic conversation about our living arrangements unaided and convincingly.

Gunjan gathered us in the living room one evening and told us we would be going to work. We were excited, until she said "cleaning". We were always cleaning the house. Gunjan was a filthy creature. She'd leave crumbs, spilt tea and used tissues everywhere. After dressing us in jeans and making sure our hair was up in high buns, she led us outside for the first time since I'd arrived. It was still magnificent to me. It didn't smell of a decaying rubbish-mound like Drovane. In fact, there was hardly any rubbish – just a few crisp packets.

We sat in Gunjan's car as she drove us to our "workplace". She told Rayaan to get out when we pulled up to the first house. We hadn't considered the possibility of being split up. Rayaan climbed out in trepidation, and Gunjan got out too. She went to the boot and pulled out a bag full of cleaning supplies. Leading Rayaan, she walked to the front door. A black lady answered and beckoned both of them inside. Gunjan reappeared five minutes later, alone. She got in and drove to the second location, which was my chosen house.

She handed me a bag from the boot and walked me to the front door. The door opened and a white man stood in the doorway.

"Hello, please come in." He had an accent. It was foreign. It was different to the voices on the television. We hadn't heard any other white voices apart from the van driver, and this man didn't sound like him.

Gunjan came in and told him I was a new employee; a school-leaver, she said.

"16? Wow, they look younger each birthday I have," he chuckled, and winked at Gunjan who did the fake-laugh that she used whenever the phone rang. Gunjan left and I stood there staring at the man. "What's your name, love?"

"Eliska, from Slovakia," I answered. Nobody had told me I couldn't speak to him. What was the harm?

"I'm Pete, from England," he said. I didn't believe him for one second.

"No, where you born from?" I was getting to the bottom of this, English be damned.

"I'm pure Geordie, me." I knew it, he wasn't from England. He was a Geordie. I didn't know where that was, but I loved the melodic accent he had.

He showed me the kitchen and the bathroom he wanted me to clean. It wasn't that bad. I busied myself and figured out which sprays to use based on the pictures on the bottles. It was uneventful, except for when I'd finished and had my work inspected by Pete. He brought out a Capri-Sun and a box of French Fancies, and as we sat eating, he asked me how old I was again.

"Sisstin," I replied, parroting Gunjan.

"You look very young; you don't look 16." He started searching for something on his laptop. "Kolkoh mass rowkov?"

It took me a minute, but I realised what he was saying, "*Koľko máš rokov?*"

"Ah, TIRTEEN!" I beamed. I'd learnt this with Dagmar and Rayaan. He looked concerned and I realised what I'd said.

"13, love? You look younger than that. Have another cake." He held the box up to me, and I had another yellow one.

Gunjan pulled up and I looked at him. If he told her that I'd revealed my real age, I didn't know what she'd do.

She knocked the door and he opened up. She told me to wait in the car. She held her hand out – I guessed it was for money.

"No, you're lucky I don't call the police. Fuck off from here." He slammed the door on her. I was only a few steps out of the door at this point, and Gunjan was looking thunderous. This wasn't good.

Back home Gunjan slapped me across the face several times. She slapped like a child compared to my family. I pretended to be forlorn, so she'd see I got the point.

*

We continued to clean for weeks after; we didn't ask questions, as Gunjan was hardly approachable or likely to give us coherent, reasoned answers. We just continued doing what we were told. I was cleaning mainly for a white family nearby, and they didn't seem to mind that I was 13. They barely spoke to me aside from a strained greeting when I entered the house. They had come from France, and would give me lots of delicious leftovers. The mother would send up her youngest child to watch me when I was upstairs, as if I would steal her ugly jewellery or something. Everything she had was too small and bland for me – I knew from Dad's various girlfriends that the thinner, plainer stuff was the most expensive. But my tastes were true to my birthplace and I loved chunky, colourful things.

Rayaan was the most fed up out of the three of us. She cleaned for a lady with two cats. She couldn't stand it. She'd come home smelling dreadful.

One night as we sat eating rice and the lumpy red soup that I learnt were called "baked beans" and were a vital life-source for many English people, Gunjan came in from the living room and told us we'd eaten enough. The three of us exchanged looks. We were hungry to the point of delirium, and so tired that our eyes were barely open. She went to the sink and grabbed a permanently sodden rag. Even in these snatches of peace we had, she couldn't let us be.

I'd be working in the morning, given a meagre packed lunch to eat in the car on the way to another job, and then picked up to complete ironing or washing that Gunjan had taken in from neighbours or elderly people around the community. I often thought about my dad and if he knew what I was doing. I knew Ma wouldn't care. She'd be happy I was doing something other than "staring at the sky like an idiot". Gunjan couldn't let us eat our dinner without reminding us we were nothing. Insignificant street-urchins rejected by their families.

It seemed that sleep was another English luxury that we weren't able to afford yet. I went from being a young-looking early teen to a dishevelled, beaten shadow of myself. For the first time in my life I looked the part of a Drovane street-urchin. England had ground me down. It had made me long for the decay of my home. At least there it was the buildings that rotted and not me. I had my ma's resistance to folding under terrible living conditions, but I was starting to waver. I was growing angry with this grey, busy hell I'd been banished to. Full of multipack fibre cloths, spray bottles, stained tabards, choking chemicals and looks of disdain that my entire arsenal of products would never eradicate.

Many of the families were indifferent to us. Some of them I knew were used to young girls coming to clean for them from back in their respective countries and cultures. It wasn't sinister or illegal. It was just a way for the poor to earn extra income. I knew it well: many of the families in my own community would try to earn extra money this way too. But then there were other families who revelled in the degradation. Who had amassed nothing of importance in their life, but were able to scrape together the fee for one of the skinny immigrant girls to come and clean for them as they sat on their faded sofas munching on bumper packs of crisps and biscuits, watching us as if this were the colonies and we were put on this Earth to serve them and them alone.

I cleaned their literal shit, and yet I was the one they sneered at, the dirty fuckers. It's as if they refused to even bother flushing when they knew I would be working for them that day. I completed my work to the same high standards I expected of myself for everyone, regardless of how they treated me. I rarely worked back home, as the clouds were too enticing to tear myself away from. I'd let my stomach grumble for hours before I'd drag myself to hunt out a scrap of food. But I always knew if a job was worth my attention, it was worth my effort. After all, I didn't have education, possessions, family or those types of things to be proud of. My pride came from the shiny bathrooms, twinkling floors and polished surfaces I left in my wake. That was my legacy. Not how many big words I'd memorised, times tables I'd learnt, or science formulas I knew. It was how fresh and clean a room looked by the time I was done with it. But it wasn't enough for Gunjan.

She said we were to refrigerate the rest of our plates to eat tomorrow evening. She tossed the rag on the table for us to clean up. Sighing, I moved to grab the slimy mass of fabric. But I was too late.

Rayaan stood up and threw the balled-up rag at Gunjan's face.

We were as taken aback as Gunjan, until she leapt forward and dragged Rayaan by the hair across the table. Rayaan started flinging her arms around madly. We watched as she dragged her nails down Gunjan's face. Letting go of Rayaan, she swore at all of us and ran out of the room.

We waited to hear the bathroom door shut before we laughed as quietly as we could. We were in awe of Rayaan. She'd had this wild look of complete abandon ever since she'd arrived at our little "home", as if the horrors she'd seen were etched on to her eyeballs for evermore. As if Gunjan and her hollow scowling were nothing compared to what she'd already endured.

Gunjan stayed in the bathroom for almost an hour, while we were lolling on the sofas in the front room and skipping with a tatty old rope that we'd found in the bathroom cabinet. We froze when there was a banging at the door. If it was the neighbours, we were dead. Dagmar and Rayaan looked at each other and then at me: who was going to answer? The banging started again and before we could react, Gunjan had flown from the bathroom to the door. The three of us huddled together on the armchair.

In came a husky, angry man. Dagmar grabbed onto mine and Rayaan's T-shirts; she must have recognised him. He had bulbous eyes, a wet bottom lip and the remnants of a full head of hair clinging to his sweaty scalp.

Gunjan pointed at Rayaan and we huddled tighter. She snapped at us to go to bed. The three of us got up in sync.

Gunjan held a hand in front of Rayaan. The three of us stopped.

The man grabbed Dagmar and me by our hair and dragged us out of the living room. The three of us were silent throughout.

Gunjan yelled something to him, and he carried on dragging us to our room. He threw us down on the mattress and we scrambled backwards into the corner. He gave us a surprised look mixed with mild offence, and gave us a small shake of his head. He held a finger up to us, pointed to the hallway and shook his head again.

He left the door ajar. We heard him and Gunjan speak in their own language again, and then we heard him shout at Rayaan. He sounded terrifying. Then it was silent for a few minutes. The television was switched on loud.

Dagmar and I heard Rayaan being sworn at again, and the slaps that followed. We held hands and stared at each other, wide-eyed. We could hear thuds and slaps mixed with Gunjan speaking through gritted teeth. Rayaan would yelp and scream every so often, causing Dagmar and me to push ourselves closer together.

"Shall we do something?" I asked Dagmar.

"No! Do you want to be next?"

"But they're hurting her!"

"She shouldn't have argued with her. Doesn't she think we all want to say no? I'm glad we aren't all being punished because of her." Dagmar squeezed my hand. "It'll finish soon."

It was a while before the man appeared in the doorway, holding Rayaan around the waist. He tossed her to the floor and left without giving us a second glance. She was red all over. Her face didn't have a mark, but her arms were covered in grazes and her hair was raised in random spots where she'd been dragged.

The three of us were silent. Rayaan hobbled over to our mattress as Dagmar and I made space for her between us. She lay on her back. We cuddled her as close to us as we could as she held our arms.

The next day the man came back and took Rayaan away. We never saw her again.

The commotion of that evening had brought questions to the door. Who were we? Why didn't we go to school?

In the days that followed, Dagmar and I cleaned houses in the evenings under cover of darkness, and spent our days sitting silently. That suited me fine; the daylight in England was as harsh as German daylight. There was less grit and gloom to pierce through in comparison to Drovane, and so the full force of the brightness would beat down through heat, rain, and wind. It made me feel ill. But the night sky was exciting and soothing for me. I was safe in the darkness. I felt calmer.

Unlike Gunjan. She was unravelling, fast. She pulled our hair on the few occasions we spoke too loudly or slammed a door. She was growing more impatient with us every hour. Whatever we did was wrong to her, and it seemed to take a lot of self-control to not murder us.

There was almost double the number of phone calls since the neighbours had started asking questions. Gunjan told us never to open the front door, and to stay away from the windows; she'd even started to keep the curtains and blinds closed during daylight.

Her paranoia was starting to rub off on to Dagmar and me. We would be scared to run the taps too much, in case it could be heard by the neighbours. We'd sit on the floor under the windowsills as an extra precaution. Gunjan had taken up smoking, and her window ban meant she smothered us with her smoky haze. Her nerves were shot.

I wondered why she'd got involved in all of this if she was so weak-willed. Ma would have found her pathetic. Watching Gunjan with a cigarette hanging from her lips, leg shaking, eyes glued to the door, I wondered how shady our entire setup actually was. What would happen if we were found here? Would we go to jail? Would Gunjan slit our throats before whoever she was waiting for burst through the door? I always made a point to keep the knives in a pot under the sink in case her manic fretting manifested itself in a more physical manner.

It felt like we'd been living this way for years when the door finally swung open. Gunjan had been on the phone all morning. She was spilling the ash from her fags everywhere. Dagmar and I had given up trying to keep the place clean. We would spend our time whispering stories to each other – long, rambling stories about princesses murdering their own captors. Dagmar used to take the lead with the stories. My own request was for a magic cloud to follow our protagonist, speak to her and carry her away in times of great duress. The man who had taken Rayaan came walking through the living room. He'd seen me and Dagmar sitting under the windowsill, and turned to argue with Gunjan. She was half whispering back. She turned and told us to get our "shit".

We collected our belongings (a handful of faded leggings and T-shirts) and stuffed them into the black bags the man threw into the room. He told us to go with him.

It was a relief breathing clean air.

We got into his van and drove away from my first English home.

We drove for hours, jolting back and forth in the van. Dagmar laughed every time I bounced up and down, clutching my backside. The man had put on a CD of Bollywood songs. It was the craziest, most bizarre moment of my entire stay in England so far.

I was asleep when the man gently shook my ankle. He looked mortified to be touching me, and I remembered the offended look on his face when Dagmar and I backed away from him on the mattress. Poor guy can't even help a human trafficking operation run smoothly without being thought of as a rapist. He half-carried me to a house.

It was almost evening.

"Where are we?" Dagmar asked. I shrugged.

"Sheffield," said the man. "Yorkshire."

We were none the wiser.

The woman at the door looked cruel. She had a furrowed brow and an expression that made me feel like we should apologise for being late.

"In." She looked around and dragged us both inside.

SEQUINS, SHIMMIES
AND SALIVATING MEN

I personally haven't done much to combat the "Dancing Gypsies" stereotype. Honestly, I've never met any Gypsy that didn't adore dancing, or at the very least know how to dance. I'm sure there are some out there, just not in my universe.

From a very young age I've been dancing. Watching my aunties, my grandmas and especially my beautiful Ma – I learnt how to lose myself in movement. It started when I'd be shouted at by Ma and to stop her seeing me cry, I'd start spinning around with my arms out. I must have looked ridiculous, but it worked. The spinning eventually morphed into me using my feet to turn as I swung my hips around. I was obsessed with Ma and everything she did, so when she'd walk with her hips shaking to an invisible beat, I'd do the same. When my family were drunk enough, they'd always start a dance-off and I'd be fervently drinking it in and practising in secret for the weeks that followed.

Ma caught me one rainy afternoon and instead of blowing up at me for looking simple, she sat and motioned with her hands for me to continue with a smile on her face. When I'd finished, I fell on to the floor exhausted, with my legs in the air. Ma shrieked in laughter and came and lay next to me.

"You're very good, Eliska!" She patted my puffed-out belly.

After that day she'd spend a small measure of every evening showing me different dance steps and different ways to move my body. I couldn't have been very old, but I picked it up very quickly by all accounts. I was never adept at useful things like helping out in the markets for food, but I could spend hours dancing just like my mother. I spent two years being "trained" by Ma. Every evening she was at home she'd set aside time to dance with me. It wasn't much, but it was special – millions of kids had that evening-time for a bedtime story and a bubble bath, but I was luckier than all of them, because Lenka Zlatkov was teaching me the art of Gypsy dancing, belly dancing and escapism.

It was important for me to find something I could do well so I could help contribute to the home. I was always shame-faced when my cousins were showered with praise for bringing home bags of bread. I'd feel like the odd one out when they came back with treasures dug from the bins outside retail shops: shoes, tops, lipsticks. So, knowing I had a bankable dancing ability opened up a whole new world for me. Ma would take me along with her when she was working and make me dance for her clients. Sometimes they'd pay her extra if I took my clothes off. I'd be dancing naked and shivering slightly, overjoyed that I could help earn money with my dear ma.

My time in Drovane taught me so much, from the political to the personal. I realised that I'd always have to be platinum standard to match white mediocrity, something I picked up whenever I'd stay in Germany. Anja would be praised for basic tasks, whereas I'd need to be superhuman to garner a bored smile from my grandad. I realised that my heritage was more of a medical status than a badge of honour to most of the world. I realised that without an education and self-care I'd forever be a feral "Gyp-ling". I learnt that most people's idea of "helping" was seeing us as frightened, meek little things who needed stuff explained to them v e r y s l o w l y as they took notes on their pads and found the grubbiest kids to photograph. I learnt that having pride wasn't allowed when you were poor and wanting to make yourself look nice was equally frowned upon. If you had the misfortune to be born into a pit like Drovane, you had better make sure you spent your life looking like you were a ghetto-dwelling peasant. My time in England reinforced this same idea – the anger people would feel when a family on benefits had a widescreen TV! People who've never had to live on "handouts" have the grandest ideas about how one should live on "their tax money". And people with media-enforced judgements tout the loud minority as the norm, instead of the silent majority just struggling through each week without sinking. I learnt not to try to change people's minds.

I also learnt to utilise every scrap of talent I had to earn money. Hobbies are for the rich; the poor have side work. My dancing has proven over the years to be the best skill Ma gave me; it's fed me numerous times and given me the peace of soul that years of therapy couldn't have achieved.

I don't really consider myself Slovak. Slovakia never considered me Slovak, and when the world looks at me, they don't see a Slovakian girl. My whole goal since leaving Ma behind has changed from earning enough money to buy a house in Slovakia, to earning enough money to never have to return.

Dancing has earned me money faster than anything else could have. I rarely feel like I'm "working" when I'm dancing; I enjoy every part of the process, from the costuming to set-designing if possible ("set-designing" just meant telling the darbukah player where to sit, but I digress), to music, to choreography.

My dancing-for-money journey started when I was still with Gunjan and her nerves. I never count the times I danced in Drovane, because that was just me helping my ma and her clients. In England I found real work, instead of dusty "freelance" dancing.

I first met Yadira before we were taken to Sheffield. I was in Gunjan's front room with Rayaan and Dagmar, showing them various dances I'd learnt, and I bathed in their admiration. Gunjan wasn't in the room, so we'd taken the opportunity to have some measure of fun. Yadira cleared her throat and I stopped mid-shimmy. The three of us turned to the doorway and saw her.

She was at least six foot, with a majestic mane of thick curly black hair, and she towered gloriously over drab, scared

Gunjan. Yadira was an Egyptian woman in her fifties, but looked older to me; her makeup was thickly caked on, and her pencilled eyeliner was always thicker than her pencilled eyebrows. Her signature artificially plumped lips were always painted Barbie pink.

The first time I saw her, I was struck by her size and the presence she commanded. She was a woman you couldn't ignore, from her hair to her height to her makeup to the outlandishly patterned flared trousers and mustard-yellow blouse she wore. She was looking at me with her tongue sticking out to the side, as if she was caught midway licking her lips. I felt smug; Yadira's interest was certainly piqued.

She pulled out a packet of cigarettes from her large handbag and asked me where I'd learnt to dance. I didn't know how to answer; technically, I learnt in Ma's front room. Did I tell her that? Or did I tell her I practised alone in the cold whenever Ma was working? I didn't have the English capacity to tell her either of those things, it turned out, so I simply said, "Home."

She raised her ashy, drawn eyebrow and nodded slowly. She turned to Gunjan and spoke in a low voice for an age. She finally stopped and faced the three of us again. Blowing us a kiss, she turned and left.

I spent days thinking about her. She was such a… woman! A vibrant and colourful woman. I imagined Ma would dress like Yadira if she was rich enough, although Ma's makeup would be far superior.

From the way she looked at me when I stopped dancing, to the way she spoke to Gunjan afterwards and jerked her head in my direction, to her full lips pushing us a kiss, I was excited. I knew she was impressed with me, and I knew it meant I would benefit somehow from it. A smile was as good as a contract in the seedy worlds I had been raised in – both Ma's and Dad's.

Rayaan and Dagmar would mention it sporadically, and I'd feel a re-energised rush of pride and excitement. I almost asked Gunjan when we'd see Yadira again, but that idea always dissolved whenever we saw her miserable face.

After so long hoping and wishing she'd come back, and even daydreaming of her whisking me off to stay with her – I imagined her home to be huge, with a garden and vivacious patterns draped throughout – I eventually saw her again.

It was the week after we were driven away from Gunjan's care by the man in a van. He had taken us from South Shields to Sheffield to live with another gloomy woman with a pre-ordained grudge against us.

The woman, Mrs Maktoub as we had to call her, was hellbent on treating us as if we'd pissed in her rice. Her irrational loathing of us quickly started to wear thin – at the ripe age of 13 and a half, I was thoroughly done with her type.

Mrs Maktoub called me to the front room, and my mood lifted instantly when I saw Yadira standing there. She had a baby pink blouse on under a huge white coat, and white jeans tucked into a pair of red boots. Her hair and makeup looked exactly the same as it did the first time I'd seen her; in fact, it looked rock hard, like it hadn't been touched since our last meeting.

She stood up and gestured for a hug. I was desperate to smell her perfume, so I let her and her coat envelop me. She smelt as great as I knew she would. Floral and peppery.

She let go and took her seat on the sofa. The whole room felt unworthy whilst she sat regally with her legs to the side, pushing a cigarette to her lips.

"I have some work for you, little one. If you want it?" Her voice was hoarse and rough – had I noticed that in South Shields? Or did the softness of rose-tinted memory sweeten her voice in my head?

I didn't know what to say – I was enthralled! Of course I wanted to work; I wanted a house for Ma and a pair of red velvet boots just like Yadira's.

"Yes, of course!" came my desperate reply. I've never been one to play games if offered something I need or want.

"Yes… what?" She raised her head and eyebrows as she waited for me to speak.

I had a brief flash of fear as I struggled to think of all the words we'd learnt for endearment in English. I wasn't as vocally challenged as the months before, but I still had moments when I'd forget basic rules and pronunciations.

"Yes… Yadira?" I spoke as slowly as I could, searching her face for a clue as to what she was waiting for.

"Na. Not 'Yadira'." She mimicked my high voice. "You say 'Ya Umi'. Repeat 'Yah Oomii'."

After two goes I managed to grasp the basic phrase – I kept trying to add an "r" in between the "u" and "m". She was surprisingly patient.

"It means 'mother'. Your mother isn't here, is she?" She nodded as I shook my head. "So someone needs to look after you. I will. I'm going to be your mother now when you are in England." She smiled.

The next week I was waiting in the kitchen, in a fresh T-shirt with a palm tree saying "MIAMI DREAMS" and blue jeans. After hearing my name barked out from the front room, I knew Yadira had pulled up. I was so nervous that Dagmar had to put her hand over my mouth to stop me vomiting.

"Why are you so scared? This is what you wished," she half-scolded.

I shrugged dumbly and did a little shake to try and force the nerves out of me. I walked down the hallway and opened the door meekly. Yadira was in the back of a black car. She waved at me. I felt better instantly. Just me and Yadira? This would be fine.

As I got closer, I saw the outline of a thin, bald man in the driving seat. I reached the car and opened the door, ready to greet Yadira. I was face to face, however, with another wide-eyed brown girl.

"Hello! Are you ready to work? It's the first day for both of you!" Her arm reached over the other girl and she gently tugged me into the car.

Neither of us spoke to each other – or at all, save for answering Yadira's questions or chirpy statements.

Yadira spoke to the driver in a fast tongue; I couldn't recognise the language. The other girl looked from Yadira to the driver every so often, as if she could understand what was being laughed or gossiped about. I felt extremely self-conscious, wondering if I was the butt of the joke.

I scowled out of the window for the last 20 minutes of the trip, annoyed at them for being ignorant and speaking about my faded "MIAMI DREAMS" T-shirt and laughing at my baggy jeans that made me look like I was extremely well endowed in the crotch. All this, of course, was what my paranoid arse had decided they were saying.

We pulled into the car park of a hotel. The name was illuminated in giant letters and I was morbidly wishing one of the letters would fall onto one of the cars below. I wanted to see if it'd completely flatten it, people and all.

We exited the car and Yadira held each hand out as we both clung to her. We walked in a horizontal line through the automatic doors, like a normal woman and her daughters. We stood patiently next to her as she giggled with the young woman at the reception, and I remembered the Gypsy lady at the hotel my dad took me to when he'd hoped I'd be going to school. I imagined him being proud of me today, standing waiting for my new job. I hadn't needed school after all!

Yadira motioned at us to follow her as she made her way to a steel door. The door opened and we walked inside; it was a lift. I'd seen one before in Germany, but had been too afraid to go inside. Now I had no choice. The doors closed and I pressed my back against the wall, hoping to brace myself against whatever was going to happen without Yadira and the other girl noticing. The lift moved and it felt as if my whole body was being forced down by a heavy pressure. It stopped abruptly, and I stumbled a little before regaining my balance.

Stepping out, Yadira seemed to know exactly where to go. I couldn't take in the environment, as I was having to half-run to keep up with her brisk walk. I knew it was a stark contrast to the hotel Dad had taken me to in his bid to make a schoolgirl out of me – that "hotel" had odd doors, mismatched décor and the faint aroma of dalliances past. We reached a room door identical to all the ones we'd passed. I was impressed that she knew which one to stop at, until I saw the number plate. Wondering how thick I really was, I went inside and gulped down the smell of fresh linen and lavender.

"Do you need to use…" Yadira pointed at the ensuite. I shook my head and the other girl copied. "Ok, then let's start!"

She took off her coat and started to reach into her handbag. There was a knock at the door, startling me and the other girl, but Yadira got up with her eyes still fixed on her handbag and smiled at us as she walked past. It was the driver, carrying two large suitcases. He had a white shirt and black jeans with sandals. His toes were gnarled and hairy, nothing like my dad's feet. They made me feel sick.

The both of them were in conversation as they unpacked the suitcases. They pulled out four identical long black bags with hangers poking out, and a small beauty case with little polka dots all over.

"So, my little ones..." Yadira had a small speaker and was messing with the sound knob. Suddenly there was a ripple of music through the room and my skin immediately prickled in excitement. It was a simple drumbeat with a couple of bells every so often but in that moment, it was the best music I'd ever heard in my life.

Yadira asked us both to dance in the middle of the room after making the driver sit in a chair facing the window. The both of us were reluctant to start with, but she turned the music a touch higher and then off we went. I closed my eyes and pretended I was on a stage with Ma in the audience and Dad clapping for me. The music faded out and we stopped dancing. Yadira looked self-satisfied as she surveyed us both.

"I have something for you both!" Her eyes twinkled as she rose to her feet. She went over to the bed and began unzipping the black bags. The first one she unzipped revealed a flash of teal and gold that mesmerised me. It took all I had not to fling myself on it.

After all had been revealed, I was transfixed by the sheer opulence of the outfits. Teal and gold, orange and silver, green and purple, and blue and gold. All four outfits looked like works of art. The fabric, the cut, the trims and the detail were all so utterly impressive that I felt afraid to touch any of them, lest I destroyed them in some way.

"Don't be shy, pick one!" Yadira pushed my shoulder forward. I couldn't believe I was allowed – actually, ordered – to wear one. I wished Ma could see me deciding which outfit to wear. She'd be jealous of me, for a change.

I knew straight away I wanted the teal and gold; thankfully the other girl picked the orange and silver one. Yadira helped us one by one into the outfits. As the other girl stood in her outfit, I was awestruck: colours sparkled in the daylight pouring through the window, making her look like a little disco ball. It was finally my turn! Yadira showed me how to wear the skirt correctly, so the fabric fell in all the right places and the seam at the back was covered, and how to carefully tie the top so none of the sequins or beadwork would be damaged.

As I stood in the middle of the room, I had never felt more beautiful.

We practised in our outfits again to the music from before and Yadira looked happier and happier. She sprayed us with some perfume and then dabbed tiny touches of lipstick on our lips and cheeks with her finger. We were ready.

"The party is downstairs, so we won't need to go outside. You will dance for a little while and then come upstairs and have loads of food! Yes?" Yadira beamed at us and we beamed back like little hungry hyenas. This was shaping up to be the best day of my life.

The walk downstairs to a large, decorated room was uneventful, as was the actual party. Nobody really noticed us until we went into a smaller room with about 15 or so men. Yadira handed something to a man sitting at the back, and then the song we were to dance to rang out. I hadn't felt scared or ashamed until the moment I started dancing and saw the panting face of an overweight, sweaty man stuffed into a suit. His pink skin was glowing almost, and he was gradually leaning forward more and more as the music progressed. I tried to shut my eyes, but was scared of him grabbing me and running away, so I forced myself to look at anything other than him. I focused on a tall bottle of Fanta and felt my stomach tighten. The music faded out as it had three times earlier that day, but this time a wave of relief came over me instead of disappointment that it had finished. I looked at the other girl, who was smiling and laughing with a hand on her chest. She obviously had a better time than me. Yadira beckoned us to the door and off we went, back through the larger party and to the lifts. Again, nobody noticed us in our finery. We must have looked like all the other people at the party: colourful outfits that were boring after the first eight people passed through the lobby.

Back in the room, she counted out an envelope of cash into three piles of varying thickness. The thickest pile stood next to two miniscule piles, as if a couple of notes had been blown off the top and happened to lie perfectly alongside the main pile.

"Now, I can give you this…" Yadira held out the little piles towards us. "But where will you spend it? Will you even be able to keep it? Or I can use this and buy you even more beautiful costumes and your OWN makeup!"

We were two silly girls who'd had a day of surprises, a jolting moment downstairs in my case, but then a meal that shamed every other scrap of food we'd ever eaten, and now were lazing on the bed watching television. Well, the other girl was watching television. I was watching the tree outside making shadows on the walls (I was never that bothered with television – back then, I had no idea what *Emmerdale* was, so not only did I not realise what greatness I was missing, but my sexual awakening was also delayed until the joyous day I saw Cain Dingle for the first time). So of course we wanted our own makeup and costumes. We played right into Yadira's hands – though honestly, I doubt she'd have given us those two notes even if we wanted them.

That week kicked off a long working relationship between me and Yadira. I never saw the other girl again; Yadira had mentioned how she wasn't really liked because of her "over-eagerness". I guess the men we would regularly dance for only liked girls who looked half-scared. Maybe a girl looking comfortable and as if she was enjoying herself wasn't what they were into.

WHO WANTS YOUR MAN, MRS MAKTOUB?

Yadira had whisked me away for my first ever dance job a couple of weeks after arriving in Yorkshire, and returned me two days later. Dagmar greeted me with a tight hug and whispered in my ear, "It's pure hell here."

Mrs Maktoub was one of those women who thought they'd married such a gift to the world that every woman with the audacity to breathe near him must be stealing him. How the hell you can steal an adult man I'll never know. Nobody is "stolen" – people go willingly. There is no thievery, just adultery. Ma had never stolen a man. Maybe their money, but never the man. *They* came to *her*; she didn't kidnap men and force them to sleep with her. Dad was a different issue – I've never seen a woman resist him apart from me. Even then, I was fickle. Sometimes I'd have the stomach to be immune to his charm offensive, other times I'd melt into his lop-sided smile.

"This isn't your wedding, go and get dressed. You have work to catch up on." That was Mrs Maktoub's favourite line – "it isn't your wedding".

I dressed, did my chores and then went and cleaned the Indian restaurant I was allocated to. I was scrubbing a particularly nasty toilet – it must have been some brave soul who ordered a spicy dish and regretted it instantly – when I caught myself thinking, *Why? Why risk the potential jail time, the stress, the hassle, just to keep two immigrant teens as cleaners?* It didn't make any sense. I knew Mrs Maktoub was getting a cut from Yadira when I was dancing, but even so, it surely wasn't worth it.

I found out why sooner rather than later.

Mr Maktoub was as miserable as his wife, but he enjoyed watching Dagmar and me doing the most menial of tasks. I was a very young 13 when I'd left Drovane: I hadn't had enough social interaction to fully mature, nor any schooling at all. Emotionally, I had grown a lot since we drove away from Drovane in the van, but I still didn't fully realise what I was: a lonely teenage girl with basic English skills. Though after Gunjan's intensive school experience at the kitchen table, perhaps I'd reached an intermediate English level now.

I never saw myself as a sexual being. To me, a sexual being was an overtly vulgar-tongued person like Ma. In my mind, I was still the little idiot of the Zlatkov family.

So, when Mr Maktoub told me and Dagmar that he had a few friends who were excited to meet us, it took me longer than it should to be reminded of Rosa's story of Karl and his "friends". I was appalled. If I'd somehow managed to survive being Lenka's daughter and not sell myself in Drovane, then I'd be damned if this moron was going to make me a prostitute.

I told Dagmar we should find something to hit him on the head with one day and then run away. The plan stalled when we realised we didn't have a clue where to go, and the threat of being captured by the police, or any of the weirdoes we'd encountered on our journey thus far, was too much.

Instead, Dagmar decided we should tell someone. Mrs Maktoub, for example. I disagreed: the type of woman she was, she'd blame the foreign sluts for trying to lure her husband into a wayward life. What if I told the Indian family I cleaned the restaurant for? The owner, whenever he was there, was nice enough. He'd always have a chat with me, no matter how brief or mundane. But, as Dagmar pointed out, he knew I wasn't 16 and he probably knew something was iffy about me working when everyone else my age was at school. So why would he have an issue with what Mr Maktoub did when he was perfectly happy for me to scrub his restaurant?

We both agreed on the final option: Yadira.

The Maktoubs always seemed on edge when she was around, and from what I'd witnessed from Yadira, their uneasiness was well justified. I always had a performance to do, or to attend as an assistant, so I saw Yadira regularly. She came by after I had washed the stench of the restaurant off me and walked straight into our room. I had one leg in my pyjamas and the other raised in the air.

"Eliska. I have some work for you." She sat on my bed.

"I need to tell you something!" I whispered as I hopped over to shut the door. I knew the Maktoubs would heighten their senses when Yadira was around. "The husband, he is going to bring his friends to 'visit' us!"

"Visit you?" She acted dense sometimes.

"Visit *this*." I pointed to my knickers. I finished pulling on my pyjamas as Yadira got the message.

"You weren't for that, though."

Come again? I wanted to ask what the fuck I was for then, because I had originally thought I was here to learn how to read and write. Not to learn the difference between Cif and Mr Muscle or learn how best to get shit stains off a bathroom wall.

"What shall we do?"

"Nothing. I'll speak to *Ukhti*."

Yadira didn't fill me with the greatest of confidence, but it was better than nothing.

She clearly didn't speak to Mrs Maktoub that night, because Dagmar and I had been asleep for a short while when the door creaked open. Mr Maktoub's heavy breathing announced his arrival, and the panting of another man announced danger's arrival. This wasn't good.

Dagmar was facing me as we stared at each other from the opposite ends of the room. I clamped my eyes shut before they saw I was awake. I held my eyes shut as I heard them approach, as I felt the bed sag under one of the men's weight, and as I felt an arm either side of me.

It was Mr Maktoub. His signature stench of sweat and dry roasted peanuts was overbearing. I still kept my eyes shut. This wasn't happening, this wasn't happening. He started to smell my hair and move the duvet off me. He had turned me onto my back and straddled me when both of us jumped at the sound of a foghorn wail emitting from Dagmar. I watched her in wonder as she managed to keep her mouth completely still, with the sound still going. The man was trying to push himself off the bed as Dagmar sat upright, with her arms straight behind her, clenching her fists. She had that stance that Olympians have before they jump into the sandpit.

Mrs Maktoub came running in and Dagmar shut her mouth instantly. I wanted to laugh so badly. One minute she was in that ridiculous stance wailing with her mouth wide open, the next she shut her mouth and pursed her lips, still in that dumb pose. Mr Maktoub slapped me around the face, climbed off me and started blubbering to his wife, but the snot and tears dripping off his face did nothing to appease the enraged woman standing before him.

There was a knock on the door, and Mrs Maktoub told Dagmar to go and answer. I was left alone watching the stranger trying to inch past Mrs Maktoub, and her husband on his knees sobbing. Mrs Maktoub broke her ice-cold stare to flicker her eyes over me. I blinked at her, clutching the duvet back over me.

She bent down till she was inches from Mr Maktoub's face and whispered something. She waited for both of them to leave the room before she looked at me, mumbled "Sorry", then turned and left. Leaving me unsure whether to laugh or cry. My lifelong habit of bursting into stupid laughter at the most inappropriate of times threatened to rear its unwanted head when I heard footsteps coming back to the room. Dagmar poked her head inside and padded to my bed to explain what had happened outside.

She told me a neighbour heard her war-cry and came to investigate. Dagmar made up some story about me starting my first period and the horror of the situation causing me to turn into a banshee. I asked if her story had convinced the neighbour. I wasn't concerned about her accent, because she had the same knack as I did for mimicking people's accents. "She was fine. Half asleep." She joined me in my bed; we didn't speak, but we knew we'd be moved now. We didn't know if we'd stay together.

Yadira arrived the next day, after I called her secretly from the house phone. She had given me her number for emergencies, and I dialled the numbers written elegantly on a clean piece of paper. It wasn't as secret as I'd hoped, because I was still getting the hang of phones: I dropped it first, then yelled down it as if we were in different countries. Mrs Maktoub was busy in the middle of the marital bedlam taking place in their bedroom, so she wouldn't have heard me anyway.

I let her in and explained once more what had happened. She laughed at my impression of Dagmar, then went upstairs.

That evening, Mrs Maktoub sat sullen in the kitchen. She'd told her husband to leave – he had – and now she was upset.

Yadira must have had some strong words, because we were told that we'd be going to school. We'd been given temporary IDs and were posing as Mrs Maktoub's relatives from Lebanon. This covered the mixture of accent and "spicy Euro" look we had going on.

This was all I had ever wanted. School.

*

We were in the school for half a year, and it was a woeful experience. We spent our time together, eating and trying to help each other with our classwork. We'd be harassed wherever we went – the playgrounds, corridors or toilets. But with each other it wasn't so bad. Many times we'd held hands so tightly that we left nail imprints in the other's skin.

Dagmar and I were both bullied for the haphazard uniform we had, the way we spoke, and the way we smelt. Mrs Maktoub only allowed us one five-minute shower a week after her husband left. I believe she thought we were to blame, but was too afraid of Yadira to do anything about it. I was earning Yadira a lot of money, so disrupting where I was staying would inconvenience her.

For good measure, I was racially abused too. It baffled me that Dagmar wasn't teased over her race – not that I wanted her to be, because she could barely handle the bullying she did get, whereas I was used to it from Drovane. We were the same shade, but she had more European features, while I had a longer nose. It wasn't just the white kids that made "Paki" comments: I was regularly called "dirty gyppo" and "pikey" by every race. I never understood what a "pikey" was; I still kind of don't.

Mrs Maktoub didn't help. She encouraged us to go "shopping" in the school lost property boxes. Dagmar caught headlice when she found a headband with "HOTTIE" stitched on in glitter, and I howled with laughter as she wept, combing her hair with a nit-comb we'd bought at the chemist. The humiliation when Dagmar and I wore our "found" clothes on non-uniform day was so bad that I swore never to go back there ever again. The next day I was sitting in double science in the immigrant class, marvelling at how wrong I had been about England. This dumbass place was no different to Drovane. Just richer and cleaner. The people were as poisonous, and the bigotry was as strong. Of course, it was a dramatic over-reaction, but I couldn't fathom how different England was to the fancy biscuit-boxes in Dad's kitchen. I felt cheated.

Still, I flourished with Yadira. We travelled to hotels and grander venues before long. I'd dance with two or three other girls – one of whom I became good friends with, Himma. The pair of us were Yadira's "good girls". She'd brag after each show that we made her the most money.

Then we moved on to bigger things. Himma and I went to Istanbul in an air-conditioned van with soft, comfortable seating. Yadira sat in the front as Himma and I watched the world go by through tinted windows in the back. Yadira had a set of passports for all of her girls, none of which had our actual faces or names. She'd always deal with border crossings or anything official as we sat in our plush seats smiling sweetly, and eventually seductively, at whoever popped their head in to check our identity.

We would dance for private parties on boats, in grand houses for weddings, birthdays, and any other event Yadira orchestrated.

They were always private affairs; she never allowed pictures or videos to be taken.

"Do you see who you're dancing for? They aren't the type of people who want to be caught watching dancing women." She'd always look around when saying that. "Anyway, it's against the faith. You can't make pictures or videos of yourself. Any good Muslim knows that." The hypocrisy didn't pass her by, and she always said that last part with a smile on her face.

When pressed, she'd elaborate on how private everything was kept. "You and Himma are the only ones who dance. The rest work extra. I can make more from you two just by dancing. People ask for you personally now. You are exciting to watch."

We were making enough by dancing to avoid being prostitutes, was what she meant. She'd say it gently, as if we were special to her, but there was always the lurking threat of what would happen if we ever stopped being so profitable from dancing alone.

Yadira had started asking me to perform at more and more private homes, as opposed to just "special occasions". I'd be in someone's small front room, dancing and sweating to a generic song played on Yadira's phone whilst groups of people, not always solely men, would be breathing heavily and leering at me.

England wasn't supposed to be this.

More than a few times I'd been pawed at by men who wanted more than just a dance. Yadira would watch for a while as I tried to bat hands away from me, and then lazily intervene when she felt they were getting more than what they paid for. Squeezing developing parts of my body was okay, but when they tried to tug my clothes off, that was too far. There was a price structure and I was only factored in for Yadira's cheap deals on dancing girls.

I thought of all the times I had danced for the men who Ma said "couldn't work properly unless there was a child in front of them," and how they would look at me whilst Ma was on her knees in front of them. The same weird feeling of being "wrong" would wash over me, and I would close my eyes, waiting for it all to be over.

Each time it happened, Yadira would placate me afterwards in the car, telling me how beautiful I was and that men couldn't help themselves. And what did I expect when I was such a cute little thing? Only as an adult do I see the parallels between

Yadira and Ma. Both had tried to sell their work to me, and both had inadvertently drummed into my head that men were sexual beings with no self-control and women must beware of such beasts. It was up to a woman to ensure men wouldn't froth at the mouth at her and lose all reason.

I suppose even then I knew she was chatting shit. I've never been beautiful, and certainly not some otherworldly vision of attractiveness that would cause men to lose their minds. But what could I say? Was I in any position to argue with the woman who was feeding me? I knew she was dangerous because she would walk into these rooms of "beastly men" with no qualms, trepidation or hesitation. As if my ancestors were speaking directly to my mind, I told myself to be grateful it wasn't worse.

And so it continued.

I would go to school, then go on my various cleaning jobs, complete the list of chores Mrs Maktoub set for us each day, and dance whenever Yadira summoned me. It was routine – we didn't resent it because we had no time to. We just followed instructions.

Dagmar and I were the closest we'd ever been to another human. I never thought about Anja and Arne, because it would hurt too much. The idea of them wondering every month where I'd gone and then playing with each other as I was working, working, working here in England would break my heart. My family were distant memories to me, as I convinced myself I would never see them again. But Dagmar was my family. She was my mother, father, sister, brother and confidante.

From the stories we made up together in South Shields to the secrets we shared about our families to the dreams we hoped would materialise in England, we were each other's most trusted allies.

I knew Dagmar only had a grandmother back home, and she wanted nothing more than to be able to get her a small cabin. Her grandmother took care of her, and was disowned by Dagmar's father and the rest of the family. Dagmar was a "lovechild", although it seemed there was very little love from either parent. Her mother had other children and couldn't afford another, while her father didn't want his wife to find out about Dagmar. Whenever she spoke of her parents, she would scowl until she was almost unrecognisable, but when speaking of her grandmother her freckles would glisten and her eyes would seem alive and determined. She wanted that cabin more than anything. To be able to go back home and tell her grandmother that she didn't need to spend her last years eking out a living in the Laundromat – just to pay for a dilapidated apartment with a severe case of damp – was the ultimate goal for Dagmar.

All of our impromptu stories about our futures ended the same for Dagmar: living in a cabin near a lush, floral field with a dog and her grandmother. In her stories, her aging grandmother's health complaints seemed to vanish, and she'd live forever with Dagmar. I thought of my own grandmother and how death seemed so far from her – she was more mobile than Dagmar's grandmother from what

I could make out. I'd never live in a cabin with Vera. I'd irritate her to death, and she'd pimp me out to any nearby farmers within an hour.

My stories weren't as predictable. Sometimes I'd have a home with a garden just for me and Ma. Sometimes I'd have a bigger home for all of my Zlatkov family and my siblings. More often, though, I'd live in Dad's house and he would be good to me, he'd let Ma come and stay, and we'd all have a fulfilled life with no violence or prostitution. He wouldn't beat me so ferociously, or coach me what to say when the hospital staff asked me what happened, and Ma wouldn't stare at me with the hateful eyes she'd have sometimes when she was sore from working, before launching herself at me.

At night we'd lie together in my bed, crying silently or making up the stupidest stories about killing Mrs Maktoub by pushing her down the stairs or caving her head in with one of the ugly, scratched pots she'd use to make rice in. The violence we'd conjure up never alarmed us. We imagined the ludicrous schemes and antics we'd have to pull to convince people Mrs Maktoub was still alive; we ended up stuffing our sleeves in our mouths to stop laughing. On each of our respective journeys thus far, we'd been threatened with and been on the receiving end of so much aggression that we were desensitised.

We were able to keep each other smiling as we huddled in the small bed. Me watching the dark sky, longing to feel the wind on my face as Dagmar and I flew away from this place, and her staring at the plain wallpaper wishing she was as close to the cabin as her grandmother was to death.

She was the only reason I smiled most weeks, and I was the same for her.

But it all ended when I received news from a smirking Mrs Maktoub.

I was leaving. A permanent ID had been found for me. Hours away from Sheffield. In the Midlands.

Dagmar was to remain in Sheffield.

The move came almost instantly. There hadn't been time for it to sink in that this was it. It had been under a year, but Dagmar and I felt like we'd been together for decades. Decades of uncertainty, fear, risk and fragile hope condensed in a whirlwind of a few long, frightening months.

I was gone in less than a week. The school was told I was going back to Lebanon. Nobody cared. None of the teachers even knew which one I was.

The same man who had dropped us off in Sheffield arrived in the same muddy van to take me to the Midlands. I was to stay in Leicester and carry on my schooling there.

Yadira had decided she wanted to come along. I had worked in Leicester a few times before at parties, and she knew a few of the Muslim sisters over there. They'd keep an eye on me, she said. She arrived an hour later than planned, which I was grateful for. It gave me and Dagmar more time to cling to each other and promise we would one day meet again. We fooled ourselves into believing we'd make it in this country. We fooled ourselves into thinking neither of us would end up on the streets or selling ourselves. She grabbed my hand and told me our favourite joke in Slovak.

"Eliska… *Keď policajt povie 'papiere' a ja 'nožnice', tak som vyhral?*" – Slovak for "When the Policeman says, 'Papers' and I say, 'Scissors' does it mean I've won?" Dumb as hell joke.

Our faces were pressed together, and our tears became one. The man cleared his throat and then tapped me impatiently on the shoulder. I never saw her again.

The scar that day left on my heart has never healed. I've never had such intense friendship, companionship and support from anyone else since. I've had no interest in forging the same type of relationship with another person either.

The last I heard of Dagmar, she'd died of heroin addiction at the age of 18.

THE KHEER
TO THE SOUL

Yadira and I sat at the front with the silent brown driver. We had been on the road for a little over half an hour when Yadira glanced over at me. I was leaning back with my eyes closed. She assumed I was asleep, rather than fossilised with terror at the motorway. I never sat in the front on the motorway when I was in Germany.

"So, how you get these IDs?" Yadira asked.

"You know how." The man had a sweet voice when he wasn't shouting.

"No, I don't. I move girls around; I don't bother with paperwork." She giggled. She wasn't flirting? Oh god. I bit my cheeks to stop myself laughing.

"It was easier before, it's got harder for the others coming over," he began. "It was easier to register births before, now they want to see the stitches to prove you had the baby you brought with you. Can't pay people off like before either."

"So... you... I don't understand."

"One baby gets registered all over about five times. Then when we need IDs, we have them. They make passports, cards and stuff over the years and then we have a proper ID pack to sell."

I would have called bullshit on the whole thing if I hadn't been brought over in a washing machine box myself.

"Who is 'they'?" Yadira was fascinated, I could tell.

"They. Just 'they'. The ones who organise everything. My uncles used to do it until they got caught, then a bunch of random Bengalis, Jamaicans and stuff popped up. Now you've got Bulgarians and Europeans doing it. It's not smooth like it was before. I remember in the eighties you could just drive someone down and say, 'they can't speak, they've got a sore throat' and pretend to look for the passport and drop an envelope down. That's how everyone got over here." The man had a nostalgic lilt to his voice.

I must have fallen asleep for real at some point, because Yadira elbowed me awake.

"I said we're almost there. Fix yourself up."

I sat up straight and stretched. My heart was broken for Dagmar, and anxious for this new place I was going to.

The scenery wasn't as pretty as it was when we first left Sheffield. It looked more like the journey to my grandparents' house in East Germany.

We drove into Leicester and I recognised a few shops. Maybe being here wouldn't be so bad. The community was mostly ethnic – I wasn't sure how many Gypsies were here, but I loved all the different food shops around. I wasn't as enamoured with British food just yet.

The van pulled into a cul-de-sac and onto the drive of a posh-looking house right in the corner. I loved it straight away.

Black gates kept the rest of the street away, and the clean drive looked welcoming.

We tumbled out of the van and stretched. I was happy to be here. I didn't know who or what lurked behind the door, but the Franz Volker in me just loved the exterior.

"Hello Dhruv!" A bald, happy man was walking out of the house with his arms outstretched. Who the fuck was "Dhruv"? I saw the van driver go and embrace the house-owner. His name was Dhruv? He didn't look like a Dhruv.

The bald man turned towards Yadira, clasped his hands together and said hello. He then turned to me and held out his hand. I shook it limply.

"Can she understand English?" he asked "Dhruv". I was never going to be comfortable calling him that.

"Yes, I can," I piped up.

"Oh sorry! Please come in, Alissa!" Wait, who the fuck was Alissa? Yadira elbowed me in the arm, passed me a plastic wallet with a passport and other forms in, and told me to go inside. I looked at the passport. It was my picture from the first day in Gunjan's room; she'd made us stand against the white walls as we had our picture taken. The name said Alissa. That was my new name. I didn't mind it, I liked the name, though I didn't like having my only possession taken from me. But if I wanted to make it in England like I'd promised Dagmar we'd do, then I had to make it as Alissa Kaur Boparai. Not Eliska Zlatkov.

I stepped inside the house and met the bald man's wife. They had a warmth to them. I was surprised to hear I was the only one in this house. No other immigrants to share with. I speculated how much it had cost Ma to send me to England. I'd encountered so many people on the way – they'd all need their own cut. Had what she paid really stretched this far?

That evening I sat eating *roti* and *bhindi masala*. The bald man, Haroun, and his wife, Usha, explained that they were paid to be a "foster family" for people like me until I could stand on my own two feet.

I didn't believe them for a second. He looked too eager to have me there, and his wife couldn't hide her displeasure at the situation. I swallowed their bullshit alongside my *roti* in front of their faces, but my heart was sinking faster than Haroun was sinking the beer he'd pulled from the fridge. After offering me one, which I declined, he sat and watched me eat the rest of the food.

I turned 14 a few weeks after arriving in Leicester. I got a card and then a lift to the factory where Usha worked at night. The factory employed several immigrant women to sew and do laundry. It was less a factory and more a massive room with some washing machines and dryers in one corner and sewing machines in the other.

Usha taught me sewing basics, which I'd already half-learnt from Yadira, and put me to work in the factory. I worked slowly at first, trying to master the sewing machine, but as I got more comfortable, I began working confidently. I'd sew the Asian dresses with such ease that I felt I'd finally found my calling. I didn't interact with the other women, simply because they didn't like me. They didn't care that I looked just like them or that I could speak 85% of their language. I wasn't from India, Pakistan or any brown country – I was from Slovakia, and so I was automatically an outsider to them. I didn't care. I had bigger problems at home.

Haroun – at least, I assumed it was Haroun – kept trying to get in my room at night. I'd noticed something off about him, so I began moving the dresser a tiny bit in front of the door. Just over the entry point. I'd hear the doorknob turn, but nothing else; he wasn't able to move the dresser.

I tried to tell Usha, who slapped me around the face and threatened to burn me in my bed if I made another accusation against her husband.

One night when I was shattered from sewing, he managed to get in. I tried to scream like Dagmar, but my body wouldn't co-operate.

"I just wanted to say goodnight, sweetie!" He always called me sweetie. I hated it. I hated the word, and the way his accent would make it sound even sleazier.

I was watching him swaying in the doorway when a brown arm dragged him backwards. Usha. She shut my door without a word, and the next day we all pretended nothing had happened.

I spent the next two weeks door-watching and snatching pockets of sleep when I was unable to hold my head up any longer. We still carried on as if her husband wasn't trying to attack me in the nights. Some nights I'd hear him breathing outside the door and some nights I'd see the door handle turn. Every time I felt as if I could get a grip on my life and get past the nasty things that had happened, I was always reminded of my insignificance in the world. This man would remind me every night how easy it would be for me to be raped and killed without anybody knowing.

I sank into the routine of moving furniture across the door and sleeping in belted trousers in case I fell into a deep sleep and he managed to find his way in. For months, time passed in a tired haze of sewing, school and staying awake every night. My eyes looked horrendous, and my skin looked grey in daylight. I hated looking in the mirror; I saw every struggle I'd overcome in my sallow skin and sunken eyes.

Despite being bullied for my accent as usual, school was also a special place for me. I made friends with the Punjabi girls. We compared our cultures and the similarities of our languages. I felt a bond with them, but nothing compared to mine and Dagmar's. I never told them where I lived, as Usha told me I'd be arrested. I'd make a vague hint about living with relatives whenever I was asked. Which was fine with most of them, as they weren't allowed to go to each other's houses or have people over themselves. I was thankful for our strange cultural restrictions whenever the subject of "sleepovers" or "come round for tea" popped up from some of the girls with more liberal parents.

School had been a lifelong dream of mine ever since Slovakia. It was a place where I was convinced I would be given the golden ticket out of the life I was born into. My disappointment with my first experiences with school back in Yorkshire was enormous. I never refer to that first fiasco when I speak of my schooling. Why would I? I didn't learn much, apart from better English slang and how to beat up racist girls. The shock on a racist bully's face when I reached boiling point and squared up to them was surprising to me. How can you say things like that and not expect retaliation? It's as if they were outraged at my audacity.

In Leicester, though, school was everything I dreamed of. I had always had a burning desire to succeed. Not just out of desire to overcome the poverty I was born into. But also out of spite. Many of the greatest achievements of my life have been born out of spite. Slovakia told me that I deserved Drovane, so I left (well, my parents made that decision, but still). That cruel man at the school told my dad and me that school wasn't for Gypsies, so I would do my utmost to work hard and complete my schooling. Mrs Maktoub and all the other "Mrs Maktoubs" told me I was nothing but a cheap slut here to leech off the government, so I would make sure to work as hard as humanely possible to make something out of the dirty peasant girl who would nod obediently whenever those women started berating her.

I had to do my schoolwork, regardless of the bullying and indifference from the teachers. I didn't really blame the teachers, as I would get frustrated with myself when I couldn't grasp written instructions. The classrooms were always full to the brim, so how could I expect the teacher to forego all the English pupils just to break it down for my slow arse? I would secretly take textbooks home and try to drill them into my head so I wouldn't need to keep asking the teacher what to do.

I loved learning. Remembering a random fact in the middle of my sewing work would fill me with such delight that I would glide through the rest of the day in an elated haze. It was working! Learning was working! It renewed my vigour for education each time it happened.

I was slowly ambling toward a point of happiness in England for the first time. I was improving in my schoolwork week by week. I had discovered the absolute saving grace of my life: reading. I might have been reading books that the rest of my friends had already read at eight years old, but I had found the single, consistent coping mechanism that would aid me through Haroun-dodging nights.

I had managed to claw my way from the "immigrants and teens who still eat glue" sets to first and second sets in core subjects. I was even called "gifted" and "talented" in Art and Textiles.

It was a relief to be able to express my creativity in ways that were actually praised and seen as "good", instead of being locked away to dance for old men or sewing until my back ached. I enjoyed learning about various artists and the way they'd painted the same world in different ways. I thought about my classmates and how differently each of us saw the lesson we were sitting in. I was drinking it in as if it was an elixir, while half of them seemed bored to tears and were doing everything but listening to the teacher. Not for the first time, I wondered why this was a piss-take to them. My cousins would have done anything to have a seat in the back of the class. They wouldn't sit tearing pages out of their school diaries, flicking them at each other or at diligent students. My cousins would be furiously making notes and moaning at me for staring at the pictures like a simpleton.

As wonderful as I could make my school experience, I just couldn't do the same at home. Haroun made another pass at me during the Christmas before my GCSE exams. He'd been drinking too much as usual, but this time he was angry. He swore at Usha and called me.

I went inside and asked what he wanted.

"You," he slurred, "I want you to dance for me."

I rolled my eyes and turned to leave, but he reached forward and grabbed my arm, spinning me around.

"I said, dance for me. It's Christmas. You're in my house. Fucking dance." He dropped his empty bottle to the floor and grabbed my hips, shaking them.

"Get off!" The Franz Volker in me took over and I elbowed him in the nose, then picked up the bottle, ready to smack him over the head.

Usha grabbed my hand and told him to leave.

He spat on the floor, staring at me. "When I get back. YOU GONE!" I'd elbowed his English skills out of his head, apparently.

He didn't need to tell me twice. I was going. A school friend lived nearby and I knew she would help me. I only had a few things to pack up. Some clothes, books and toiletries. I put them all in one black bag. I remembered doing the same thing years before at Gunjan's house, but I was stronger now. I wasn't afraid to leave. I would prefer to be arrested than to stay with ol' Chester the Molester and his enabling wife.

I gave Usha a peck on the cheek before I walked out of her door and her life. She had let me stay there, after all. She patted my arm, with tears in her eyes.

I wasn't free in this lovely country. I was working for an unknown source who would collect the money I earned from whomever I was staying with at any given time. When I first arrived in England, I had assumed it was the van driver who was in charge of everything. Then I thought it was Gunjan. But as her paranoia kicked in, I realised she was in as precarious a position as the rest of us. Then in Yorkshire, I wondered if maybe Yadira was the one in charge – but she never concerned herself with anything that wasn't dance-related. If anything, she'd have preferred me not to clean, but just to travel with her and dance, dance, dance.

It was at Haroun and Usha's house that I resigned myself to never finding out who I was working myself ragged for. All that remained the same was a plain brown envelope that my cash wages would be shoved in and every so often collected by a different driver. My wages from the sewing job I had weren't paid to me directly. They were kept in the makeshift office tacked on to the "work room" in the same brown envelope. I figured that as long as I continued working, where I was staying wouldn't be such an issue, would it? All that mattered was the money I earned. Yadira seemed to have a tracker fitted to me so she could hunt me out whenever she had another dance job.

I walked out of the black gates and out of the cul-de-sac. I knew the way to my mate Ranjit's. But would I really be welcome there? A random girl showing up at her house? I decided to go anyway.

I got there in under ten minutes. I regretted knocking instantly. It was stupid. Why had I come here?

"Alissa! What's up?" She had a huge smile on her face, and the smell of *roti* dragged me indoors. Her mum came through from the kitchen with flour on her hands and the same smile as her daughter on her big, round, happy face.

"Hello!" She had a strong accent. I smiled back at her.

"Hello, Mrs Sarai." I became ever so shy standing in this lovely person's house.

"What's wrong, Alissa, why have you got that bag?" Ranjit looked worried.

"I've left. I can't go back there. Can I please stay here for a little while?" I felt stupid.

"Oh! Why you can't go back?" Her mum looked like she was going to cry. "I speak your mum!"

"I don't live with my mum…"

"Then who?"

"I live with relatives, nearby."

Ranjit looked more and more concerned. "Where do they live, Alissa?"

I told them the address. What was the use of hiding it now?

They both looked horrified. My head turned from mother to daughter and back to mother.

"What?" I asked.

"They are fucking weirdoes, Alissa!" Ranjit apologised to her mum, who raised her hand as if she was going to slap her one, though I couldn't imagine it actually happening.

"They take girls. Make prostitute. Haroun is a *kutha*, a dog! *Haram zaada*." She turned to Ranjit. "Tell her! *Haram zaada*... er... bastard!"

"I speak some Punjabi, I understand," I stammered. "I know he is a bastard, that's why I left. He wanted to do things to me."

She began wiping her hands on her apron the moment I finished.

"You can't stay here because her dad is not nice. He is throw you out." She looked helpless; I hadn't realised Ranjit had a mean father. "My sister is stay at *Gurdwara*. Is rooms there."

"What about social services, mummi?" Ranjit asked.

"*Nahi*! Those *haram de* will..." She glanced at me, then finished her sentence in fast, low Punjabi to Ranjit.

*

I finished my secondary schooling at the Gurdwara, the Sikh temple. The room was sweet. It was small but the thought of being in such a special place was humbling.

Ranjit's auntie helped me set my bag in the rickety wardrobe in the corner of the room. I was so amped up with adrenalin that I couldn't help pacing the floor like a moron for at least an hour. Then I felt the weight of the night's decisions come crashing down on my shoulders. I felt scared and lonely, and I wanted more than anything for my dad to come and scoop me into his car, play "Strangelove" and drive me away to his warm, safe bed.

Not for the first time did I wonder if he knew what was happening to me. I had only been able to ring my family a handful of times after Yadira allowed me to use her phone. I never knew any phone numbers by heart, and so it was an arduous process trying to track down a number for the Zlatkovs or Volkers. I had a short five-minute conversation with Ma as Yadira sat opposite me, after briefing me on what I was allowed to mention and what was best to leave out. "So your mother won't worry," Yadira said.

Ma asked me if I was behaving myself and whether I was living in a house yet. I said yes, "but it isn't my house". I asked her for Dad's number so I could try and speak to Anja, and she said she'd call me back with it. She must have rung Yadira because a few weeks later, Yadira said I could ring my father this time. Ma hadn't asked if I was okay or safe or if I was being treated properly, so I hoped against hope I'd get these questions from Dad. I wanted to tell him that I was tired and needed his help. But he didn't answer.

It was at the temple that I learnt the importance of balancing routine with spirituality. I would wake up to the sounds of the morning prayers being half-sung by a man with a low, soothing voice. I'd use the small bathroom opposite my room, and use a facemask Ranjit gave me for my "panda eyes" as I sat on the floor of my room, reciting the parts of the *parth* (prayers) that I had learnt by ear. I didn't quite know what I was saying, but I know my malnourished soul craved it. It was the facemask my spirit really needed. Then I'd get my things ready for school, walk to the *langar hall* (food hall), and help the ladies with anything they needed doing to prepare the *langar* that day.

The concept of a *langar* – fresh food made daily for anyone who came to the temple regardless of colour, gender, sexual orientation and so on – was so touching to me that I was always honoured to come home and find people eating food I'd helped make that morning.

I'd have a bowl of Indian rice pudding called *kheer* that smelt the way I imagined the Waltons' home to smell. Warm, inviting and comforting. Then I'd be off on my way to meet Ranjit to walk to school.

I'd come home from school and be asked by three different "aunties" how school was. Something I'd never experienced from my own family. I could be gone for hours on end, even as a six-year-old, and walk through the door without anybody noticing I'd been away at all. But here I wasn't bothered or asked what I was doing there – I was just checked on and almost fed to death by caring grannies who had nobody to fuss over but the skinny girl in the "homeless" rooms. The priests, or *paathi*, as I learnt they were called, always gave me a smile, and some of them would pat my head like a little child. The first time it happened, I recoiled, as all the distrust and fear of men I'd built up took over my body. But the *paathi* didn't look offended or angry. He just smiled sadly and put his hands together. The next time he tried, I'd been in the kitchen helping out and I didn't jump back. I didn't flinch. I smiled back at him and carried on with my task.

It was peaceful and just what I needed. I went along to the Punjabi classes that were held there every Sunday and learnt to read and write Punjabi. I was chastised every week because I kept forgetting to wear the orange *chunni* that was required.

Ranjit's auntie, Jasdeep, was in her mid-forties and had been staying at the temple since her divorce. Ranjit's mum, Harbans, wanted her to stay with them, but it turned out Ranjit's dad was a bigger dickhead than I thought. He forbade her to come to the house because she was a divorcee and he didn't want her "bad luck" to rub off on to his own three daughters.

This was the only downside I found to staying in the temple. There was always a small group of loud-mouthed harridans who would make it impossible to kill the "shame" aspect of Indian society. The gossiping and the blaming of divorces, childless marriages, alcoholism and even death on the wife/daughter/mother involved forced many women to cease coming to the temple altogether. There were so many invasive questions and judgemental looks from women claiming to be God's right hand because they spent all day at the temple. The simple fact was they were so rancid that their own families wanted nothing to do with them, so they spent all day together spitting venom into the same bucket. During these moments, I was reminded that Gypsies really are bastardised Indians. Our habits were exactly the same.

Ranjit's auntie eventually went back to India to stay with her brother in Punjab. I was the only one staying in the rooms when I finished my GCSE exams.

I knew it was time to move on. Heartbreakingly, I knew that if I didn't go then, I'd never go – I'd stay there forever. Part of me wondered what was wrong with that, but the other part of me saw the lonely old women who had nobody or nothing and would sit listening to the prayers all day, waiting for death. I couldn't let my family's efforts to get me educated, to give them a way out of prostitution and poverty, be in vain. They were depending on me. My time in the temple refreshed my soul, and I needed to go and build on that.

Harbans told me about her friend who lived with her two daughters an hour or so away from Leicester. In Birmingham. Or Wolverhampton, as it turned out. Harbans' friend was struggling to pay her mortgage after her husband had left, and she couldn't work due to crippling health issues. I had been working and cleaning ever since moving out of Haroun's. My money for sewing was still collected in a brown envelope kept in the office, with the exception of a few notes given to me directly. Each week, Usha would collect my cleaning money directly from the two families that I was still working for. I never bothered her, and she never bothered me – she took the money to keep whoever I was working for happy. I was happy to not be in Haroun's grip or hunted down by people demanding my wages. Yadira kept me with enough work to sustain me, not knowing I was living rent-free. I saved the small portions of money I was allowed from my various jobs, knowing I couldn't live at the temple forever, despite wanting to.

I explained my decision to Yadira, who inhaled sharply.

"Have you told Usha?" She asked.

"No. Why do I need to?" I shrugged.

"Because you work for people, Eliska. You can't just decide to go wherever you please. Have you got your own paperwork?"

"Yes. I kept it when I needed it for school. Usha and Haroun haven't got anything of mine."

"It's up to you. You can work for me whether you're here, there or in London. It makes no difference to me. You will give me your address." She said the last bit as a statement. Not a question. "Do you trust the people you'll live with? Have you met them before?"

If Ranjit's family trusted them, then I would too. If my time at the temple had taught me anything, it was to let go of some of the distrust I'd let build in my heart like congealed fat. I told Ranjit's mum I could pay for a room, and I could help with the cooking and look after her friend's kids. She laughed and told me the daughters were older than me. She'd have a word and see what could be done.

Her friend was the dearest thing, and said I absolutely could come and stay. She offered me the room for £200 a month. I got the train over to Wolverhampton and was greeted by two stunning Punjabi girls. They introduced themselves as Manjit and Hardeep.

"Hiya!" Manjit put her hand out and I awkwardly shook it like it was diseased. She seemed so happy, and I wasn't sure why.

"She's always this loud. Don't worry, you'll get used to it." Hardeep was effortlessly casual, and I felt so aware of myself standing on the train platform with meagre possessions and a desperate desire to be wanted.

"Shall we go to ours, then? Or actually, it's yours too." Manjit grinned wider than I thought possible. "Let's go home, ladies!"

As we piled into Hardeep's car, loud rap music came on suddenly, making me jump, clutching my bags.

"My taste isn't that bad is it? Bloody hell," Hardeep laughed.

"No, sorry, I wasn't expecting it this loud," I mumbled.

"She wants an even bigger speaker system than this," Manjit moaned. "She's gonna have it so loud that the bass will take us home. She won't need to drive."

The two of them squabbled like me and Anja as we drove to my new home.

Wolverhampton was rather beautiful. It was less busy than Leicester and I appreciated how easy it was to breathe there.

The house looked like every other house on the street, but there was a little string of fairy lights above the garage door.

"Every house needs a bit of magic, doesn't it?" Manjit laughed when she saw me staring at the lights as I pulled my bag out of the car. "I believe in all that. I hope you don't mind living with some nutjobs."

"I hope you don't mind either!" I smiled.

The house was beautifully decorated inside with golds and reds. It felt Christmassy to me; I loved the winter-warm feeling of the colour scheme. It didn't take me long to settle in; the room was larger than I'd had before and made up nicely with patterned wallpaper and a large, soft bed with an abundance of pillows.

Within the month I'd become firm friends with both girls. We would have movie nights and go to the drive-thru in our pyjamas in the evenings. I felt as if this was what the temple had prepared me for. I was living the happiness I'd been eager to get to the night before I left for England – the night I was curled up next to Jani, dreaming of the biscuit-box life I'd envisioned England to be.

*

I've found in life that happiness often equates to mundaneness. True happiness is doing the same thing day in, day out, to the point where whole months pass you by and you barely realise. You carry on with your menial daily tasks – "Oh, is it my turn to cook again already?" "Yoooo I swear I did the food shop last week, was it really two weeks ago?" This was the true measure of how content I'd become in this little Wolverhampton home.

Before I knew it, I'd been living there for two happy years.

It was a slow-paced two years if I consider what I had done. When I first arrived in Wolverhampton, I made sure to seek out any cleaning or sewing jobs available. Given the community that I now lived in, I found few women who needed outfits tailored, but an abundance of cleaning opportunities. It was when I was cleaning that I found a brochure for A-levels.

I wasn't immediately sold on the idea of A-levels. My love for education had never waned, but the idea of juggling my work, school and Yadira's jobs, which were consistent and time-consuming, tired me immensely. I had only just managed to get my skin right, my life right and my routine right. But something within me wouldn't let me rest.

I kept thinking of which classes I'd take if I was to enrol. I even went as far as circling five that I couldn't decide between.

I had been speaking more and more to my family on the phone now that I wasn't shackled to strange families or to work that I never saw any money for. To all intents and purposes, I was as free as I'd ever been in England so far. I spoke to

Arne at great length about whether to continue education. I wanted to – I wanted to desperately. But I was having to deal with practicalities. I was paying £200 a month for my room, which was a bargain in my book. I had a warm, safe environment, with a private room complete with a lock. But I was still working hard to get the money together each month, with general living costs on top. Would I have time to do all this if I wanted to study alongside? Would I be able to afford books? The college I'd found was outside of Wolverhampton, so I would need to travel. Could I afford it? I didn't drive and had no plans to learn, as I had no chance of getting a car with all the expense they came with.

Arne told me that it was all I ever wanted to do, so I had to make it work. He was right: education was the only gift I ever wanted to give myself. I'd give all my money to those unknown people collecting brown envelopes, or my family back in Slovakia, or whoever else; I didn't care. I would give my youth to cleaning toilets and sewing for hours; I didn't care. But one thing I did want to give myself was the gift of dignity. I wanted to be able to walk through the streets of eastern Europe that saw me as vermin, with an education in my back pocket and a head full of knowledge. That would give me the greatest satisfaction. Spite – my greatest drive.

I rang the college and asked what I needed to enrol. My paperwork was solid, stating that I was born in the Midlands. I was an ordinary English girl. I needed my GCSE results, which

I had – I thought I hadn't done that well, but my friends were pleased regardless. My Bs and Cs and a rogue A in Textiles were disappointing to me. I felt as if all the work I'd put in had resulted in a middle-of-the-road selection of grades, so what was the use in continuing? If this was all I could manage? After seeing other pupils in sets higher than me being disappointed in not getting A*s, I realised how ungrateful and stupid I sounded complaining about my results to my friends, some of whom hadn't received a single B or above.

Digging out the results of my GCSEs and the paperwork I needed, I took the buses to the college.

It was a huge building, all shiny glass and glossy posters of smiling, beautiful people holding books. There I stood in a floral skirt, a Metallica T-shirt I'd bought at the charity shop in town and tied at the waist, and my trusty black boots. I felt so uncouth when stood in front of the smartly dressed posters. Fashion was never my strength: I always managed to look like a cross between a belly-dancer and a 1980s Hell's Angel. All bangles and biker gear.

Nevertheless, I enrolled. The woman who I spoke to was stunning. An older brunette lady with her hair in a beehive, puce lipstick and rose eyeshadow. She congratulated me on my results and asked what I wanted to do. I told her I wasn't sure. I had five courses in mind and couldn't decide which ones.

"Well what is it you want to do after this? Do you want to go to university?"

"Yes, that sounds nice."

"What do you want to study?"

"I'm not sure. Anything."

"Ooo, you'll have to pick better than that! It's a lot of money and time wasted if you're not a hundred percent sure!" She smiled.

"I'll think about it."

We spoke at length about the pros and cons of each course I had written on my little piece of paper, and settled on my final three. She explained the classes and which days they fell on. A large part of my decision was based on what I could lump into two or three days, so as to free up as much time as possible for working.

Yadira had been giving me consistent work at the weekends, mainly in Turkey. Which struck me as odd, as Turkey would surely have an abundance of belly-dancers?

But the truth was that I wasn't just a dancer. I was something dirtier: I was entertainment for all the dodgy men Yadira knew. Either way, I was at least able to meet the rent requirements, and the cleaning jobs coupled with the odd sewing work I'd get was ensuring I could feed myself and buy the odd book I needed for college, if I was too slow to find them in the library.

I consciously stayed away from people at college. I wasn't interested in making friends. The first week I was hit with how much older I was emotionally than most people there. Many were living with their parents and had their first tastes of freedom at college. Wearing their own clothes and coming in at allocated hours, instead of the standard nine-to-three hours of a typical school day, was so alien to my classmates. That, to them, was freedom. How could I relate? I was kind of glad that this was the most exciting, unsettling thing they'd ever experienced. But I knew I couldn't ever be close to them. I had strange habits born from childhood damage, abuse and paranoia. I wasn't teased, but I was regarded suspiciously at first and then weirdly afterwards. People rarely included me in group tasks, and when told to "Join up with whoever you want!" I'd just pick the closest person, shame-faced.

Anja would get teary when I explained I didn't have any friends. I told her honestly that I didn't want any. I was better off alone. But she didn't understand. She was constantly surrounded by three or four girls who had the same taste for expensive things and slower-paced lives as she did.

Arne understood me perfectly. We were both loners. Me in the middle of a bustling college and him in the serenity of the Black Forest. His friends were like him: sad boys abandoned by various family members and rejected by society for daring to acknowledge their feelings.

I spent an awful lot of time in libraries, both on college premises and in the town library. I loved it. The peace, the stories, and the feeling that I could go anywhere in the world just by picking up a book.

It was during my library retreats that I discovered an intense passion for folklore and mythology. I'd always heard stories from both sides of the family – fanciful urban legends and the like. I was thirsty for more. I felt the contrast between

German mythology and the Gypsy tales I absorbed described me perfectly. I felt the duality of my heritage in so many ways, and my tastes in art, music and books reflected that. Unlocking the rest of the world's tales was a life-changing moment. I had only experienced the harshness of the real world, the seedy side. But the glory, heroism and beauty in the world's mythology and lore began to open my pessimistic eyes.

A teacher read a short story I'd been tasked to write and commented in passing that Gothic fiction might appeal to me. This was the beginning of a lifelong passion. I read everything I could get my hands on, from *Frankenstein* to *The Mysteries of Udolpho*. I read the dark origins of fairy tales to the sickly-sweet Hollywood versions they'd morphed into. I read, read, read.

My obsession with Gothic fiction inevitably guided me to a fascination with history. In particular, Victorian England. I couldn't get enough. I fiercely wished I had picked history as an A-level. I even saw the history teacher and asked if he could recommend any books on Victorian culture.

I had never felt so hungry for knowledge before. I'd be cleaning and laughing to myself like a dork about living as if I was in a workhouse. Then reading about an actual Victorian workhouse and shitting myself that I'd put that into the universe.

From the Victorian era, I travelled on through the other periods of English history. I filled my head with subjects I enjoyed, and I felt so fulfilled. I was finally feeling normal for the first time since I'd arrived in this country.

When it was time to start thinking about university, I pored over lists of degrees for hours. Willing the best one for me to reveal itself. It did.

I had been scrolling down the list for Wolverhampton University, and found the perfect degree. Creative Writing. From cloud-watching alone in Drovane, to huddling with Dagmar, to my assignments – I loved creating stories. I would rewrite history, so to speak, when I'd be lying alone on the ground telling the clouds about the names Ma had called me.

My imagination was always alert, because we had nothing else to stimulate us. I could make even the most vicious arguments sound sweet and hilarious to my siblings, and my *Oma* always said it was because I was a good storyteller like her. So why not try this degree? Anything that reminded me of Dagmar was a positive thing. I kept her in my heart always, and if anything good could come from our shared horror, perhaps it could be earning a degree?

I spent weeks poring over my personal statement and UCAS application. I sent it off with a prayer and an impassioned speech to God about all the vices I would give up if I could just get onto this course.

I thought the badness in my life had finally passed. I was waiting to hear from university and smugly thought, "this is the only worry I have. I'm an English teenager now".

I was wrong.

THE REAL
ESMERALDA

CLARITY

I believe what happened next was my karma for clutching Dagmar's hand and curling up against the wall when Rayaan was being beaten.

I had been working in the city that night. I was dancing at a Punjabi lady's hen night, and was on a high. It was brilliant. I'd been given a brand-new costume courtesy of Yadira. It wasn't really mine, because I shared costumes with two other dancers, but I was the first one to wear it. And I felt beautiful. It was orange and red with black embellishments. I was so proud of it that I decided to wear it on the walk back to the taxi rank I'd arrived at a couple of hours earlier.

It wasn't cold enough to scare a Slovakia-raised girl like me, so I didn't think twice, wrapping the veil I performed with around my shoulders. My bag carrying my clothes, phone and purse was gently swaying with the breeze on my shoulder. It wasn't quite dark yet; the sky was that purple hue between dusk and night. I'd been the first part of the entertainment for the excited, happy bride I'd left back at the venue. There was a male dance group for when things got too improper for my virginal eyes.

I was a corner away from the taxi rank when I heard a whistle. I ignored it and carried on walking.

"OI! I SAID *KIDDHA SONIYEH*!"

"Dickhead, that's not Hindi, that's Punjabi." I heard a second voice drawing closer. "You been listening to Harps' man dem too much." I heard footsteps, but I wasn't scared. This was England. There were laws for me too here.

They caught up with me. They moved in front of me, and I still wasn't scared. There was a dark-skinned black man dressed in sports gear with a cap, and next to him in an almost identical outfit was a brown man. He was obviously the one who chided the first about speaking Punjabi and not Hindi. He was staring at my outfit and fiddling with a gold "om" sign hanging off his necklace.

"Yo, you Indian?" the Indian man asked.

"No, I'm Gypsy." I tried to step to the side but was blocked by a third man; he was wearing black sports gear too.

"Gypsy? Wha' the fuck is dat?" He had such callous eyes. At this point, I started to feel uneasy.

*

There were six of them. Two black men, three Indian men and one who looked like a mixture of both. Dressed in sports gear like it was their uniform. I wasn't supposed to be this, Ma sent me to England so I wouldn't be this.

*

My hands were scratching at the floor, trying to find anything that could help me.

"Nah… allow it…"

"I knew you were bent, man. Stick it in her mouth, a mouth's a mouth innit."

"I ain't gay, dickhead."

"Prove it, innit."

"He ain't going to, pussy." The light-skinned black one spat at the floor, near my hand.

"Nah, you're the one learning Punjabi to impress the top-knot crew."

This was met with jeering and laughter by the other three, while the one whose turn it was on me carried on grunting away, pushing me deeper into the gravel.

*

I had such a talent for screaming loud in Drovane. Ma would swear she could hear me when she was in the alleys. On her knees. With a man in her mouth. Like mother like daughter. Could Ma hear me screaming now? Nobody in England could. Nobody fucking came.

*

"Take her top off, Kam."

My costume was torn beyond repair. One of them pushed himself in my mouth. I couldn't breathe. I could smell sweat and cheap body spray. His belt buckle was digging into the flesh under my breast. I wanted my dad. My dad and the heavy fists he'd used on me time and time again. Where was he?

*

The lady whose hen night I danced at was called Dhanveer. Such a pretty name for such a pretty girl. I always knew I found women as attractive as I found men. Ma threatened to beat it out of me, but then would point out random women and ask if I found them attractive. I just thought Dhanveer was pretty. I didn't want to be with her. She was classy – she had that air about her. She had long dark hair, straightened for the occasion, but I could tell it wasn't naturally that way. At the bottom her hair had already started to curl up. Her eyes were brown and twinkled when she said goodbye to me. Her long, hooked nose was shiny when she air-kissed me after I declined her offer of a lift, and she said, "Be safe."

*

My hair was being pulled back with such ferocity that my whole body rose up, then let go, and I slammed into the ground. I could taste the blood at the back of my throat. A shoe prised my mouth open, thrusting in and out while the men laughed from all angles.

"I no say she's had worse in her mouth." I heard a zip, and then there was something pouring on me. Their laughing was almost deafening. It was piss. I tasted it as soon as it mixed with the blood pouring down my face.

"You know you're called lower than untouchable in India?" The man had squatted down, so he was looking at my wet face. He smelt of the mustard oil I had once rubbed into Jani's hair.

"How do you know?" another voice asked. As if this was a lesson in Gypsies.

"Some of them moved into my sister's street. Her father-in-law told us. Fucking dirty cunts."

"No way."

"Yeah, they walk around with their tops off. Begging for money and shit."

"Did you know that?" The one with the mean eyes was looking at me as he held a phone in front of his face. "Did you know that you're a slag? Look at her, she's loving it."

"Nah, what was that film? The Disney one?"

"OHH I KNOW WHICH ONE YOU MEAN!! FUUUUUUCK WHAT WAS IT! THE UGLY GUY AND THE GYPSY WITH THE TAMBOURINE!!"

"HUNCHBACK OF—"

"NOTRE DAME!" "ESMERALDA!" they shouted in unison.

They were high fiving each other and celebrating their Disney knowledge.

"HAVE. YOU. GOT. A. TAMBOURINE. IN. YOUR. BAG?" The dark-skinned black one joined the other two squatting in front of me. He was gesturing with his hands as if this was a normal conversation.

I tried to speak, but choked on the piss and blood in my mouth.

My bag was emptied out. There wasn't a tambourine. Just the carefully packed bag that I had neatly folded my clothes into, ready to go home. I felt worse as I saw the Galaxy Cookie Crumble chocolate bar I had been saving as a treat for the taxi ride.

"Where you sending it?" the Indian man asked the other Indian one with the mean eyes who was making the recording.

"Same as before innit. I'm calling this one The Truth bout Gypsy skets."

"Nah, call it Esmeralda."

"Allow that, call it The Real Esmeralda."

"We captured a live one here mate – crikey!" The mock Australian accent tickled everyone's funny bones, and they were off again.

Such hilarious banter and wide-ranging discussion of Romani-Indian relations, all while I was being anally raped with one of them pulling my hair back and another sporadically kicking me.

*

Dhanveer was marrying a man she'd been with for 12 years, she told me. I asked her why she waited so long to marry him. She said she wasn't sure. When I'd finished dancing, she showed me a picture of her wedding outfit. It was blood red: mesmerising. I ached looking at it. I wanted to wear it and spin around for hours.

"It's not much, but it's what my parents could afford. Indian weddings can get expensive." She smiled.

I used to eat from bins. I wore hand-me-down underwear. I was washed with a filthy rag. I was lying on the ground being raped by six men. The ungrateful bitch.

*

After the last one was finished, my body quivered with his. He was lauded by his friends for "making her cum".

*

She liked it. She never said No. She just feels embarrassed now. She was into rough sex. She was dressed provocatively. She's not from here. Who cares? Gypsy, isn't she? They're all prostitutes anyway, they're coming over here more and more, fucking pickpockets and thieves. What?! She's stripped?! Come on, she's a stripper, take her statement then send her on her way, bad night at work. Her mother's a prostitute? She must be, too. She orgasmed, she obviously consented then.

*

It had been maybe a year since I'd settled in England. Using my new ID, I flew back to visit Ma and see Drovane. Yadira had granted me this little treat, as I'd become one of her top earners in a very short space of time. Yadira drove up with me, again in a plain van. She said she had "business" and would come to collect me again in a few days.

Ma saw me and gave me her signature look.

"I'm going to take you somewhere tomorrow, Eliska. Be ready."

I wasn't sure where we were going, but it was Ma: I had to go willingly or be dragged. The next day we walked up to a dirty little building with music blaring out. I went in and saw half a dozen near-naked girls walking around and swinging round poles. It was the most bootleg strip club ever.

After speaking to one of the girls, Ma told me to step up. I looked at her like she was insane. She slapped the back of my head and told me to get up. She half-dragged my T-shirt off and then watched as I pulled down my skirt.

I stood in my knickers freezing. I was 14, but still looked malnourished and frail. Something about this look turned the greasy men on, and they started throwing screwed up notes at me as Ma kept encouraging me to walk around the pole. When the ordeal was over, Ma was ecstatic as she counted the scrunched notes. She made me go back a few times over the next couple of trips.

*

After a final kick to my breasts, driving the wire in my costume through my flesh even further, I was old news to them. Even they didn't want me anymore. I was covered in their sweat, piss, spit and cum. They didn't look back as they walked off. The wind was blowing more strongly than before. It was dark. My shredded costume was whirling around. I felt the air around my exposed areas. I wet myself. It poured out. I had no strength to do anything but lie there, waiting to die. The moonlight wasn't shining on this alley. I could see bright streaks of light far away through my blurred vision. I was glad the moon hadn't shone over here; I didn't want to be seen. I wanted to be absorbed into the earth. The way I should have been when I was born a Gypsy. A mistake. An unwanted result of two selfish people who should never have been allowed to have children.

Where were you, Dad? So controlling over everything – how I would sit, speak and smile. So aware of how "ethnic" I looked that you would force me to take out my nose rings, resulting in Ma drunkenly and painfully re-piercing it every few months. You would make me take out my plaits. You'd bring Anja's plain, bland skirts and T-shirts and make me wear them as we travelled back to Germany. Where were you now? I screamed your name in my head and my heart over and over, like an invocation. You didn't appear.

I don't know how much time passed. Eventually, I tried to get up. I was on all fours when I was sick.

*

Dhanveer had sent a tray piled with delicious food to me in the back room. I sat happily eating *aloo tikki* after *sholay* after *samosa*. Following that little starter, I practically inhaled the naan, rice, *moth dhal* and *tindo sabzi*. Still high from dancing, I'd wolfed it all down.

*

I looked at the brown sludge on the ground. I was disgusting. My blood ran cold, and I was grateful – this was death, I was sure. I passed out.

*

I came around to find two crying women knelt beside me. White women. One had a Monroe piercing and her hair scraped back in a bun. She had a cigarette in her hand and was pulling strands of hair off my face. I could hear the other woman; she was mumbling, but kept stopping to cry and say "Oh my god, Jade. Oh my god."

"Georgia, where are they man? What the fuck." Back to me: "Babe, you'll be okay, it's alright."

*

I woke up again briefly when I was in the ambulance. Jade was still clutching my hand. I had something wrapped around my legs. I felt dizzy and sick again. And sleepy. So sleepy.

*

"Lovey… lovey." I was numb. I couldn't move anything. "Lovey, stay awake for me. Can you hear me?" I opened my eyes and saw the brown watery eyes of a black woman with the clearest skin I'd ever seen. I was staring at the face of *Sara e Kali*. Our patron saint. The Black Sara. We had little in my family's room in Drovane, but we had small figurines of her, small drawings on the wall. I didn't know where the statues came from. I needed to know.

Within seconds of my brain recalibrating, I realised it was a nurse. I wasn't face to face with my patron saint. She wasn't greeting me at the doors of the afterlife.

The nurse was asking me if I could hear her. I looked at her. Ma would love her. Ma was obsessed with clear skin – she didn't care about wrinkles, because to her they showed a long, lived life. But blemish-free skin was the most attractive thing in the world to her. It made the difference between looking like you came from Drovane and looking like you had a home with indoor plumbing. She stressed to me how important it was to never look like you came from Drovane; she would rather have died than wear the hand-me-down rags she forced me to wear. She managed to buy or steal a new scarf every month. She'd have a few men who would buy her skirts. She never let me have a skirt, and she never let me have her old scarves. She never let me have anything, but expected me to look as immaculate as she did. Well, as immaculate as anyone could be in Drovane.

*

The nurse was speaking to me and stroking the side of my head lightly. She had that look in her eyes, the "poor little thing" look. I felt offended. I was not a poor little thing, I was Eliska Zlatkov. I survived Drovane and all of its violence, so there was no need to bring me here and treat me like a delicate young girl. So obsessed with their fancy NHS in England that they'd brought me to hospital over... over... I couldn't remember why I was here. What had happened?

The pain between my legs was starting to push through the numb feeling. I remembered the smell of cheap aftershave and mustard oil. I could feel them in me, in "every hole", as they had laughed to each other. I felt the pain in my head when my hair was pulled back. I remembered Dhanveer telling me to be safe. I tried to move in a panic. I knew they weren't there anymore, the men; they had thrown me away like a used condom and walked away. I saw them walk away. But I wasn't rational in that moment. I was convulsing, trying to move and trying to speak, but ended up making animal noises. I saw the piss and blood dripping down me. I saw the phone in my face taunting me. I wanted to go back to Drovane. I wanted to die. I wanted this day to have been a horrible nightmare. I wanted so much to fall asleep and never wake up. This was England. This was the safe place. This wasn't violent. I was human here. Touching me without my permission wasn't okay here.

The nurse must have called for help, because two others came rushing to the bed, soothing me. I tired myself out and lay there waiting to die. I wanted to die so passionately in that moment. It was all I could focus on. The throbbing, stabbing pain between my legs kept reminding me of how disgusting I was. I was everything that the judgmental bigots in Europe thought about Gypsies. I was used up and tossed aside, because that's what we were for. My kind. My people.

"Sweetheart! It's okay, you're safe here. Nothing's going to happen. Shh." A white lady had a hold of my hand, telling me I was safe with a quiver in her voice. I wanted to ask her why this had happened in this country. I thought of Rayaan and the conversation I'd had with Dagmar. We didn't help Rayaan. Deep down, we were just glad it wasn't us. I knew this was my punishment. I deserved this because I didn't speak up for Rayaan. I wondered if Rayaan would be pleased that this had happened to me. If she would feel placated that I was the one screaming now. I was ruined. My unique selling point was my virginity, as Ma had reminded me several times. Now I was nothing. Ma wouldn't even care if Vera sent me out to work as soon as I saw them again. I was done.

I felt the nurse move my hair fully out of my face and pin it back. She had a tattoo of a broken yellow lightbulb with a smiling cartoon face, smoking a cigarette. I would have laughed before all of this happened to me.

I tried to breathe in but couldn't. My throat was hurting. It hurt to swallow. It hurt to think. I was exhausted. I could feel my eyes drooping again; the familiar dizzy feeling returned, and I felt my eyes roll to the back of my head.

*

I woke in a gown. I couldn't breathe through my nose, my tongue felt swollen, my ribs were aching, my not-so-private-anymore area was in excruciating pain, but worst of all, I was still fucking alive. I felt tears sting their way down my cheeks. Gypsies seem to be born with a resilience like no other; we're thrown into the worst conditions but survive and, in some cases, thrive. I wished I didn't have that fucking strength. I wished I could have died as soon as they threw me on to the ground. The first man who approached me had pushed me and someone else had their foot out behind me. I landed on my back, and like hyenas they were on me. One pushing apart my legs, one tearing at my costume and others groping, kicking whatever was left.

"Hello…" The white nurse was back. "How are you feeling… sorry, that was silly. I mean, is anything hurting?" She looked apologetic after asking the second question too. "Can you speak, bab? Can you tell me your name?"

"Elithka." My voice was hoarse.

"Hi, Emily! We've been wondering what to call you." She was so soft and sweet. I felt bad for thinking "Bitch, in what world do I look like an Emily?" All we had in Drovane were our names, but I couldn't even correct this lady. In a way I was glad she didn't hear me clearly; I wasn't Eliska anymore. I was a revolting thing. I was a dirty thing. I didn't deserve my name.

We continued in the same manner for a while: she asked me basic questions to get me talking, I guess, and I answered in a hoarse croak. She looked at me as if I were her own daughter. I would stare at her tattoo instead of her face. That cartoon lightbulb. She smelt of softmints, and I suddenly became thirstier than I'd ever been. I could have drunk an ocean's worth of water. My mouth was parched, and I imagined the inside of my body all shrivelled and dry. If I could only have something to drink, this pain would be washed away. I was convinced.

"Watha." My heavy, swollen tongue was taking some getting used to; I hardly had the energy to move it.

"Okay, a little bit." She looked around, as if she wasn't allowed to give me water. This was England. Surely I was allowed water.

I was impatient as she poured half a plastic cup's worth. I wanted her to give me the jug. She brought it to my lips and immediately I spluttered. I tried again and managed to get a tiny bit into my parched mouth. It stung all the way down my throat.

I watched her as she cleared the water away. She had dyed blonde hair brushed into a bun, tied at the base of her neck with a large clip. Her eyes were warm brown with a few wrinkles around them. She had bags under her eyes that were visible through her worn-off concealer. Her lips were starting to dry up at the sides. She looked like the sugary mothers in children's cartoons. She wouldn't have looked out of place in a chunky-knit cardigan, taking a batch of fairy cakes out of the oven. I heard someone call, "Linda!" and she rushed off.

I was asked if I wanted to report what had happened to the police. It turned out someone had already called them. They came the same night, but I was too hysterical to talk with them. The next day they came again and, as I was awake, I was expected to talk.

Nurse Linda explained that my costume – what remained of it, anyway – had been bagged up on arrival. There had been tests, and I needed to consent to further swabs being taken. I didn't understand any of this, but agreed, because Linda was telling me with her eyes and little nods that it was the right thing to do.

I had stitches everywhere between my legs and in my arm. They had torn me to shreds, just like my costume. I went from being a virgin to being haggard and stitched up all in one night. I wanted to shed this body and move on to another one. This patched-up, abused shell was no longer mine. I always had "ugly tits", as Ma so eloquently put it, but I was still content with myself. I was short, but wore heels. I danced like a dream and earned money. I had imperfections, but they were all mine, and they were what made me so lovely. But now, these stitches, scratches, bruises and scars weren't imperfections – they were stamps. They were tokens left by six men who now held a claim over my body. They had marked me with their violence, piss and sperm.

My experience with the police wasn't good. There was a woman who had read a "How To Look Sympathetic" handbook and decided to practise all the techniques at once: she looked like she was having a slow-motion seizure, with her sluggish nodding at every other word and closing her eyes whenever my voice dipped. The man she was with was as useful as the bus timetable in Drovane.

Nurse Linda had told them what I was wearing when I came in as she handed them my costume. His face went from *It. Is. Ok. I. Do. Understand.* to *You're not serious?* I felt the judgement radiating off him. Nurse Linda must have too, as she exchanged annoyed looks with her colleague.

My heart sank. It was true what I was always told in Drovane. The police would never help people like us. Because we were the ones they spent their days locking up. We didn't fit "victim". We only fitted "suspect" or "guilty".

I was allowed to leave a few days later. I'd suffered painful oozing after I used the toilet for the first time following my stitches, so I was kept in an extra night. I called Manjit, one of the girls I lived with, to come and pick me up. She didn't know what had happened, and I preferred to keep it that way. I told her I had been mugged. She was gracious enough not to ask why I still had my belongings except for my costume.

Back at home, I hardly got up unless I was taking the recommended salt baths for my stitches. Manjit would make me food and soups, which I was grateful for. I spent my days wishing I was dead. I skipped painkillers, hoping the pain would shock me into a heart attack or whatever happened when pain was unbearable. All I achieved was lying in agony with tears streaming down my face.

My physical healing was uneventful. I told nobody what had happened; I missed half of my check-up appointments. I didn't refill prescriptions, and I waited ever so intently to not wake up at all. I'd eventually fall asleep in the early hours, and every morning I opened my eyes, I swore to myself. I didn't want this. I didn't want the pain, the shame or the inevitable "getting back to normal" bullshit that was sure to follow. Still, life persisted, and I continued to heal.

It was when I started to walk around more easily that I first had a flashback to being raped. During my physical healing, I only focused on the pain, not the cause of the pain. I had started to believe my own story that I was mugged and kicked around on the way back from Dhanveer's hen party.

I hadn't heard from Yadira at all since I texted her the night I was attacked. I'd finished eating after performing, and was in that drowsy lull that you get when you've eaten too much and the sofa is too soft, and the heating is on and there go your eyelids. My phone was on loud and the stupid message notification made me jump. Yadira asked if I was finished; I let her know everything had gone well and Dhanveer would be paying the rest of the money either tonight or tomorrow. I hadn't pressed the issue because it would be rude, and besides, we were used to waiting a day or two after an event for payment. Yadira responded promptly with an "Okay. Talk later," and that was it.

I had been home for just under a week when I had a phone call from Yadira.

"Eliska, I need the costume for Gahlmi. Wash it and make sure it's fresh for her. I will pick up tomorrow. I have a wedding for you next week in Leicester, can you go there yourself?"

My stomach felt uneasy. How was I supposed to tell her? I made a kind of squeal sound as I faltered. Yadira took it as a "yes" and continued talking. "The lady paid the next day. She messaged me and told me she was very happy with you, well done." Her tone was abrupt. Complimenting someone seemed to cause her physical pain.

"*Ya Umi*, I need… something happened." I wished I didn't have to tell her. It shouldn't be causing me this much stress.

"What happen? She paid; everything is fine *inshallah*." I could hear her nails tapping on something. She was getting irritated.

"I had a… some… I mean, I was walking to the taxi rank and something happened. Some men, they had… I was assaulted." I couldn't bring myself to say the word.

"Assaulted? What you mean, assaulted?" She snapped.

"Sexually assaulted, *Ya Umi*." I said it softly, as if it would have hurt more to say it louder.

"Where's costume?"

I had to take a couple of seconds. I knew it wasn't going to be an emotional moment, but I wasn't expecting that.

"It got ripped, then the police had it. I don't…"

I was in so much trouble.

"What?" Her voice was lifeless, somehow. "Do you know how expensive it was? Do you know it was made for me special?"

"I'm so sorry Yadi… erm, *Ya Umi*." I was feeling dizzy again.

"You're going to pay me back for it and pay for a new one for Gahlmi and Sertab. Stupid girl."

"I didn't—"

"*SHUT UP!*" I half-jumped. I was sure I'd pass out. "You owe me two thousand, you'll work when I say. I will call soon. Stupid girl."

She hung up. I was so relieved she was off the phone that I didn't process what she'd demanded of me until hours later, when the nausea and dizziness passed.

I stood up slowly. I owed her £2,000. How? The costume wasn't more than £800. I knew because the fabrics and embellishments weren't earth-shatteringly expensive. A good portion of the £800 would have been labour. Getting another one made would cost the same. I had just under a grand saved, and thanks to the lump sums I was paid after I danced, I'd paid for my room months in advance. I was okay for rent for the next few months, but I needed to buy food, and as I stood, all stitched together, I knew I wouldn't be working for a while. I barely looked out of the window; I was not ready to leave the confines of my room. Yadira valued her costume more than me. I don't know why I was surprised.

I walked gently over to my laptop. I needed to check my bank account. I was almost at my desk when I felt a sudden flash of pain between my legs. With the pain came an image of my legs being forced open. I snapped my eyes shut and began breathing rapidly. I felt myself vibrating in panic. I tried to feel my way back to the bed, with tears dripping off my nose.

The stress of Yadira kept me mute for the next two weeks. I just wanted to shut my eyes and never wake up.

I had lovely dreams of being dead. I could hear Ma telling the other Zlatkovs, "I don't know why I bothered tearing my pussy open to have her." Then I'd wake up to the bandaged nightmare I'd become.

*

In the months after I was raped, I shut myself in my room and ate my way to three dress sizes bigger. The extra weight made the remnants of pain ache even more.

I didn't leave the house. I barely left my room. I was getting by on the shoebox of cash I had stuffed in my wardrobe. I still had money in there from dancing, and it was that money that kept the roof over my head and the cheap frozen meals on my plate. I got used to online grocery shopping, and the £1 meals that were half legit food and half poison. I'd spend £20 a week on groceries and eat like Henry VIII. Instead of trays of pheasant and boar, I'd have overladen plates of chicken nuggets (although for 50 at £1, I'm not sure what the fuck I actually ate), chips, pizza and whatever was on sale that week. It was during this time I also discovered my love of the neon orange nectar that is Irn Bru.

I felt the weight sticking to me like whale fat. I didn't mind. I was thin and easily overpowered when they took their turns on me: the first one robbing me of my virginity, the rest robbing me of my dignity. I was determined not to let that happen again. Being bigger was better. I wouldn't make it easy for anyone to push my face in the ground and force themselves in me.

How stupid I was for thinking my size was the reason it happened. As if there were no bigger victims. But in desperation and frantic rationalising, you will cling to anything to comfort yourself and try to steel yourself against future threats.

The cute outfits I'd started collecting for university mocked me on the rare occasions I'd open my wardrobe. I generally stuck to the same three T-shirts that Arne gave me at various points when he'd visit me, and pyjamas. My hair was thinning and falling out in clumps. Eventually I stopped brushing it. The psoriasis I'd had as a little girl seemed to have come back with a vengeance: I had patches on my face, between my breasts and all over my scalp. Fervent itching did nothing for my weak hair.

I had the curtains permanently drawn. I didn't want daylight to shine on the pit I'd created. I covered any mirrors – why would I want to see this shaggy whore hobbling about the room? It was hard enough being her. I didn't want to see her.

I was filthier than I'd been in Drovane. At least some attempts were made there to keep me somewhat presentable, even if it was only the rag Auntie Mala would clean me with after cleaning her own daughters. I imagined my family walking through the door and witnessing what I'd become. Impure. The strict rules our grandmother had drilled into our heads about purity and cleanliness, which despite our dire living situations we genuinely tried to follow, had been broken. I was disgusting.

I had been suffering from stiffness in my right hand for weeks. At first, I thought it was nothing to be concerned about: I had no recollection of hurting it, so it couldn't be broken. But when my finger swelled to twice its normal size, I had no choice – I would have to leave the house.

I had nothing that fitted me. I found a pair of leggings that I affectionately used to call my "period leggings" because of the comfort they gave me when the blood on my knickers was the first tell-tale sign of a dismal week. I wiped the T-shirt I'd been wearing for the past three days with a wet cloth to remove visible stains. I put a cardigan over myself, wrapped a thick woollen scarf around my neck so my misshapen nose was hidden, and ordered a taxi. The thought of the bus was giving me heart palpitations.

Everyone was staring at me. They could still smell the piss, blood and cum on me. I still had it running down my face, my back and between my legs. I was still wearing my costume, so everybody knew I was asking for it.

I walked through the spectators to the doctor. Everybody knew what had happened. I was the lesson they would tell their sisters, daughters, nieces and cousins. "Don't act like a slag. I saw this tramp in town and she was ran-through. Don't be a slag like her."

I was ordered to have a blood test the following week. Great, another day out. I spent the entire week preparing myself mentally to go. The blood test came, and I sat there, aware of the state I looked and hoping I could somehow drop dead as soon as she pushed the needle into my fat arm. I didn't. She took the blood. She looked me over and asked me if I was okay. I nodded and left. I had to book another appointment the week after, when my results would be back. I only had one of Arne's T-shirts left that I hadn't worn – one with "I ♥ SAUERKRAUT" printed on.

I had pre-washed the T-shirt, as the Lenka in me wouldn't allow such a deep depression to let me look ghastly this many times. I set off in the same leggings, which had worn in the crotch with my newfound fat after only two trips outside. The doctor's waiting room was almost empty. There was an old Punjabi lady whose eye I caught a few times; she beamed at me each time. I wanted to tell her I wasn't worth it. I was *ganndi*, dirty, a word I'd learnt from my Punjabi friends. I wanted to tell her I was a *kanjari*, a shameless whore. I didn't deserve her suspiciously straight, white-toothed smile. Eventually I was called in to see the doctor.

"Hello Miss Zlatkov, take a seat." She was a middle-aged lady with short "boy-hair", as Vera would call it.

I sat. She gave me some line about looking over my results and she was happy I could make it.

"In a nutshell, your iron and vitamin levels, especially vitamin D, are very low. Very, very low." She looked at me as if I was supposed to do her job.

"Okay…" I didn't know what she wanted me to say.

"You also have a lot of inflammation."

How she could tell that from blood, I didn't know. I marvelled at science. We continued in this so-awkward-it-could-have-been-a-comedy-sketch way until she finally took over the conversation and explained she thought I had arthritis. I vaguely knew what that was, and I looked at her, confused.

"I'm not old, though."

"Arthritis can happen at any age. I've seen children with arthritis." She was nice, Dr Green. I let her talk as I looked at the lipstick on her teeth. This meant I'd need to buy more T-shirts. I was sure to have more appointments now.

*

I can't pinpoint a moment where I thought, "Right, back to life now" – because honestly, I'm not sure if I've ever had that moment, even today.

But having to go to those appointments and return to my rank room afterwards made me realise what a state I was living in. I hated catching my reflection in the shiny glass doors at the hospital where I'd started receiving treatment for psoriatic arthritis. I dug out my box of makeup and tried to cover up some of the blemishes and scars I still had on my face. Many were faded already, some were gone altogether, but there were a few I'd got into the habit of picking and prodding whenever I was worried. My original concealer was too dark for the pasty ghoul I'd become, but I didn't care. I'd rather look like I had pigmentation spots than walk around like a grizzled war veteran.

I gradually left the house more, if only to run errands. I did a shift or two with Ljuba, the Polish girl I cleaned with, at night when there was hardly anybody around. I bought a supply of black leggings and baggy tops to wear to university. I had to go to university to get the loans I needed to live on until I could work again.

Yadira had costumes sent to me to repair, make and clean. I wasn't paid because of her costume-debt. I needed money to survive.

I prepared myself for university. My striving for education had vanished. I no longer felt the energetic motivation that the prospect of gaining a degree had woken in me. Now I was just going so I could get the loans.

*

I was still healing from surgery after the attack when Anja called and asked why I was barely phoning, and why I hadn't been to Germany or Slovakia to see anyone. Was university keeping me that busy? She asked if I had died. "Obviously not," I bitterly replied.

Anja wanted to come and visit me. I didn't want her here; I didn't want to see anybody. I wanted to be left in peace to pretend I was just an ugly, unhealthy girl, instead of someone still wearing those men's brutality on my face and comfort-eating my way to death. At uni, I would sit in the back and barely interact with anyone, apart from one girl who spoke to me on the first day. I don't remember her name, just that I kept her sweet in case I needed her to write my name on the register that was passed around each lecture. I would hold a fake smile for as long as it took her to leave for the train and then I would go home, lock my door and hate myself.

Anja was Franz's daughter, though, and when she made a decision, it was final.

The day she came, I'd made my way to the airport to greet her. I spotted her instantly. Maybe it was my bias, maybe it was just her, but she was the loveliest one in the entire crowd of people. She'd dyed her hair honey-blonde, and was wearing our father's tartan hoody and my shades. I didn't realise the shades weren't tucked away in my room until I saw her.

She was coming closer, and I was almost in tears waiting for an "Anja hug". She'd cuff her arm around your shoulders, then hold the back of your head on her shoulder. It was just what anyone needed.

She drew closer and walked right past me. I was angry for half a second, until I realised she didn't recognise me. My big sister *wouldn't* recognise me.

Anja was looking for the short, petite, brightly dressed girl in too-high heels. She would never be on the watch for a fat, Penguin-from-the-Batman-movies girl with a box of Ritz Crackers stuffed under her arm. When I waddled over to her and called her name, she spun around with a smile on her face that contorted into horror when she saw me.

"*Mein Gott*, Eliska! You've been enjoying university life too much! You look like a little brown pig!" Her school-learnt English gave her the same bluntness that I originally had, until I learnt the small talk that English people love. She chuckled until she saw my face. I was looking at her with a pinched expression. "*Schwesti*, what's wrong?"

"I was mugged."

"Mugged? What's that?"

"I was robbed." I couldn't bear to tell her the truth. I wanted to stay clean in her eyes. I didn't want her to know how revolting I was.

The week passed too quickly for her, but too slowly for me. I wanted her gone, because my story of being mugged wasn't holding any weight with her. I snapped at her to stop asking about it on the third day, and she begrudgingly agreed. We had a nice time watching movies and eating nachos in my room. Anja didn't force me to go out, but she had a weird silence about her at random times, when I'd catch her watching me.

She'd been back in Berlin three days when she phoned me out of the blue.

"I want you to tell me the truth, *kein witz*." She was using her serious voice. Anja, Arne and I would always say "kein witz" ("no joke") whenever we wanted the truth from each other. It always worked.

"What?" I had just woken up, and that was only because the neighbour had decided five past eight was the perfect time to use his ancient lawnmower.

"Something bad has happened, Eliska. Tell me what it is, and don't tell me you were robbed."

I wasn't surprised she'd worked it out. My hips and belly had spread like rumours, and I'd flinched every time she brushed against me unexpectedly. I'd gone from the both of us clinging to each other through the night on past visits to almost jumping through the roof when she'd toss her hair back without warning me first.

I told her.

She was inconsolable. "I knew! I knew! You… I… No!"

I spent an hour comforting her over my rape.

Finally, she managed to whittle down her juddering sobs to a hiccupping sniffle. "You have to tell your mum, Eliska."

"You are insane, Anja."

"No! You have to. She can comfort you. You're her child. This is different from stealing food!" she pleaded.

Maybe she was right. Maybe that was exactly what I needed. Ma's comfort. I pondered Anja's advice for a week or so. Anja paid for my ticket, and so it was settled.

I was going to Drovane.

I was nervous going back with the extra weight I'd gained. I took a few extra £1 slabs of chocolate with me. They'd laugh at me on first sight, but I'd make some of them a pound or so heavier before I left. Although fattening them up a little bit would be less revenge and more kindness.

I arrived in Drovane on a cheap ticket. I had the same small bag I'd always take with me when I visited. I never took clothes or phones or iPods. Ma would either sell them or smack me for showing off. Whenever I returned to Drovane, I was expected to wear the second-hand skirts my cousins had outgrown. I was on the randomly appearing bus to Drovane, daydreaming about telling Ma that I was used and dirty now. The trek to Drovane, coupled with Bon Jovi's "Blaze of Glory" (since getting to England I've constantly been a decade and a half behind in music and TV tastes – I've been catching up slowly) blaring through the earphones of my cheap MP3 player, pushed me into fantasies of Ma softening and cradling me. It was soul-affirming.

The bus turned the corner onto the beaten dirt path and stopped. I stepped off and saw the bus driver look towards Drovane out of the corner of his eye and lower his head. I half-wanted to shout, "THEY'RE COMING!" and watch him shit himself, but that was cruel. Apparently, I'd become a nicer person since I'd been raped.

Since reading *Mildred Pierce* by James M. Cain, I'd been astounded at the use of rape as an exclamation point when dealing with disobedient women. In his book, the line "What this needs is the crime of rape" during an argument between former lovers made me realise that I was somehow supposed to be subdued forever – a politer woman because I'd been raped by bad men. The same way cancer survivors are expected to be kind, gentle souls because they lived when they were expecting to die. If I was to carry on being the irritating, sarcastic little shit that I was pre-rape, then I wouldn't get understanding nods or a sympathetic ear; my attitude would somehow justify my attack. The same way that, to the bus driver, my being a Gypsy meant I deserved this life in Drovane.

I got off, giving him a filthy look for having the same prejudices everyone else in the country had. Poor guy. I wanted to run to Ma, but I already had an ache in my back and needed a sit down. A few of the neighbourhood kids ran over and hugged me, and my need for a constant five-foot barrier around me dissolved as soon as they pushed their faces into my tummy and tried to wrap their arms around me. I felt home. The stench of the "neighbours" was sweeter than I remembered. I took the appropriate care to avoid the hepatitis-infested puddles and picked up one of the kids whilst the others fussed alongside me.

"ELISKA?! NO! YOU'RE PREGNANT?!"

"*AN*! YOU LOOK SO BEAUTIFUL BUT YOUR FACE IS BIG ENOUGH NOW!"

"HOW HAS THAT HAPPENED?!"

The random shouts came with a smile on each face. I was glad it wasn't harsher. I asked where Ma was and one pointed to our block of flats whilst another lady grumbled, "She's giving herself a rest." Nice to see their disdain of the Zlatkovs was alive and well.

I set the little girl down and handed some of the chocolate out, and after covering my face with dirty-mouthed kisses, they ran off, overjoyed. I began climbing the stairs to get to our floor. It was as noisy as usual, and I was glad. That noise was what I'd longed for as I lay in hospital listening to a symphony of beeps and bed creaks.

I found Ma in the middle of a blazing row with Auntie Masha. She had her back to the door and was screeching about stolen bangles. Auntie Masha saw me first and her face burst into an affectionate smile.

"Shut up! Your daughter is here!" I thought I saw a tear in Auntie Masha's eyes. Ma spun around and stopped with her hands in the air.

"What have you done to yourself?!" She looked shocked. Not sickened. That was good, I guess.

I felt a lump in my throat. I silently grabbed Ma by the hand and dragged her to the stairwell. Ma swore at the kids playing hide and seek and they slinked off, with hateful looks at us both.

I sat her down as she asked over and over what was wrong. I felt my stomach flitting about.

I took a deep breath and told her everything. From Dhanveer's shiny long nose and her divine wedding dress to the race of the men to the taste of them to the stitches between my legs. She let me talk and talk, a neutral expression on her still beautiful face.

I finished, and breathed hard. I waited for her hands to clasp my shoulders and pull me towards her.

To this day I wait.

Lenka Zlatkov, with her lined eyes, coral painted lips and brown skin, looked at my overweight body. She clicked her tongue. "For free? You let them do that for free?"

No, no, no. That wasn't how this was supposed to go. She was supposed to tell me it was okay. It wasn't my fault. It was going to be alright. I was going to get through this.

She shook her head and walked away, leaving me in the stairway desperately holding back tears, whilst my body trembled at what had just happened.

The sour smell of the trash, wafting through holes in the wall that were windows once upon a time, made me feel sick. The constant chattering and din from the other families was making my head throb.

I left the next day and phoned Anja at the airport. I had to pay a charge to get my flights changed, but luckily for me, tourism around Drovane was pretty much non-existent. So, I was able to get back to England.

I hadn't said goodbye to Ma. She was busy working.

*

I had been back roughly a month when there was a knock on the door. I heard Manjit answer and shut the door again.

"Eliska! There's someone here for you…" Manjit sounded bewildered.

"For me?! Er… okay." I was about to put away toiletries I had purchased earlier that week. I always stocked up on toiletries to take back to Drovane, so I had bought packets of toothbrushes, leave-in conditioner, and so on. But I'd come back far sooner than planned.

I wasn't expecting anybody. Perhaps it was Yadira with more sewing. I had finally managed to pay her off, but I enjoyed making the costumes so much that she let me continue. It had taken months of back-breaking work on a cheap, basic sewing machine I'd managed to get second-hand. I'd sit there, crouched over the machine, until I fell asleep at my desk. I would painstakingly hand-sew embellishments. But I'd managed it eventually. I'd managed to make back the money and please Yadira. She only extended her sympathies to me when she first came to pick up an outfit herself. Prior to this she'd send her driver, who looked as if he'd be better off working in a haunted house scaring people. She saw me, and her lips snarled instantly. I was numb. It didn't do much to damage my confidence, because I was already dead inside. She picked up the outfit and patted me gingerly. She pushed an extra £20 in my hand and told me to relax.

It wouldn't be her at this time, though.

I reached the door. I wasn't able to run down the stairs in my old wildebeest manner yet. Even a year later, there would be days I'd have a dull ache below. I fixed my hair in the mirror and opened the door slowly.

It was Dad.

I felt my eyes well up when he saw me.

I say "when he saw me" because I had spent my life until that point seeing *him*, but he never *saw me*. He never saw me the way I wanted him to. He was the first man I loved. He never noticed me the way I did him. In that moment, as he stood on the doorstep with his blue eyes, tall frame and muscled body, looking at me, I felt solid gold. I felt beautiful in the way girls feel when they have their daddy's whole attention. His face was fraught. He nodded at me and lightly edged me out of the way as he walked in.

"*Your room?*" He didn't make eye contact with me.

"Upstairs." I was an idiot. "I'll show you."

I walked upstairs and led him to my room. I sat at my dresser, trying to take in this surreal moment.

He shut the door and looked around. He saw the bag I borrowed from Anja a few trips ago. He reached down and emptied it on the bed. He began stuffing clothes inside. He opened my wardrobe drawers until he found my underwear, and shoved handfuls inside. I remembered the day he dressed me to go to school – he was so embarrassed touching a pair of knickers – and now here he was, unashamed. My toiletries were still on my dresser waiting to be put away. He grabbed the pack of toothbrushes and threw it in Anja's bag. He finished silently ransacking the room, and motioned for me to leave. I was on the landing, confused, but following his instructions, when he turned back, pulled four books off my bookcase and dropped them in the bag. I was touched that he knew I couldn't be without a book.

He pushed past me, leaving his aftershave in the air, and walked down the stairs. I followed.

Manjit mouthed, "Who is that?"

I told her it was my dad.

She told me to text her.

I walked outside to see Dad standing by a taxi. Had it been there the whole time? He was going to get the shock of his life when the time came to pay up.

The taxi ride was silent. I had never felt so safe. We pulled up to the hotel he always stayed at when he was visiting for under a week.

He paid the taxi driver the astronomical amount without a word. I got out and followed him to the hotel room. I wanted to hold his hand.

He let us into the room and carried my bag inside. He sat on the bed with his back propped against the headboard. He stared ahead.

"Eliska, come here."

I was freezing in my leggings and the India cricket shirt Manjit had given me last Christmas. I inched towards him and slipped out of my flats. He patted the space next to him. I sat down awkwardly with half of my bottom hanging off the edge. He gently lifted me onto him sideways by my waist, so I was sat in his lap with my head buried in his neck. I felt like a little child. I felt his chest heave as he nestled his chin in my patchy hair.

I felt so safe in his embrace. His big strong arms were wrapped around me the way Anja's slim, toned arms did. I couldn't help crying. I was weeping and wailing as he softly rocked me, kissing the top of my head. We stayed that way for hours. His tears dripped down my balding scalp, which made me cry even harder. How dare I make him cry after so many years? How dare I reduce my strong father to tears?

We fell asleep eventually, with me holding on to his arm as tight as I could manage with my arthritic hands.

The next morning, I woke up to an empty room. Dad had unpacked some of his things and set out some of the clothes he'd stuffed in my bag. In his haste to pack my bag the day before, he'd grabbed a crop top and maxi skirt. I hadn't worn anything like that since I was attacked.

I took my toiletries and used the bathroom. I had to use his towel to dry, as I didn't have mine. His towel was huge, and it felt kind of good being able to feel small for once. I was rooting through my bag trying to find something I could pull over my underwear when Dad came back. He was carrying several bags.

"What are you doing?" He was probably having the same flashbacks as I was. Me running around the hotel room naked. Thankfully I had knickers and a bra on.

"You didn't bring proper clothes. I can't wear those." I tried not to sound ungrateful.

"You used to love wearing stuff like that, like your mother. Eliska, put them on." He set down his bags.

"I can't, have you not seen the way I look?"

"Put the fucking clothes on."

He won. Minutes later I was stuffed into the crop top and maxi skirt looking like a shitty tribute to Octomom. I complained to him that I felt fat and ridiculous. He told me to shut up and look at the women of England.

"You're so rude sometimes. German women aren't some otherworldly beings. English women are pretty."

"That's not what I meant. You're so determined to argue. I can tell you've been to university. I meant women here dress how they want, not how someone thinks they should." Oh. I wasn't expecting that.

After I'd drunk the juice he'd brought me, I was presented with the funniest image of all time. Dad had a bag from an Indian super-market. That wasn't the funniest part. He had gone inside and asked the woman about what "shit" his daughter should put in her hair for it to stop looking so dead. He'd brought me a selection of oils and shampoos on the say-so of an Indian lady "with a fucking accent. I could barely understand her, and she could barely understand me".

"She told me what to do. Rub it in your scalp and hair. She could have rubbed it on me." He smirked a little. I couldn't help laughing.

That night he filled the bath up for me and popped the bath bomb that he'd bought earlier under the running water. The bath turned a serene pink.

"Eliska, it's ready." He was pulling off his T-shirt.

I was impatient as I took off my clothes. The bath looked so inviting. I sank into the bubbles and felt like I was floating. Dad came in and sat with his back against the bath, his head resting on the rim.

"Tell me what happened, *schatzi*." He had obviously been working up to hearing the full story. I sank a little further into the bath; he reached behind, and I held his hand. I told him everything, the way I'd told Ma. He'd squeeze my hand harder during the parts that hurt me the most. I told him about the stitches I had to have. I told him how I had wanted to die for so long.

"And now? Do you want to die now?" He squeezed my hand.

"No. I don't know. I want it to stop hurting. But I don't think I want to die." I had stopped wishing for it so vehemently, but a life with this shame and pain wasn't appealing to me either.

After that night, the conversation flowed more easily. We discussed everything: how I was moving forward and how I would continue to move forward. I wanted to dance again eventually, I wanted to lose the weight, I wanted to finish the surgeries I needed to get back to how I was before that night, and I wanted my hair back. He had warmed up the coconut oil in the microwave and was painting my scalp with it, instead of rubbing it in the way he was told. I wrapped my hair up in a towel and sat against his knees as he watched television.

One of the main discussions we had was my fear and repulsion of brown and black-skinned men. I couldn't help it. Whenever I saw a group of boys, I would be terrified. I'd begin panicking if they weren't white. I hated feeling this way. It happened when I went to Drovane too. Boys that I'd grown up with, men I'd called "Uncle" since I could form coherent words, I now viewed as a danger to me. My colour of flesh on a man sickened me.

I half expected him to come through with hundreds of anecdotes about "animalistic" ethnic men. But he didn't. He listened instead.

"Look, you live in England and you want to keep dancing. So you're going to go to more countries filled with these people. You have to stop being stupid." Well, damn.

"Dad, I'm not being stupid."

"You've spent all your life telling me Gypsies aren't all the same. I don't care either way. These countries that they were from—"

"They were English, Dad."

"The countries their parents came from then, those countries are filled with rapists." He cleared his throat the way he did before he started a rant. "That's what they're taught women are for. In India especially, you know they kill baby girls because they don't want daughters? They worship their sons – they treat them like kings. They let them have anything they want: money, cars, clothes, anything. Men can go and work abroad, or study. A man can have as many girlfriends as he wants, but it's his right to marry a virgin. The women are stuck at home and can't even look at a man. No wonder they rape women. It's not rape over there. The women don't have a voice. And the blacks, don't talk about them. They *all*—"

"Can you please stop?" I felt duped. I thought I could share my feelings with him without all this extra bile. I refused to be the validation for Volker bigotry. "Stop, please. This doesn't justify your and *Opa*'s racism. You're acting as if white men have never raped anybody. Are you insane?" This was something I would have to work through without him.

"This doesn't justify it? I've always told you about *them*." He meant ethnic men. "They don't see women the way white men do."

I was aggravated now. "How white men see them? Do you mean you? You've had babies with everyone except for the poor bitch you married!"

"All of the sex I've had in my life has been consensual."

"Even the 13-year-old?"

"LENKA TOLD YOU SHE LIED!"

"YOU CAN'T TELL THE DIFFERENCE?"

I had nothing else to say. I wasn't going to break through decades of indoctrination. We spent the rest of our time together skirting around political and racial discussions.

It was the day before he was due to leave when he brought up university again. I had told him I was only there for the loans. I had started with such new energy during the first few weeks of lectures, meeting professors, and so on, but depression had seized me again and now I was back at square one. I had no desire to do anything.

"You're too smart to waste this chance. You need to stop all of this now." He gently stroked my back. We were lying in bed watching television and eating grapes.

"I can't help it. It's not that easy to just 'stop'," I snapped.

"Well, you need to try. What are you going to do? Cry for the rest of your life? Eat and eat until you can't leave your room? How will you work? What will you do? You're not like Anja. You wouldn't be able to live on my money."

"I'd love the chance to try," I grumbled, and he laughed. His laughter warmed me, and I thought of all the times I'd lain in the garden of his Berlin home in the middle of the night. How he'd call me a "weird Gypsy witch" but still sit at the back of the garden chain-smoking until I was tired. Sometimes I'd fall asleep outside and I'd wake up to find him drinking coffee, watching me. These moments sounded so foreign to some people, but to me they were normal. Ma would make me dance for her paedophile clients, and Dad would stay up all night to let me sleep under the moonlight. I knew who I was safe with, and it was always him. Even when he hit me, I knew I'd rather it was him that taught me the lesson he always thought he was teaching me.

"You get that degree, *schnucki*. Show me one of you idiot kids got my brains." He sighed.

As we drove back to where I lived, Dad had his hand on my thigh and was absentmindedly fiddling with the thick hoop in his ear. The warmth was comforting. He was the only man I'd ever allow to touch me. He was the only one I loved. I wasn't going to let anyone else touch me again.

He put my bag in my room and kissed the top of my head. He observed me for a while.

"I do... you know." He took a deep breath. "Buy a book." He handed me two crisp £20 notes and gripped the sides of my face. I stared up at him, wishing he'd stay.

"My sweet little Gypsy girl, behave." He kissed my lips and kept his face against mine, the way Dagmar had years earlier. He pulled away and held me, looking at me as if I was everything he needed, and smiled at me.

I wanted to tell him to take me with him. But I had a degree to finish.

He waved self-consciously before he got into the taxi. He left.

Dad phoned me a month later to tell me to make sure I was still using the oils on my hair. He phoned me a month after that to tell me I'd better tell Anja I was doing okay now, because we were both getting on his fucking nerves with our depressive moods.

THE EDUCATED GYPSY

LIFE IS TOO SHORT
TO READ SHIT

I had received my university acceptance email on the way back from a work trip to Istanbul. I had been elated. The ride was stuffy, sticky and sickly from all the Turkish pizza I'd stuffed in my face. Opening the email on the shaky wi-fi the cheap café provided was enough to send Bob Ross into a murderous rage. The heading of the email took an age to load, and then my insistence on refreshing every five seconds "to make it go faster" slowed the whole process down even more, to the point where I was ready to launch the computer through the window when I saw the glorious words "Congratulations Eliska". The rest of the ride home felt like bliss as I mapped out my new university life. I was beyond excited to get my reading lists, shop for new notebooks, and figure out what my university look would be.

Then the rape happened. Then I sank into functioning depression and couldn't care less about trivial things like notebooks. Then I didn't care whether I went to lectures or whether I died on the way there. Nothing mattered.

My first day came hurtling forward. I went to the introduction week. An Albanian girl I cleaned with, Era, had left me a bag full of clothes she didn't want anymore as she prepared to return to Albania. She'd kissed my cheek and told me to go back to Slovakia, as there was nothing for us here.

I walked to the assigned room. It was already half-full. I didn't have a chance to stop and breathe before entering, as there were three other people behind me. There was an empty seat right next to the door. I made a bee-line straight for it. Sitting with my back to the door wasn't the best choice. With every person entering, I flinched. I sat staring straight ahead until a voice rang out. I jolted slightly. The room was full now and there were three people stood at the front.

There was a man with a smile on his face, a natural smile – it looked as if his eyes were smiling with him. The lady who had spoken stood front and centre; she had the shiniest, gloss-iest long hair I'd ever seen on a white woman. I was shocked to hear she had an American accent. Her name was Jackie. I remember thinking she hadn't told us her surname, so what were we supposed to call her? I hadn't realised that first-name terms were the norm at university. The man introduced himself, and he had an English accent. Then back to Jackie. I couldn't understand much due to the blood throbbing in my ears; I was overwhelmed. The room was too hot, Era's trousers were cutting into the fat around my waist, and I felt out of place.

A blonde, tanned woman stepped up and introduced herself as "Candi". Her accent wasn't English; I couldn't decide if it was very posh London or something else. The girl next to me told her friend it was a South African accent. I had found a white African woman: university had already paid for itself! My world was broadened instantly between the English man, American woman and now the blonde South African woman.

"Life is too short to read shit," she said.

I was scandalised.

I had an idea of what university would be like, and worried whether I'd fit in or if my trashy background would stick out. I perfected my Midlands accent. I practised not swearing. I contemplated trying to pass for a different race, just in case these educated people knew about the way Gypsies are forced to live in Europe. Instead, I found a group of people from a variety of backgrounds. They didn't care if you swore, they didn't care if you had an accent, and they even had the "boho dream" idea of Gypsies.

From that day I was in love with the judgement-free atmosphere in the multi-coloured building. I'd see women with green hair, men with lipstick, and instantly I was in love with English people. The freedom in this country suddenly struck me at university.

But I was struggling to deal with the volume of people I was faced with every day.

Since being raped, I was on autopilot. I drifted through each day and painted on a smile. I couldn't stop. I couldn't afford to. I carried on eating and shaking through the night, then got ready to attend classes during the day. On the days I had to work for

Yadira, I'd drag myself out of my room and go through the motions. I didn't dance; instead I did makeup for other dancers and fixed costumes. I'd feel myself withdrawing further and further into myself, but forcing myself to carry on as normal. Whatever normal was. I didn't talk to anyone at university. I just wanted the three years to be over.

I did terribly in half of my first-year modules. I barely remember my first year. At one point I got an email from my lecturer asking if I thought this was a distance-learning module. I dragged myself to that class the following Monday; my sole purpose was to scowl at the one who sent me the email. But as I sat there, I realised I didn't know who the hell the guy was. There were three men in the room, and I had no idea which was my lecturer.

By some miracle, I scraped an overall pass through the year. I had two resits, but I just didn't care. It was a constant battle to get up in the morning. I would lie awake all night then be hit with a sudden rush of suffocating fatigue as soon as my alarm went off. My alarm was one of my favourite songs, "*Naj Naj*" by Toše Proeski. I'd listen to the full four minutes, wishing I was back in Drovane, singing along squashed next to Jani under some nasty rug dug out from the "neighbours".

The Gypsy lady who ran the "convenience store" in Drovane was originally from Macedonia, and she still kept abreast of all the Macedonian pop culture. She'd been playing a Toše Proeski CD on one of mine and Jani's trips to her. We recognised the lady singing instantly – Esma Redžepova, a legend amongst Gypsies. Esma didn't have a shy voice; she was proud and emotive. She could hold a note and really make you feel it. I'd get chills whenever we huddled in the convenience store listening to Esma's multi-faceted, soulful voice booming out. She'd sing of Romani struggles and love and pain and everything else we wanted to say but didn't have the voice to. *"Chaje Sukarije"*, possibly her best-known song, was everything to us growing up; we learnt the words from Vera and made up dances to perform to our family in the evenings.

Jani and I asked the shop-lady who the man singing was, and she showed us the CD cover. It was the handsomest man we'd ever encountered in our 12 short years. He had spiky hair and a thin pencil beard. You couldn't really see what his face looked like properly, but he was our popstar. We'd hatch plans of going to Macedonia and marrying him. Shop-lady would laugh whenever we'd go to her and ask her to play his songs. His song with Esma was called *"Magija"* and remains my most treasured song. It always reminds me of my family in Drovane.

The Midlands of England were a far cry from Drovane. Toše Proeski was a far cry from the music that dominated English radio and television. I was always fonder of heavy metal and rock music than I was of the softer pop music that I heard everywhere. Lying awake in the morning listening to *"Naj Naj"* and reminiscing about Drovane made it even harder to pull myself out of bed. It was as if my body was made of lead. I was a dead, depressed weight, and there were days when I was just paralysed. Even if I wanted to get up, my depression held me to the bed. I would lie awake for hours, starving, aching, silent, until Manjit or her sister would pull up outside, returning home from work or bringing their mum back from an appointment. Then I'd make my way to the bathroom and emerge pretending I'd done a full day at uni. I don't know whether they believed me. I didn't care.

I had enough doctor's appointments and surgery follow-ups scheduled to see me through the first few weeks of our summer holiday.

For the rest of the summer break, I tried desperately to pull myself together. I tried laughing therapy – a group of us sat in the middle of a woodland area laughing on the say-so of an ageing woman with a passion for crocheted shawls. My laugh was more of an awkward "he-he" compared to the wide-mouthed guffawing that went down in those woods. The laughing therapy made me even worse, because I started thinking about how easy it was to fake laughter. I wondered if anybody I knew really laughed from their heart or whether it was all a charade. I moaned myself back into my pit.

I just couldn't do it. I couldn't shake the feeling that I was never going to be happy again. I couldn't stop feeling scared whenever someone passed behind me. I was dreading going back to university and having to use the crowded lifts or climb the stairs which left me breathless and embarrassed. I'd have to pretend I was on my phone or go and wait in the toilets until I got my breath back, before saying hello to the two or three polite people who would greet me.

I never had enough time to process what happened to me. The time I spent holed up in my room was spent feeling disgusted in myself and wanting to die. Before being raped, I would lie in my bed and break down the day's events, think about whatever needed thinking about and making any decisions that needed to be made. By doing this, I could take in the day and move forward with the next. But I didn't do this with the assault. I never wanted to think about it again.

As I began to rise from my food-fuelled stupor after Dad's visit, I started experiencing flickers of hope for what having a degree would do for me. Maybe I could move away from this place. Maybe I could live in a different country in a small village in a small house, writing stories. My appetite for bettering myself, for education, was slowly rising again. I dared to let myself feel some semblance of excitement.

Second year started. But as soon as I set foot in the building, I was worse than the first year. For one of my modules, I didn't attend a single class. That particular module was led by Jackie, the American lady with fabulous hair. I think I sent one or two emails with weak excuses explaining my absence. But the week before the assignment deadline, I received an email from Jackie. She asked whether it would be better for me to take some time off due to what had happened, as submitting assignments in my current state would inevitably lead to failing. I remember the way I felt when I read that email in bed. I was angry and upset. I thought to myself, *Of course I can handle this. I don't need time off. Nobody believes in me*, but by the end of that week I'd put in for a leave of absence. Jackie was right: I didn't need to hand in sub-par work just to make a deadline and get this degree finished. What I mistook for her irritation and lack of faith in me was concern and good advice.

The first week of my self-imposed "holiday" was spent the usual way: wallowing in bed.

The next week I had a post-surgery check-up. I went. Everything was fine, and I left. On my way home, I decided I would go into town and get a pair of earrings. The thought came out of nowhere. I didn't try to argue with myself. I ignored all the voices inside telling me I would run into one of *them*. I watched my stop approaching, and I didn't get up. I was going to go all the way to the bus depot, which was right in the middle of town. The bus waited at my usual stop for what seemed like an age. I was on the verge of accepting defeat several times, telling myself to just get up and go home. I waited. Finally, the doors shut, and the old bus creaked into life and trundled off again. This was it. No way out now.

We arrived at the bus station. I inhaled sharply when I saw the people crowding, ready to get onto the bus. *There's going to be some shoving*, I told myself, *someone will probably touch you, but it's okay*. I repeated it over and over until I was suddenly in the middle of town.

I had made it. I had walked through that small crowd without jumping, flinching or being overcome with fear. I had just walked through like a normal person.

The next task was walking into a shop and buying a pair of earrings. I was looking around, taking in the bustling noise and choosing which shop to go to. My stomach wasn't twitching the way it usually did. It was strange: I was stood in the middle of town with people rushing around me, and I was okay. I went into the shop with the fewest people at the entrance and walked to the earrings display. I looked at the earrings. I was just like any other customer. I found a lovely pair. Blue and gold, £4.50. I bought them and walked out of the shop.

The fresh air was soothing. I took a deep breath and it felt like the first time I'd inhaled properly for months.

On my way back to the bus stop, I stopped at a charity shop. I'd always bought books from there before I was attacked, and I felt the need to buy one to celebrate my little outing.

"Hello! Haven't seen you in a while!" The grey-haired lady beamed at me as she hung up cardigans.

"Hi… yeah, I've been… busy. Uni." I felt a genuine smile form on my face, not the one I'd been painting on my lips for months.

We chatted for a while. Like normal people. I felt normal. I didn't have "RAPED" on my forehead. She didn't care that I looked shocking. She was just talking to me like I was anyone else.

I picked out a book, paid and left. I got on the bus and went home.

That day was the turning point. I pushed through with each day, and it became easier.

Soon I was planning to go out the day before, instead of "seeing how I feel on the day". A day before turned into a couple of days before, which turned into a week before, which turned into me making solid plans for weeks ahead.

My break from university was the most peaceful time of my life. It sounds clichéd, but I really did find myself. I explored who I was, and it was enlightening.

I read more and more. My English got so much better in those months, and I was proud of how my writing improved.

I've always felt stronger connections to English that any other language, as it's the language in which I learnt to read and write. In some ways, it feels like my first language. In those months, I read piles of Philippa Gregory novels, which re-ignited my love affair with English history. I began reading as many novels set in Tudor times and Victorian times as possible. I was insatiable – I adored everything about those periods. The greed, gluttony and unapologetically trashy attitudes of the Tudor period was like a white, rich version of Drovane. The art, literature and revolution of the Victorian period was inspiring. For once in my life I had a hobby that I could enjoy without having to earn money from it.

From the costumes I had sewn for myself and other dancers I worked with, I became known to a dressmaker who worked predominantly with Asian and Middle Eastern women. She contacted me and asked if I would like to meet up and bring some samples or pictures of my work. I agonised for days over what to show her. Even on the day of the meeting I was scrambling about for pictures of past work.

I had built her up to such a Versace level of notoriety in my head that when I saw her in the café we'd arranged to meet in, I was underwhelmed. She towered over me, pulled me into a tight hug and kissed each cheek. She was a curvy woman with a smile that reminded me of Auntie Mala, but with more teeth.

"Hello Eliska! You're early, that's good!" She spoke with the faintest hint of an accent.

"Hi, I was too excited to wait!" *Play it cool, fool*, I scolded myself.

We made small talk over the strongest pot of coffee I've ever had. It was Turkish. I knew it straight away: it was the same stuff I always steered clear of in Istanbul. I was not a coffee person at all, and this stuff had me riding lightning, but she'd paid for it, and it seemed impolite not to.

She told me the café was her sister-in-law's brother's café. They always made her fresh Turkish coffee because she was family. I loved how other cultures consider even the ricketiest links to people as strong family ties. I'd thought it was only Gypsies who would have an "intimate gathering with close relatives" and invite their cousin's brother-in-law's grandparents' niece and her kids, because not to would be bad manners.

Her name was Banan. She was originally from Dubai but married a Turkish Muslim, then moved to England after living in Edirne for 21 years. I was pleasantly shocked when she told me she knew all about Romani people. I usually have to explain that we're not from Romania or Rome, and we don't actually have a country of our own, and yes, we really do exist. But Banan was giving *me* the education! She told me about a festival that was held in her city each May called *Kakava*. It was a celebration of Romani people. I had been to Istanbul and Ankara many times for work, but had never known that our people were *celebrated* in Turkey. It was a beautiful fact to find out, and it spurred an hour-long conversation about *Kakava*, Romani people and European attitudes towards Muslims and Gypsies. By the time we got onto the topic of my sewing, it was well into the afternoon.

I pulled out a dress I'd made, and put my phone in front of her so she could browse through other works. I saw her eyes widen at some pictures, and she looked very pleased. I was smug as hell. It could have been the excitement of the day or it could have been the tit-tingling coffee, but I sat in that café as if I was Balenciaga. I was on top of the world. I couldn't have asked for anything better. Banan loved my work, I could tell.

"This is so good. The beading is very nice! Did you do it yourself?" She was talking about a costume I had made for a show in India. I'd sat for hours threading pink beading to sew around the belt of the turquoise costume. Hours hunched over the fabric with an increasingly warm lamp millimetres from my face. Afterwards, I was lazily browsing sewing forums and found something called a Bead Spinner, which would have threaded all those beads in minutes. Now, I can barely look at the costume without back pains.

"Eliska, this is really good. There are some things I will need to work on with you."

Bitch, what.

"But it's only small things."

Better be small things.

Eventually the day ended. Banan asked me to go to her house the following week, as she had a workroom at the bottom of her garden. I imagined being shut in a garden shed. But it was paid work, so I didn't care that much.

When I rolled up to Banan's house in my best eastern European velour tracksuit (a.k.a. trash-suit), I was stunned. I expected a standard house with a grotty shed in the back, so I didn't wear anything too impressive – it'd only get ruined, I thought. So when the taxi pulled up at a large redbrick house with a big, clean drive, my heart fell into my velour-covered arse. Banan failed to tell me she lived in a nice, expensive house in a decent part of the neighbourhood.

I knocked on the door and smiled sheepishly at Banan when she answered. I saw her die a little inside when she looked down at the Gypsy girl dressed in a hot-pink velour tracksuit with matching leopard-print gilet and wedges, clutching a huge leopard-print weekend bag and an Irn Bru bottle. The weekend bag was a touch too much leopard, maybe.

She ushered me in and led me into the kitchen, where three other women sat around a table drinking tea. They weren't as polite as Banan, and looked at me like I was the Russian hooker I was dressed as. I grimace-smiled at them and muttered a "Hello". The stupidest moment of the whole situation was setting down the Irn Bru bottle on her pristine table, next to the expensive tea-set.

The walk to the shed, which turned out be practically an apartment at the end of the garden, was awkward. I had been introduced to the ladies: Kanika, Manu and Banan's business partner, Harpreet. They weren't convinced I wasn't going to give them an STD if they so much as spoke to me.

It took a few more trips to Banan's, in more appropriate clothing, for the other three to warm to me. Once I'd proved myself with my sewing abilities, I was welcomed into the fold. I didn't tell them straight away that I was near-fluent in Punjabi and Hindi and could understand exactly what they'd been saying about me for the past three weeks. I decided to let the "whore, filthy, she has a round nose" comments slide. I was thinking worse about them. I eventually told them a month or two in, and thankfully it went down well.

The sewing got me out of the house and into a routine that kept me busy with work that I enjoyed.

It was soon time for me to return to university. I had changed so much during my time off that going back felt like my first day. I had been reading relevant texts, correcting vocabulary issues

I'd had in the past, and this time I was ready. I had such a fierce determination to get my degree and show myself and the world that I wasn't defeated. I was going to be something other than a raped Gypsy girl from eastern Europe. The importance of education was ringing in my ears: every ambition I had, and every dream of mine I wanted to make come true, all required an education. If I was to spend my life writing stories, then I'd need more than just a notebook and an idea. I needed to know how to structure my work, manage my career and learn how write like a professional, instead of churning out a series of amateur short stories with no direction or purpose.

What happened to me was devastating, yes. But it hadn't killed me, despite my prolonged wishes. It would have been worse to give everything up and either return to Drovane or spend my life scrabbling for odd jobs whilst watching life pass me by in a room I paid £200 a month for.

My strength was gaining momentum. I wrote out the next 12 months on a fresh piece of paper and stuck it to the inside of my wardrobe door. I decided I would achieve something each month and write it down. Then in a year's time I would have 12 things to be proud of.

My second year started well. I paid attention to my classes and enjoyed them. I was taking notes and learning. It was amazing. It was such a difference from the experience I had in my first year. I would do the recommended reading, and even bought a Kindle in case I was too late to go home and collect my bag on the way to university from work. I didn't mind paying double for a digital copy of my textbooks. I would have poured every penny I had into ensuring I was armed with my literary arsenal whenever I attended my lectures. I viewed my degree as a war. I had been through battles: rape, depression, and so on. But I would emerge victorious like all of the historical wars I'd read about.

My attitude had improved no end, but I still had my wobbles. The joy on my face when "Victorian Culture" cropped up on the module list was indescribable. It's as if the universe sent a little gift my way by having my dream subject on the list.

However, the reality was disappointing. I barely showed up, and left early when I did. I couldn't understand why, but the windowless room gave me terrible anxiety out of nowhere. Sometimes I'd be dressed and ready, but turn around and walk straight home after getting within five minutes of university. I felt trapped in the room, and I'd be laughing away with a friend whilst feeling as if I wanted to pass out. I tried hard to keep a confident façade up, but I knew I had disappointed myself. That module should have been my best grade out of my full three years. If nothing else, I got more resources to browse during my leisure time. I've done all the reading for the module twice since the class ended.

In general, attendance was difficult for me. I'd either be working or having an "off day" that would see me unable to leave the house, convinced that someone would come and drag me into another alleyway. Despite this, my resilience held steadfast with university. I wouldn't let the horror of my life so far be in vain. Ma sent me here to be educated, and educated I would be, come what may.

It wasn't just my anxiety; I'd become a very flaky person in general when it came to timekeeping and appointments. I'd fix a time to meet people and stumble through the doors 20 minutes later with an apologetic smile. To this day, my dad absolutely hates this about me, and often lectures me on how you only have your word in this world. When I show up late, I'm showing that I can't keep my word. University attendance was no different: I'd be armed with my motivation and determination, but still manage to be late.

These were only gentle bumps in the road compared to the boulders of the past. I always think of university in two parts. The depressed melancholy pre-break and the lighter, freeing time post-break.

During my time at university I had the epiphany that I no longer wanted my main source of income to be dancing for Yadira. I didn't want to use my body. I wanted to use my brain now. I had got to this point with people using my body and taking advantage of my young age. But now I would dance when I wanted to, not because I needed to feed myself. My sewing was going great, and the cleaning work I did was fulfilling, surprisingly. Making as much money as possible wasn't important to me. My father had money, Anja had access to money, Arne had a sizeable inheritance from his mother's family, but how happy were they? I found joy in books on loan from the library, not in expensive shops or cars.

That was how my German family lived, and it was nice enough for them. I never judged them; if bags, shoes, cars and gadgets brought them happiness, then load up on them! Happiness should be snatched at every possible opportunity, however you find it.

For me, though, knowing my Gypsy ancestors were looking down upon me, being literate and educated gave me all the delight I needed. My heart was full when I thought of my family that perished in the Holocaust and who were not even recognised in the subsequent re-telling of the horrific events in schools. Now, they were living through me as I forged a new life in this land. Gypsy blood wandering a sophisticated country with a degree and a fully dressed career.

I owed it to those lives lost to make the most of mine. The prospect of life after university was both daunting and exciting. I knew I was going to throw myself into whatever I did. I would carve out a respectable life for myself however I could. Telling Yadira this was easy, as she only ever half-listened to what anybody said to her anyway. I could have told her that I'd decided I would be dancing in a chicken costume from now on and still got that placating "hmm" from her.

I was preparing for a great future, a vibrant future, with all the deliciousness that unpredictability brings.

I felt myself changing. I wasn't afraid, I wasn't a victim and I wasn't beaten.

DRAG YOURSELF UP

As third year was drawing to a close, I had two things on my mind: my dissertation and graduation.

I had gone to the library and hauled in extra books on grammar, critical writing, dissertation-writing guides, and a Depeche Mode biography because you have to make this life liveable.

As if I needed an excuse to visit, I went to a couple of libraries and ended up taking out books that had nothing to do with my dissertation topic at all. They were grand-looking leather-bound books that matched the "hard-working" aesthetic I cultivated in my room.

I would sit in the evenings at my desk with my books spread out, laptop blaring Sikh *kirtans* (a lasting, soothing relaxation technique from my time at the temple) and my emergency dissertation snack-pack on my bookshelf. It consisted of a huge supply of Kinder chocolates courtesy of Arne, paprika Pringles (because I'm Gypsy/German so paprika is God), and a bottle of Irn Bru.

I had candles and incense burning with the curtains drawn. It was bliss. Cave-like environments make me feel more at home than anything else. The darker and more dimly lit, the better. I couldn't work during daylight hours – it was too bright, too naked and too intrusive. The night-time was when I could allow my mind to fully unleash itself. I could barely string together comprehensible sentences when I worked in the university library in the middle of the day, yet at home, when everyone else was asleep, my fingers flew over the keyboard like Beethoven.

Creativity and clarity come easier to me in the darkness.

Everyone I spoke to during dissertation-time sounded so stressed and told me they loathed the tedious task of putting together a coherent, quality body of work. I would join in and talk about how soul-draining the thing was, but secretly I loved it. I enjoyed the flurry of books, theories, studies, references and bibliographies. I enjoyed the topic I was writing about (Humour in Tragedy). I enjoyed reading different studies and browsing websites that would take me from my original topic to the 1984 slaughter of Punjabis at the Holy Golden Temple to how drag queens were key in the development of feminine identity.

I agreed: *RuPaul's Drag Race* genuinely was key to how I recovered from rape and reclaimed my femininity and sexuality.

I started watching the show during my depression. I watched the first episode of season two and hated how glamorous everyone looked. I started watching again during my break from university. Watching the episodes, hearing the stories from the contestants and being told how they healed and found themselves in drag was life-changing. It was during season two that they did a burlesque task with Dita von Teese featuring in the episode.

I loved it. It didn't remind me of the seedy stripping I did at 14. It reminded me of Las Vegas and the glamour of old Hollywood pin-ups. After googling furiously, I found classes nearby. It was weeks before I worked up the courage to go. But during the day when I'd be sewing in Banan's apartment-shed, I'd pretend the glitzy outfits I was sewing were part of the show.

I went from feeling as if being feminine and wearing overly feminine outfits was somehow wrong and the reason I was raped, to wishing I could walk everywhere in a pineapple dress like Manilla Luzon, or a turquoise cat-suit with a red bolero *à la* Jujubee.

Despite being "characters", the way they would speak about themselves was so confident and nonchalant that at first I was gobsmacked. But after hearing "I'm a superhero diva and my power is glitter", I couldn't fight it anymore. I was a fucking superhero diva. They weren't going to take that from me, those men weren't going to rob me of my *Charisma, Uniqueness, Nerve and Talent*. Copying the makeup and outfits created on *Drag Race* was the first time I allowed myself to think of myself as a sexual being. It was the first time after being raped that I felt "sexy" without wanting to scrub my skin raw.

Suppressing my sexual self was like admitting I deserved what had happened. This was the last part of my healing: I had to accept it was not my fault. Watching drag queens embodying the very essence of feminine sexuality gave me the confidence I needed to re-embrace who I was before what happened to me. I was someone who wore fashionably questionable outfits with my own femininity exuding through. My bellydance-biker blend was always tinged with my natural love of the human body. I loved seeing women with "skimpy" clothing. I loved seeing men topless. It wasn't out of sexual gratification – it was out of love for the world, the human race and how we're all fucking flawless. There were people who preferred to cover up and there were people who loved to show their flesh. Both were right, both were beautiful, and both were free in this world. I had grown up watching my grandmother berate Ma for wearing skirts that showed too much leg after working in the alleyways of Drovane, and I'd watched Dad walk around in boxers more than a few times. It was normal. It was life.

Why should our very bodies be sexual? The animals I encountered that night would have done the same to someone in jeans and a T-shirt. It wasn't my outfit that raped me. The policeman I'd had the misfortune to be assigned to afterwards couldn't grasp that fact. As I grew tougher, I often thought of seeking out that policeman and telling him that there were parts of the world where the women covered themselves head to toe but still suffered the horror of rape. What excuse would he find to excuse those beasts' actions, the way he excused the ones who brutalised me?

I recreated some of the outfits I adored on *Drag Race* out of the scraps I collected when making other people's dresses. I secretly wore heels in my room or around the house when it was empty. I started wearing skirts, crop tops and dresses around the house when nobody was there. I had been slowly losing weight after my arthritis diagnosis, and it had eased the painful pressure on my joints considerably. I was feeling more comfortable in my "old" clothes now that I could see the depression-weight disappearing. I was in love with the plump thighs that weren't shifting, though. I hoped they'd stay. My body was in a new phase of shy sexual acceptance. I was learning to love myself differently and intimately. I was trying to stop being frightened of touch, whether it was my own or a doctor, dentist, or optician.

This sexual renaissance roused by *RuPaul's Drag Race* taught me more about self-love, self-acceptance, and the importance of placing value on your own opinion of yourself. Who matters more than you?

My dissertation was more like a religious experience than the nightmare assignment that almost every student dreads. It was the culmination of my developed academic skills, my personal journey as Eliska, and my newfound belief in myself. I honestly felt miffed that it ended so soon. I felt like I had more to prove, more to show. It was during my dissertation that I was absolutely sure I would continue with education after my degree. I wanted to do a Masters, I wanted to do a PhD. Imagine: Doctor Zlatkov. Ma would take the opportunity to charge extra – I could practically hear her: *"This is the vagina that delivered a Doctor. This is worth more than any pussy in Drovane!"*

I handed in my dissertation, and then was left with only one worry.

Most people take their parents' presence at key life events for granted. They get to focus on how they feel about the event, instead of just praying someone from their family will turn up. Speaking to my friends about graduation was a sore spot. They were busying themselves with outfits and after-ceremony celebrations.

Manjit had asked when my parents were going to arrive in England for my graduation. She asked if they'd be staying with us whilst they visited.

"Yeah, I don't think that's going to happen."

It was the first time I'd said aloud what I'd been putting off thinking for weeks. I already knew what Ma's answer was. She told me earlier in the day that even if she wanted to waste a week with me, she couldn't. She had no passport and there was no way for her to get to England thanks to the "bastard laws they've put everywhere now".

"Come on, one of them has to! It'll probably be your dad."

I watched her compare her nail colour against the dress she'd bought that morning for work, and wondered whether this would be like the time Dad surprised me by whisking me away to the hotel when he found out I'd been raped.

I decided to call my dad when I got home. I'd call Anja first to gauge Dad's mood – I knew she was staying at his Berlin home that month – and see whether she thought he'd say yes to coming.

I had set my bag down in my room when my phone rang. Anja. Her name accompanied by her lovely face flashing on my phone always made me happy.

"Anjaaaaaa! *Schwesti*! *Was ist*—"

"It's not Anja, it's me." Dad. Great.

"Oh, why are you ringing from her phone? Is everything okay?" My joy at seeing Anja's name dissolved.

"Everything's fine. I pay for this fucking phone, I can't use it? I haven't spoken to you for a while. What has been happening?" I could vaguely hear traffic.

"I'm okay. Just working on a few dresses for Banan. I'm glad you called actually. I wanted to talk to you. I spoke to Ma earlier." I was nervous; asking him about graduation was a big deal.

"Talk about what? What did you talk to Lenka about? What's she done now?" He sounded neutral, which is overjoyed for him.

"Nothing. She never does anything for me. I don't know why I keep trying—"

He interrupted before my rant properly kicked off.

"She does nothing? You're sat in England on your fat arse because she does nothing? You're an ungrateful idiot."

Hold the hell up. I wasn't taking that from him.

"Are you serious, Dad? I got to England because she wanted me to buy her a house eventually. She slept with some guy and got me sent to England in a fucking box with a girl who shat herself. Hardly a seat in a private jet," I scoffed.

"You really don't know how you got to England, do you?"

He sounded bemused. I heard him take in a deep breath. It seemed I would be getting an education today, whether I wanted it or not.

"Lenka used to fuck an MP regularly," Dad began. "He'd come and see her all the time, twice a week sometimes. He was involved in right-wing groups in Slovakia and Ukraine. He was involved in getting people across – had been since the nineties. She asked him to take you. He laughed at her. She threatened to go and tell his wife everything. About the abortions she'd had. About how he'd taken her away for weekends in that shitty inn we went to once – remember when I took you to that fucking school?"

Dad was breaking it all the way down too fast for me to process. He reminded me of *Oma* and her compartmentalised, robotic way of telling us about her family, her very identity.

"Wait. What? An English MP? Abortions? What are you talking about?" I wasn't fazed by the whole racist thing. All racists are mentally ill, so the fact that so many of them seemed to have non-racist dicks wasn't the most surprising thing to me.

"You really do just walk around with your head in the clouds. She had abortions after you. You should have fucking been one. Anyway, she called me after he laughed in her face. I wasn't there. I called back and some old lady was talking Gypsy. I didn't try again. Then when you told me you were going to England, I spoke to Rosa. Then I offered to pay half." He was sounding impatient, but I didn't care. When didn't he sound bored when I spoke to him? He'd have to deal with it. I wanted to know.

"So, what did Ma pay? How much was it?"

"Why do you want to know? You're cleaning enough toilets to pay us back? Lenka paid as much as her pussy could handle.

I think she doubled her workload for that month. I spoke to her when you went to England. I came to Slovakia to make sure you went. She was ill. I didn't fuck her; she was too ill." The height of sympathy from Franz Volker.

"What was wrong with her?" I ignored the comments about Ma's vagina. He never tried to clean up his language when we spoke about Ma.

"She was fucking exhausted. What do you think? I made her show me what was wrong, because she couldn't move her legs. She was swollen and bruised. Fuck knows what filthy shit she did. The guys she was seeing were animals. She told me one or two of them liked to put things in her. I took her with me. We stayed in that hotel in Sliač."

"What? That's hours away. She's never told me that."

"Why would she? You never gave a fuck how you got to England. You just got there. I looked after her for two weeks. In those two weeks, did you phone? Did you care what had happened to her? It was the first time she'd ever been to a place like that. She loved the bed. Good job too. She couldn't fucking leave it for the first week. The doctor came to see her and gave her a cream I had to put on her. Then she ate so fucking much, the room service bill was almost as much as the cost of the room."

This intimate moment between my parents was bizarre. The fact that I had no idea about it was even more bizarre. I did go weeks without calling, but that's because I was never guaranteed to speak with any of my family. The shop-lady was getting older and wasn't going to dart to Drovane just to get Ma. Besides, Ma would either be in prison again or moan that I was costing her money by taking up her time. Also, I couldn't phone her in the beginning because I was busy trying not to get molested. I could hardly ask Gunjan right at the beginning if I could borrow her phone. I didn't know anybody's number, and the only people I was in the care of were mentally unstable.

"I didn't know," I mumbled like a fool.

"You never know. I drove her home after making sure she was healed, after getting some colour into her face and seeing a bit of meat on her. I fixed her up, took her back to Drovane, and she was right back to work the next day. Probably the same day. Because she doesn't have a choice. She doesn't get to go to a government office and say 'I don't want to work' or 'I'm too sick. Give me money.' You don't know how lucky you are."

"If you cared so fucking much, you could have taken her to Germany." My tone was pointed, but I was sick of him acting like a saint.

"She's the only one I would take back to Germany. But she hasn't got a fucking passport. I can't use Maike's for her like I did with you. I can't hide her in the fucking trunk either. She…" His voice trailed off. "What did you phone me for?"

"I didn't. You phoned me. I answered because I thought I was talking to my sister." I kept my tone the same. He was irritating me.

"Yes, what is happening with your degree? Have you finished?"

"I have, I'm receiving an award for Overcoming—"

"Okay. Good. That's all I wanted to know."

"Wait! Dad… Dad. Are you…? Will you… Can you please come to my graduation?"

"No, I'm busy. I have things to do here."

"Please. I really want you to come, I'm so proud of what I've done. I got a degree, Dad!"

"Eliska. Were you the only one in your class? No? So, you mean other people got a degree too? This is what I mean. Everything has to be a big event when you do something. I'm not coming. Don't ask me to again. Anja isn't coming because I'm not fucking paying for her to come. I'm sick of paying for her and Arne. All they do is talk to me about money. They even fucking send me their bills. Arne can't say more than two words to me but is okay when I pay for his car. He got all that money and he still drains me."

"Okay. I'm going to be the only one with nobody there. Dad, please. I never ask you for anything—"

"Try asking me. I'll smash your ungrateful jaw to the back of your head. Nobody is fucking coming. Bye." He hung up.

I pursed my lips, waited for my eyes to stop stinging, and then pulled myself together.

He was right.

I never thought too hard about how I came to be sat in a washing machine box. Even as I got older and more educated, I never considered what Ma did to send me to England. I was so wrapped up in myself. After all, who mattered more than me?

I could show great compassion to complete strangers. Even watching the news, my heart would break for the sad faces that flickered across the screen for a few seconds. But when it came to my own family, I couldn't do it. I couldn't muster up the empathy and sympathy, because of how they treated me. I was constantly told by both parents that I was slow, dopey and simple. Now, when I had proved them wrong and earned a degree despite the most awful things happening, they couldn't pretend to care.

It was as if Ma had sent me to England to get me out of her hair. Dad just treated me like Maike, my oldest sister forgotten in Russia. Anja and Arne weren't so easily ignored – especially Anja. She lived in the heart of Berlin, and everyone that Dad knew, knew she was his daughter.

I was proud of myself, even if they weren't. Arne and Anja were beyond proud of me, and I'm sure my Zlatkov cousins would be too.

I decided not to go to my graduation. Candi and Jackie tried persuading me, and Candi offered to go out afterwards, but it was one thing I couldn't fake. I couldn't spend that day sitting in a theatre filled with loving family members, cheering mothers and proud fathers, knowing that my mother preferred to work in the dusty alleys of Drovane and my father prioritised washing his car or sleeping in, or whatever else. I'd end up resenting everyone. It'd ruin the pride I felt at getting my degree after the hard journey.

I spent the day doing an end-of-tenancy clean. I was happy. I had gone further than learning how to read and write. I had a degree. I'd earned it, I'd worked hard for it, and nobody could ever snatch it away from me. I wasn't Eliska who failed Vera's banana classes. I was Eliska Zlatkov – the educated Gypsy from Drovane.

AWAKE

SMOKE
AND MIRRORS

February 2017.

I had gone to Drovane to see my family. It was a few weeks before my birthday, and I was never going to miss my chance at the 50-pence-sized piece of *klobasa* sausage.

It had been a fun day: I'd seen my cousins, nieces and nephews. I'd had my face clawed at by overzealous aunties, and my stomach clawed at by fat-shaming grannies. Fat, to them, constituted anything that prevented the outline of your ribcage doubling as a xylophone.

Ma had avoided me most of the day, which was fine by me. After her last prison stint I'd decided to stop hoping she'd ever be a mother to me. I ended up disappointed constantly, and I was just breaking my own heart over and over. She hadn't changed since my birth, so why did I expect her to now?

It was night-time when I saw Ma. I was finishing up a major gossip session with Jani, sitting by the trees on a wall facing the Drovane blocks. It was freezing, so we were sharing a scarf as a blanket.

Ma came over and jerked her head at Jani. "It was me that pushed her out, not you. Can I have a few seconds with the Queen of England?"

Jani rolled her eyes, playfully flicked her hair in Ma's direction, and jogged off toward the flats.

"God, you're too educated to speak to me these days. Fucked a few men with an education and now you've forgotten where you came from." She lowered herself on the floor with her back to the Soviet-style blocks; she looked like those fashion magazine photoshoots with stunning women in front of depressing backdrops. "You can suck all the English cock you like. You still used to eat from bins, Eliska." Ma threw her head back as she cackled.

"I'm going inside. My feet are aching from these bastard new shoes and I'm tired." I had no time for her shenanigans anymore.

"Wait… please."

I almost died. Lenka Zlatkov had said please to me. My shock obviously showed on my face as Ma snapped, "You look like a used teabag. Don't crease your face. You have to work harder than me to keep your skin good, you've got white blood."

"What do you want, Ma?" I was growing suspicious.

"Just to talk."

"About what?"

"You. You come less and less. Are you working too hard?"

"Wha… what?" I managed to splutter out a response. My Ma, who thought being raped was the hardest I'd worked, was showing concern.

"I said… are you working too hard? You don't come here anymore." Ma's voice was smaller.

"Erm, I… I don't. Well, I suppose I do. I'm always busy with the sewing. Banan pays me well but makes sure I work for every penny. I'm always cleaning too. Then I dance whenever I can, and teach sometimes." My heart was beating fast, as if something bad was going to happen.

"But your books. When do you write them?" Ma looked genuinely worried.

"In the nights. I like it that way, though. I—"

"You always liked the night-time better. Witch." She winked at me, and then I was sure. This was an imposter – a bloody good one, because she even had the same ripped green hair scrunchie that Ma had worn for years.

"Are you dying?" I asked bluntly. There could be no other reason for this weird chat.

"No, stupid dog! I can't fucking talk to you? You write about me when I'm bad to you, and now you act like an idiot when I'm good to you!" And there she was.

"Okay, sorry. I do like the night-time better."

"You need to live properly. Go out, have sex with lots of men, marry one, become a housewife. You've worked enough. Look at your health. How you have so much wrong with you at your age I don't understand."

I resisted the urge to explain how years of malnutrition and immense poverty led to my immune system weakening.

"Being molested and then gang-raped can take its toll on you." I didn't mean my tone to sound as sharp as it did.

"Don't blame those men, don't blame me, and don't blame your father. If you waste your life, it's your own fault. Most of the kids out there look up to their Ma. I never have. I used to look past her. I promised myself I would have something better than this. Then you happened. I can't forgive you for that, Eliska." Her eyes were glazed as they filled with tears. "You shouldn't have happened, *miláčik*."

"You can live, too. Come with me, back to England! We can live together and make a life there, better than this, Ma!"

I was babbling shit and I knew it. It would never happen, but I had to say something. Seeing Ma this way was so surreal. I hated it. She was always so strong, and deep down I think I was content knowing she was happy in the life she was leading, because it made it easier for me to live in England. If I knew she loathed her life, then I would probably die of guilt.

"No, it's too late. I love it now. I never used to. I remember when you were 11, you looked like a lollipop. Fat cheeks, but bones everywhere else. I used to think you'd end up blowing away out of the window one day, you looked… When I was your age, I was being twisted into whatever shape the man who owned me for the hour wanted. It hurt. Like your new shoes. I got used to it. If I was just raped once like you, I could have lived."

She looked haunted. I could barely recognise her as she stared at the wall with wide eyes. Ma was silent for a few minutes. I was shocked at what she had just implied.

"It hurt a lot." She pulled herself up and walked back towards the blocks of flats.

I never noticed the slight limp she had until that night when she was at her most vulnerable. It was undetectable with the way Ma usually flounced about, bouncing her hips and swinging her hair. But that night, walking away with her shoulders slumped, holding onto her elbows, I saw my mother for the abused girl she was. It had taken me 20 years.

EPILOGUE

EVOLUTION

My birthplace would have kept me a slow, lost girl who'd eventually follow her family's steps and work as a prostitute. I'd have been raped, beaten, abused and worse numerous times over the course of my life. I'd have had maybe half a dozen kids with different fathers if I wasn't dragged to the "abortion woman" by Ma. I'd have grown to be a mean-spirited, bitter copy of my ma, because the world would indeed have worn me down.

Instead I really did my "growing" in England. Yes, I was raped. Brutally. But this was an anomaly. This wasn't dicing with assault on a daily basis the way my family did. Yes, I was the only one raped out of all of my cousins; they fortunately hadn't been so violently violated. But they were taking that chance every hour of every day. I, meanwhile, went to school. I went to university. I became human.

My story isn't unique. There are many trafficked, broken, raped boys and girls out there who have darker tales of tragedy then me. So how dare I waste this chance? This chance for a settled life in a civilised country that doesn't hold my race against me. Not outwardly, anyway.

England will always be my homeland. It gave me the gift of literacy. Learning how to read and write plugged me into the world. And that gave me the gift of dignity. I may move away from England one day; I may never return. But I will forever be indebted to this country. It's as if the universe sent me here on the journey it did to discover the beauty in people. As if I had to know that the heartless, prejudiced people who sneered at us, spat at us in the street and blamed all of us for the actions of a few in Slovakia weren't the norm. That people were good. People were kind. I needed to know.

And I found out.

There was one saving grace throughout my life, and that was the desire to be educated. I wanted it so much. I wanted to be like Arne and Anja moaning about their homework when I'd see them as a child. Hating the teacher that set them such a boring reading book. Wondering why an hour for lunch seemed so short compared to 40 minutes of Maths. Apart from such a poor start in Yorkshire, school was the elixir my famished mind needed. Learning about others, learning about the topics that you needed to navigate the civilised world, and learning how to interact with other humans without violence and resentment.

My inner struggle between loving Anja, and begrudging her loving mother and her abundance of clothes, toys and all that made little girls happy back then, was the greatest shame for me at times. I felt disloyal. Anja never rubbed my or Arne's face in her maternal support network, but we felt it nonetheless. Felt it when she'd have a beautifully written nametag in her clothes, a freshly packed lunchbox bursting at the seams when she'd come to Dad's for the day, when her mother championed her most feeble efforts at education, work, life. I adored her mother, and was glad our soft-willed sister had such a tender family when she left the confines of the Volker grip. But it still stung watching her waving with her mother as they drove away happily home. Arne and I were bundled into Dad's expensive cars and sent on our silent, angry way. Him with *Opa* and me with Dad.

But school had softened that struggle. I saw things from Anja's point of view. Her mother would send extra food in her lunchbox for me and Arne. Anja would always let me wear her clothes and bring toys for me to take back to Drovane – something I wasn't allowed to do, because Dad didn't want my cousins to play with them. Her mother sent me a bouquet of flowers when I completed university. She told me on the phone that the next time I was in Germany, there was a sweet woodruff cake with my name on it. Being amongst white, black and brown people from rich and poor backgrounds with single parents, extended families, guardians and so on had taught me more than any other experience could. How everyone could sit in the same room for lesson after lesson and make unlikely friendships, enemies and relationships. In those years, in that cocoon of school, racism wasn't so ferociously rampant. Yes, there were a few times, even in the Midlands, when I'd be called racist names or someone else would be racially abused, but the merciless intolerance the school showed in dealing with such incidents was reassuring. Unity worked with kids, but it seemed to fail with adults.

As an adult, being told "Gypsies are pickpockets, they snatch up babies, they're all scum" with no consequence was disheartening. It's not like I could elbow them in the nose, either, because I wasn't a feral Zlatkov kid anymore. I had lived in some dire council estates throughout my life in England, and seen the very worst of human behaviour. From openly rinsing benefit systems to harassment, violence and the most shocking parenting I'd seen in this country, I never once assumed this was the culture of white people. Yet it was fair game to call all black people "thugs", Gypsy people "con artists", brown people "terrorists". With the government's gradual amping-up of anti-immigrant propaganda, eastern Europeans had taken the place of Asians with the "tekkin' our jobs" crowd. So these types of racist generalisations were on the rise. When challenging these folk, you'd be met with a war cry of "PC gone mad" and "can't say anything these days".

I've always wondered what it is that these people want to say? What do they want to say so badly that they haven't already? What is worse than wishing death on the children of migrants because they have the audacity to seek a better life in England? There are platforms given to people who spout these types of opinions everywhere, and yet they also complain about their "free speech" being taken away. What else is left to say? Openly admitting that death is deserved for children who have no choice, no ill intention, and no concept of their very existence being offensive to certain people is surely the lowest of the low. So what else is left to say?

There were times when I became disillusioned with England. It made me numb inside knowing that people thought this was easy. Leaving behind your family, your homeland and your words to come to a place with a different language, a different culture, and a rising wave of hate-filled people fuelled by "journalists" who make more money from ignorance than immigrants will ever see in their lives. The winding up of working-class people by middle to upper-class "journalists" who live in idyllic bubbles is the biggest joke of modern-day society. Telling struggling people that their back-breaking for a pittance is the fault of the evil, thieving immigrants, instead of the government and hierarchy, is the second biggest joke.

Doctors, teachers and other professional people come here only to be muted and despised in their search for safety. Safety from war, oppression, violence or starvation. If people in England can become homeless and destitute with all it has to offer, then what do people think happens in countries where the infrastructure is weaker? What do they think happens to Gypsies in eastern Europe?

Whenever I raised this question with an anti-immigration cleaning colleague of mine, all I was confronted with were stories of Gypsy pickpockets living lavishly in Romania. The fact she was being paid under the table and claiming benefits was lost on her. We'd have many clashes over our views. The main source of contention for her was that her daughter hadn't been able to find a job since leaving school. If her daughter wasn't white, then she herself would have called the girl a "stereotype". Her daughter had no interest in school, forever got herself suspended, and would be out in the streets until the early hours. Yet it was the fault of the Polish, Slovakians, Albanians and whoever else that her daughter was not yet a brain surgeon. Even she had to concede the lack of native English applications whenever a new position became available on the cleaning team we worked for. Only immigrants would apply. We weren't taking jobs that were being fought for.

I stopped watching the news or following any type of political platform after a nasty incident when a group of drunk white men hounded me and a friend of mine, Monica. We had gone on a rare night out after being paid in our respective jobs. Me as a cleaner, her in a hair salon. We'd met when I danced for her cousin's 21st birthday, and had been friends ever since. We had a casual relationship; we were both bisexual and single. We'd been walking past a pub when the same old lewd remarks were shouted at us, the same remarks that most women learn to ignore by the age of 15. But this time they started following us. We'd been holding hands, so of course the excitable losers latched onto that.

"Oi, let us watch!" one of them slurred.

"Fuck off," Monica snapped.

We walked on. Giving each other side-eye exchanges, it wasn't new to us. But it was getting tiring.

"FUCK YOU! BLACK BITCH!" another lad shouted.

"Don't call her that, you twat!" I shouted back. My accent rarely gave me away throughout university. I had a talent for mimicking accents, something we used to do back in Drovane. So when I was in Yorkshire, for example, I would practise speaking like my classmates. I didn't sound as fresh off the boat as I actually was. Dagmar struggled more. Her natural accent was strong, although her English was better. But on this night, all of my immigrant blood rushed forth and revealed itself, replacing of all my "e" sounds with "a", "th" with "d" and as a nod to my German heritage, "w" to "v".

And so it began. "FUCK OFF BACK TO YOUR OWN COUNTRY!" "WE'RE FULL, GET LOST BACK TO WHERE YOU CAME FROM!"

Monica actually turned to me with a mischievous smile and said, "It's coming…"

Before I could ask her what she meant, it came.

"TAKING ALL OUR JOBS AND GETTING HOUSES FOR ALL YOUR FUCKING BASTARD KIDS!" It was a skinny man whose clothing hung off him tighter than Mufasa on Pride Rock.

"YEP! TAKING ALL OF THEM!" Monica roared with laughter as I shook my head, already in stitches.

"Let's go, come on. Leave these idiots." I tugged on her hand. We looked back at the skinny man, who was bright red, trembling, with his fists clenched. He hardly looked like he was going to give chase. He looked like his body couldn't be relied on to give him an erection or a heart attack. It was as if the alcohol in him had given him false confidence, but his body hadn't got the memo. So he was shaking, breathing erratically, and staring at us confusedly.

We ran down the road as they continued to call out names and racial slurs.

After that day, I decided I'd encountered enough bigotry and bile on the streets – so why would I pay any more attention to it? It was liberating. Instead of sitting there angrily when another biased piece on immigration came on the TV, I just stayed happy. I knew that people were being misinformed, but you know what, who cared? They weren't going to change their minds. Because they were content with having a scapegoat. Many of the racists I've met in my life have nothing to be proud of. They couldn't make it through a free education, couldn't make it through their teens without getting/making someone pregnant, or make it to 20 without a criminal record. There are people who have experienced all of these things, but who have still gone on to make successes of their lives or make a comfortable living – for themselves, at least. I would know, I'm related to enough of them. Yet the ones who couldn't overcome bad decisions or unexpected children were the ones who took to the streets in their tracksuits and berated every-one "other" than themselves for the woeful state of their lives.

Sure, blame Waleed and Jakub for you not being able to find a council house. Blame me and my people for you not being able to afford a house on minimum wage. Blame us all for you not being able to find a job after an adolescence spent smoking behind the school and bullying those who wanted to learn. Blame everyone but yourselves and the government.

Going "news-free" made me infinitely more positive. It re-ignited my love affair with England. I'd always been someone who saw magic everywhere, but when I'd graduated it was even more heightened. I felt true freedom. I had carved out a wonderful little life for myself. Filled with picnics on my own in a sorry-looking field, with whichever new recipe I'd decided to try that week and a book. Painting at night with a few candles lit, facing the window. Investing in a camera, taking pictures of the sky, clouds, trees, nature and all that made England paradise. I printed out a map of England with all the cities labelled and decided before I moved anywhere, I would go to each and every one of them. I'd do my own pilgrimage around this country that gave me a chance.

Since starting towards this goal, the people I've met have been the purest, kindest people I could have hoped to meet. There have been a few side-eyes, especially as my penchant for "fashion fusion" hasn't died – if anything it's got louder and more bizarre – but for the most part I've been accepted.

My confidence grew with every conversation I had with patient old ladies, every interaction with kindly taxi drivers, every engrossing discussion about history with passionate staff. I was half-formed by university, but now English culture is carving me out fully.

There is another wave of anti-immigration sentiment splashed everywhere, and hate seems to be on the rise. But for me and *my* England – we keep going. I'll keep finding castles, gardens, and historical monuments to enjoy. I'll keep compiling my list of "dream libraries and bookshops I need to see before I die". I'll keep dancing under the English moon. Drovane didn't break me, violence didn't break me, rape didn't break me, and this new threat of xenophobic race hate won't break me. Nothing will break me.

Born into hunger, survived horror, and now gorging on freedom – I'm more than I thought I could be.

ACKNOWLEDGEMENTS

My sincerest gratitude to: Jackie Pieterick and the Creative Writing Department of University of Wolverhampton, Sally-Ann Giles and The Heart & Soul Academy, Penelope Rendall, Sam Boyce, Catherine Simpson, Joanna Swainson, Ajda Vucicevic, George Robarts and the rest of the Mirror Books team.

And above all, Candi Miller – my mentor and dearest friend, thank you.

Alles für Deutschland. All for the Gypsies.